Christ love is an everlasting love. The bounty of grace that flows like a river touches our lives and inspires us to use our talents with compassion to help others on the pathway of life.

We know the greatest need of our loved ones and friends is to know Jesus as Lord and Savior. The depths of our hearts reveal a loving Savior who forgives sins. Blessings are given for us to share so that we can help one another along the way.

Souls need to be saved before the midnight hour. My desire is the same as other Christians, to walk uprightly, hold the cross high for God's glory and live in such a way that He will be pleased to call us His children, sons and daughters.

Our best friend, Jesus will walk among us, touching our lives, giving us strength for the day's journey, and giving us the blessed assurance that He will never leave or forsake us.
Love is passed on by our endeavors. The words of praise from the depths of our hearts continue as each person uses his or her talents to glorify God.

There is one thing special about a talent; each one is specially crafted by the Master Craftsman and assigned to a certain individual, no two talents are the same. God's creative works is His signature design in us to let the light of His glory shine.

Father, help us to realize that when we use our talents to express our love and devotion to you, souls will be blessed. The sweet Holy Spirit will bring conviction on the unsaved and inspiration for the Christians. God's glory will abound.

My hearts desire is to encourage and help others know of God's great love and Jesus as Savior. Let our lives be a light that shines throughout life. In Jesus' name, amen.

Treasure
Chest
To
Life Eternal

Daily
Christian Devotion

Treasure
Chest
To
Life Eternal

Daily
Christian Devotion

David L. Hurst

All scripture is from the King James Version, Scripture quotations are taken from the Holy Bible, King James Version.

Published by David L. Hurst
Cover design by David L. Hurst
Treasure Chest border frame by David L. Hurst
Cover Photo from Pixabay

Interior Design copyright © 2018, by David L. Hurst
Published in the United States of America

ISBN: 978-1-7321750-2-0

1. Inspirational Fiction
2.   Inspirational & religious
3. Religion/ Christian Life/ Devotional

Acknowledgement
Christ our Best Friend

All through life we make friends and they stay with us for a while and then they are gone. That does not mean the end of a great friendship. The reality of life is that we will be separated for various reasons. True friends are constant companions.

Some of the people we meet along the way will be our friends for life. We have to go through a healing process when our friends are no longer with us and we wait on our hearts to mend, as we are left all alone. Solitude in life is for a season.

A good, faithful friend helps us along the pathway of life with encouraging words, kindness, and loyalty to give us strength when we are weak. When we are cast down and forsaken, a true friend will always give us a helping hand and will lift us up in times of sorrow. A discouraging word is never heard.

We may walk away from Christ and separate ourselves from the love of God, but Jesus will never leave or forsake us. If we walk away, we are the ones who break the friendship. His faithfulness is not temporary, here today and gone tomorrow.

Father, Christ is our best friend. We have peace in our souls when Jesus is in our lives; there is no other friend like Him. We love to be with Jesus and have fellowship with Him. Jesus calls us friends; He is closer than a brother.

If there are thoughts that no one cares, then we haven't met Jesus. If there is anyone here that is alone and looking for a friend? Jesus on the cross with His arms spread wide, this is how much He loves us. Seek Him for an everlasting friendship. In Jesus' name, amen.

January

February

March

April

May

June

July

August

September

October

November

December

The Old Year is Past
January 1

We are beginning a new year and the calendar has already been placed on the wall. All of the special days are marked with the important things we want to do in the days and months ahead.

Think about the old year, we cannot go back, even if we had the opportunity. Perhaps we would try to claim just one of the days, but it is too late now. There is no need for us to worry, fret or sigh; Jesus is passing by. Living in the past brings up memories we try to forget.

We want to take this time to express our sincere gratitude for your guidance and for giving us grace along the way. This year we hope to return many times to the memory trail, to receive strength for this new journey in life. The old year is a reminder, sweet memories to recall of loved ones, family members, and friends who have departed this life.

Father, the good things of the past will always fill the sacred chamber of our hearts. Each passing day compels us into a closer relationship with you. A new year is dawning with new memories to embrace.

Let's mark off the calendar days as they are gone and leave behind a trail that will help others know of God's great love. This is a new year with our commitments to God, to love Him with all of our hearts, deep devotion, and for each of us to lift up our cross high for His glory.

We do not know what each day will hold, whether sunshine or rain, sadness or joy, Jesus walks beside us. Let us rejoice in His loving-kindness for He will not leave nor forsake us to walk the trail alone. Give us grace for this year so that the memories of the past will be a trail of godly living that extends to the throne room of Glory. Help us to realize a new year begins with the pages unturned. In Jesus' name, amen.

The Miry Clay
January 2

We need to visualize for just a moment the destructive force of sin in our lives. The Bible refers to sin as the miry clay. We are standing in the middle of this miry clay, trying desperately to get to higher ground. Little children as well as adults have sins and we all need forgiveness.

When sin first began in our lives, we were standing in a shallow area of the clay. At first our sins were small and we did not think they could cause us any harm. Even little sins hindered us from walking and breaking free from the strong grip of the clay. All sins are dangerous with disastrous effects.

As it continued to rain, we found that it was impossible to escape by ourselves. It appears to me that we were in danger of losing our lives unless someone would rescue us from this horrible death tragedy.

Father, as sinners, we are sinking more every day. Whether we are in shallow clay with the beginning of sin or we've gone deeper into the mire the heavy weight of sin is dragging us down, we need a Savior.

Jesus is patiently waiting and listening for the distress calls of repentant hearts. Only a little time left before the sins of corrupt hearts emerge our lives into a perilous place of torment. Take hold of the Savior's hand and be set free.

Call upon the Lord; He will hear our earnest pleas and forgive us of our sins. The moment we believe, He saves us. This is a wonderful time to rejoice with sins forgiven.

Lord, Jesus, come into our hearts and lift us out of the miry clay. It is a blessed day in our lives when our sins are forgiven. There is still a little bit of time to make things right with God. Please heed the warning; soon it will be too late. Now is a good time to say, "Thank you, Jesus, amen."

Reset the Clock
January 3

There are many times when a storm will come through the area and disrupt the power for many hours, days, or even weeks. Tornados, windstorms, or other natural disasters can cause these power failures. These power outages can last a very long time. The length of time will vary in a more severe storm.

When the power has been restored, lights come back on, clocks are reset, and life goes back to the normal routine. Now we come to the place where all of these reset times will not help us in our desire to make heaven our home if death has come for a visit. It is impossible for us to reset the clock and go back in time to a more convenient place.

When we are laid in the grave there is no resetting the clock. We cannot go back to the time when the Lord was dealing with our hearts. The expiration of life has no return date.

Plenty of time is a false commitment that fades away when life comes to an end. Thoughts from the grave, "I wish I had time to change my mind and believe in Jesus." No doubt there are many in the graves that would like to reset the clock, go back to the hour of God's redeeming power. This is not a make-a-wish foundation to backtrack in time.

Father, help us to realize that plenty of time is not an extension of God's grace, but it is a false hope of receiving salvation at a later time. Today is the accepted time. Many sorrowful regrets, if we fail to change our minds and accept Christ into our hearts. Please accept Him now.

If we reject Jesus as Lord and Savior, all of the time in the world will not help us if we go to the grave without Christ in our lives. We need to respond immediately to the conviction of the Holy Spirit. The time is now to reset our spiritual clocks. Let's make things right with God while we are alive. It will be too late if the light has gone out. In Jesus' name, amen.

23

Asleep on Guard Duty,
January 4

We know that Jesus is soon coming in the clouds of glory. No one knows the day or hour of His appearing. When He comes, we do not want to be found sleeping on our watch. It would be a terrible thing to wake up and realize we have missed the Rapture.

When Jesus comes again, the sweet harmony of hallelujah will rise and the gates of heaven will open for all the faithful believers. Will He find us asleep or wide-awake to rejoice in the resurrection power?

It is time to get ready! Please remove all do not disturb signs. Jesus is waiting to hear our hearts pleas. Some of the sleepers are unaware that Jesus will soon appear and the Kingdom of God they will forfeit.

We don't know when He is coming, but if we have made peace with God, as long as we are not sleeping, living careless, sinful lives; we will rejoice in the resurrection power. His command is to watch and pray.

Suppose our love for God has faded and we are no longer following Jesus. Please don't despair; the call from Heaven is the same, "Repent." Join with the saints and martyrs of old and be ready to meet Jesus in the clouds. Asleep on guard duty is a serious preventable crime.

Father, we don't want to be sleeping on guard duty when you have commanded us to watch and pray. If you happen to notice that our eyelids are about to close and our heads are bobbing back and forth, please tap us on the shoulder, or give us a little nudge. Perhaps stronger force is needed to stir-up our slumbering souls. Whatever it takes to arouse us from sin, to wake us up to the prospects of heaven, grant it now, we pray in Jesus' name, amen.

The Hourglass
January 5

Let's take a close look at an hourglass and see how it represents our lives. Particles of sand in an hourglass move ever so slowly to record the time. They are not in a hurry. There will not be an alarm when the final grain falls into the bottom of the chamber. The hourglass will certainly lose its power if the glass is not turned every hour.

Watch the sand as it falls. It only takes a few minutes for the eyes to close in a life of boredom. Time is so precious. The grains of sand will fall until the last. Life will be no more when the earthly hour is past. No one is promised another day. Accept Christ before it is too late to pray.

Jesus commanded us to watch and pray. This will not be a life of boredom, but of the glorious hope of meeting Jesus in the sky. There will be joy unspeakable and full of glory when Jesus comes again. The particles of sand in an hourglass slowly pass. Soon they will be gone.

If our eyes have not closed in death, there is still time to repent. Call upon the Lord. He is not very far from each of us. Sins need to be confessed. God will hear all the cries for mercy of repentant sinners.

Sand in an hourglass is only for an hour. Peace with God is for eternity. The day is coming to an end. A strong ticking heart grows fainter. Soon it will be time to meet the Master. Christ in our lives will be a time of rejoicing in heaven.

Father, an hour of our time is so little to spare. There are twenty-four hours in a day. We do not know which hour will be the last. Our lives may expire before the glass is turned. One earthly hour or a few minutes in sincere repentance equals eternal life, last chance to repent. Jesus, come into our hearts and forgive us." This is what He wants to hear before the hourglass is turned for the last time. Thank you, Jesus, amen.

Rockslide
January 6

We need to be looking up for Jesus is coming back to earth. When He comes, we want to be ready to leave this world. Those who are waiting for Him will rejoice at His appearing because they know it is time to go home.

Also, we need to be aware of the danger if we are not looking for His return. When we look toward the skies, we are not always going to have a pleasant experience. A storm may cause us to run for our lives. There are times when we have had to run to a shelter, hoping that we would survive the storm. Unpreparedness is a time of deep sorrow and regret.

Let's just say that a storm had recently come through the area and the ground was saturated with water. We were stranded in a valley and we had to climb a steep embankment in order to get to a safer place.

The storm was over, but we were not yet out of danger. It was very possible that a mudslide would bring huge rocks down on top of us and we would all lose our lives. This is a time when we all had to be looking up and making sure the rocks had not started to come down the mountain in a mudslide. Alertness will help us to survive this ordeal.

Sometimes when we look up, we see storm clouds and hear the roar of thunder. After a while the rain causes a rockslide. If we are not looking up, huge boulders will come down the mountainside. Our fate will be a grave on a hill unless we can get out of the path of tumbling rocks.

Father, help us to be aware of the rockslide of sin that will interfere with our heavenly journey. If we keep our eyes on Jesus, soon we will be walking the streets of glory. We can avoid the mudslide of sin by grace. Let's stay alert and keep looking to the skies for in a moment, in the twinkling of an eye, we shall be changed. Glory, hallelujah! In Jesus' name, amen.

In a Little While
January 7

Jesus said that "In a little while He would go away." He was referring to His ascension into heaven. Christ would be beaten with a whip, thirty-nine times, and nailed to a cross with spikes in His hands and feet. A crown of thorns would be forced upon His brow. This was a horrible way to die.

The price of sin cost Him, His life. Soon His suffering and pain would end, as He would be laid in the grave. Three days later He would rise from the dead and ascend to Heaven where he would reign as King of kings and Lord of lords.

He told the people that in a little while He was going away. We know that He was not going on a vacation or taking a trip to a foreign country. His journey would take Him far above the clouds where His Heavenly Father was waiting for Him.

Jesus kept His Word about going away and also that He would arise from the dead, and many other promises has come to pass. There is another important thing that Jesus said would happen. "I will come again and receive you unto myself that where I am, there you will be also."

The promise is given that Christ will return to earth. It won't be long now, keep holding on, we are almost home. Jesus is coming, but we have to wait a little while longer.

Father, heart-warming inspiration is to be with Christ forever. "In just a little while," we will be walking the streets of glory and praising the name of Jesus throughout eternity.

This promise is yet to be fulfilled, but the words He left behind was motivation for us to keep pressing on. Help us to realize that soon, very soon, we will feel that resurrection power when Jesus comes again. Help us to patiently wait because we know that our flight to glory is about to take place. There will not be any regrets for waiting. In Jesus' name, amen

Prepare to Meet thy God
January 8

We see how important it is to prepare for natural disasters and other life related things. If we are going on a trip in hazardous driving conditions, we know that we must prepare ahead of time so we can have a safe trip.

The weather station announced the coming of a severe winter storm. "Snow, freezing rain, and sleet will cover the highways. Driving conditions will be very hazardous! Stay off the roads if at all possible." Warnings are given to keep us safe.

This announcement was made so we could make preparation for the storm. State trucks are loaded with gravel and chemicals have been applied to the roads.

Many travelers do not have the choice of staying at home. Before the storm comes there are a few things that we need to do. A good blanket in the car will keep us warm. An emergency kit, flashlight, and even a signal alarm could save our lives.

The sleet has started coming down. Roads are slick. The car slides into the bank. The driver and family are left alone in a remote part of the country, no other cars passing by. This family was prepared with all the safety equipment for survival. They were rescued just in time.

Father, we see how necessary it is to prepare for a storm. There is something more important. We need to prepare ourselves for the day we stand before thy holy presence. It is very important that we obey all the warnings concerning our salvation. Jesus is coming and we only have a short time to prepare for that heavenly journey.

Help us to know that if we repent, our souls will be saved and this will remove the hazardous conditions of sin. We still need to proceed with caution and commit our souls to Christ so that He will keep us safe throughout life. In Jesus' name, amen.

Is it Later than we Think?
January 9

Several months ago, I was at work, patiently waiting for the hour to pass so I could go home. Time seemed to be at a complete standstill. My watch had stopped working and I was unaware of the mechanical failure. A dead battery is a good way to stop time.

Finally, I saw my co-workers at the time clock. They were in the process of leaving the plant. All of a sudden it dawned on me that my watch was broken and I was thinking that it was too early to go home. It was actually later than what I was thinking. It looks like it is time to reset the spiritual clock.

We know that Jesus is soon coming. The hour of His appearing is unknown. Do we think He will come tomorrow, or some other time in the near future? It would be a very costly mistake if we were looking for Him later in life and He came today. What if the time is later than we think and Jesus comes today? Be ready, whether it is day or night.

A decision for Christ will be made in the morning. Death comes in the middle of the night and we are still in our sins. It looks like our timepiece of being spiritually alert is on the wrong time schedule.

Think about a broken watch, which will deceive us into thinking that it is not time to go home. We wait one more hour and Jesus comes one hour earlier than expected. Our flight to glory just now left without us.

Father, help us to realize that it is almost time to go home and that Jesus is coming in the clouds of heaven. The coming of the Lord is near. Is it later than we think? I notice people are standing at the clock, waiting to go home. Help us to get in line with the faithful believers so that if Jesus comes earlier than expected, we will still catch our flight to glory. Help us to be ready with our reservation in advance. In Jesus' name, amen.

Here Today, Gone Tomorrow
January 10

We need to be aware of the changing seasons. Their time on earth will change as quickly as the wind moves from the west to the east. Calendar pages have a hard time trying to keep up.

Let's begin our journey with spring. Fresh flowers blossom for a while. We cannot go through spring without mentioning the flowers. The beautiful array of colors is a sight to behold. This is a time of enjoyment of God's beautiful creation. If only this season could stay longer.

Summer makes a grand entrance with green grass and beautiful trees on the landscape. The leaves are full grown on the trees and their display of green can be seen in the forest and along the mountain streams. This is a good time for picnics and to enjoy family events.

Autumn wants to display her many colors. She is especially proud of her red, yellow and orange. It seems as though God took out His artist brush and created this beautiful picture and gave it to us to admire.

This season ends with winter's divine inspiration and it is the last season as the trees that held the leaves are left bare by the strong, winter winds. Snow on the ground and icicles sparkle in the trees. Winter has a variety of special attractions.

Father, we are aware that the seasons are here for a little while. There is no altering the course of nature. No matter how hard we try, we cannot prevent one season from changing its length of stay. Our lives are also on a time schedule.

We have walked through the four seasons and found one thing they all have in common. Our lives are just like all the seasons, here today and gone tomorrow. Please don't wait until tomorrow to repent. Life fades at an unknown hour. Accept Christ today while there is time. In Jesus' name, amen.

Goodness and Mercy
January 11

We are thankful for God's great love and mercy that always abounds in our lives. Two of His best representatives were chosen to follow and keep us safe from the enemy. These two companions help to build character with deeds of loving kindness. Welfare for our souls is God's main concern.

Because of their vigilance and devotion to God, souls have been reclaimed and peace restored. "Goodness and Mercy," remember their names for they will follow us all through life. As we wake up in the morning to meet with friends, peace abides where love is manifest.

Let's take a brief look at some of their qualities and we will be so glad that they are following us. Goodness is honesty, so it also must be trustworthy. This faithful companion helps us to keep our hearts pure.

Mercy is divine favor when Christ paid the price for our sins. He died in our place so we can have life. The debt we owed was paid at Calvary. Mercy is compassion for the offenders (sinners) and that would be all of us. Because of the mercy and love of Christ, our sins are forgiven.

Suppose goodness and mercy are not following us, we had better make sure all the doors are locked; all security measures are in place. Without these two loyal servants, our moral values will not reach the level of holiness, which is needed for our admission into Heaven.

Father, when you look down from heaven, we pray that you will find us with love in our hearts and compassion for the lost. If mercy and goodness abound in our lives, then the peace with God will prevail with divine favor from heaven. Help us to be a reflection of Christ. It is our honor and privilege to accept these faithful companions and pledge to live our lives with mercy and goodness. In Jesus' name, amen.

The Last Page
January 12

Suppose we were granted space in a book to tell about our life's story. We only have a small amount of space in this book as other authors have also been assigned a few pages to give their final expressions of life. This will be a time to magnify Christ.

I know this is not a reasonable request for us to forfeit the entire book and just be allowed some of the pages to tell our life's story. It certainly feels like we are being cheated of our lifetime existence. Other authors have had whole books to talk about their lives, from the time of birth to their death. High honors should be accepted with sincere humility.

We are thankful that you have given us some space to share our final words in life. This is a time that we need to be very thoughtful and choose very carefully the words that we want to leave behind.

The beginning of this story we had a chapter to give a final review. Soon our last words became a page and then two words. Our most sincere thoughts were taken from us. God knew the last two words, "I forgive," would be sufficient to cover a lifetime and that a Life with Christ would be revealed. There is no better way to end this story.

Father, what could we say in two words that would reflect a living Savior in our hearts? This is a good time to remember the teachings of Jesus and how that He taught us about forgiveness. We do not need a whole book or even a page, but two words will fully express our deep devotion to Christ. "I forgive." Other authors are still writing and no honor in sight.

This is what Jesus prayed on the cross, "Father, forgive them." Help us to learn the lesson of forgiveness so that our life's story will be revealed in our last two words, "I forgive." In Jesus name, amen.

A Time to Fast
January 13

We need to learn the lesson of how fasting can supply our spiritual nourishment for our souls. The windows of heaven are always open to give us a fresh supply of grace. There are times when our spiritual lives suffer because we do not take the time to have fellowship with God.

A time to fast is a really good time to get in touch with our heavenly Father and to draw closer to Him. The body will become weak for lack of food. We will be stronger spiritually and the Holy Spirit will touch us. God will bless us abundantly with grace. Prayers ascend to heaven.

Let us take a good look at our spiritual relationship with God to examine our spiritual health. God's blessings are truly bountiful in our lives, as He supplies all of our needs according to His riches in glory. There are times when our spiritual lives suffer because we do not take the time to be with Him. Sincere hearts are revived by a holy touch.

If we really want to have good nutrition and a healthy relationship with God, we need to give up a little food, walk away from the table, and receive an extra helping of God's loving kindness and mercy. A plate left empty can lead to a life full of grace and unwavering love.

Father, today is a good day for a fast. We are thankful for the menu with all the nutrients for our spiritual health. There are many wonderful blessings that are on the list today. Whatever we choose, we know that goodness and mercy will prevail. Praise is offered to Him.

A helpful serving of your great love will compel us to draw closer to you. We are thankful for this fast, a fresh refilling of grace, fellowship with God, and abounding love for all of eternity. It appears to me that we just received a full meal. Thank you, Jesus, amen.

Adoption in Process
January 14

Sometimes Jesus makes unexpected visits. If we knew the time of His arrival, our homes would be clean and all unsanitary items would be hidden in the closet or a convenient place where they could not be found. The Bible would be on display.

We don't know when Jesus is coming to spend some personal time with us, but let's just suppose He is coming today. I can just see us working frantically to clean the house, but our souls are His main concern.

Now all we can do is wait and hope that Jesus will be impressed with all of our hard work. This may be a day of extreme disappointment. Jesus is not coming to admire a beautiful home or check on the outward appearance of our lives. There will be no grief today; sins are gone.

When He comes and stands at the door of our hearts, let's invite Him to come inside. We want to make Him welcome because He will introduce us to His Father and if He accepts us, we will become His adopted children.

Father, help us to realize that when Jesus comes for a visit, it will be for a professional cleaning, paid for by His sacrificial love. This visit will not be as a building inspector or someone who appreciates the beauty of a home or garden.

After we have a thorough heart searching and realize that we are sinners, the soul cleansing process begins and Jesus' precious blood cleans and sanctifies our lives. As God's adopted children, we will receive our inheritance in heaven and all the benefits of a glorified life.

When the adoption process is complete, God gives us a loving embrace and welcomes us into His family. Help us to realize that when we invite Jesus into our lives and He forgives our sins, we have the blessed hope of going to heaven.

It is Suppertime
January 15

We know that Jesus has gone to heaven and that very soon we will sit down at the table, as it will be suppertime. Everything is being prepared and soon all things will be ready.

Jesus gives the invitation to come to the banquet, but there are some of the non-believers that do not respond to the call, even though they are called many times. After a while the door will be shut permanently.

Lord, we pray that you will continue to deal with their hearts and draw them by the Holy Spirit. We don't want anyone who could have a reserved seat at the table to miss heaven because of sin. Please accept Him before the invitation expires.

It's only a matter of time when the Lord of Glory will call to the saints of God. "It's suppertime." All those who received an invitation and responded with faithfulness to the Master's call will be in the presence of the King. Sinners saved by grace will be rejoicing with thankful hearts for His mercy.

All things are ready. Imagine for a moment sitting at the table, knowing that we have entered into the kingdom of heaven and Jesus is beginning to serve. This is a time of sincere devotion, love, and honor.

Father, give us a vision of the glories of heaven. Listen to the angels sing; join in the heavenly choir with words of "Glory, Glory." The voice of praise is a sweet melody that will be heard throughout eternity. Songs of mercy will stir up our souls with thankful hearts and reverence to God.

Is it possible that we are so close to the Rapture that the evening meal is being prepared for us? Listen, Jesus is calling, "It's suppertime." There is no need to check the mailbox for an invitation. All correspondence will be on a personal basis. In Jesus' name, amen.

Compassion for the Homeless
January 16

We need to be considerate of others, as there may come a time when we are begging for bread. The story is about a homeless man that came begging for food. Since he did not have a job or any financial way of taking care of himself, he had to wear clothes that he got out of the dumpster.

The owner of the grocery store where he was begging, turned him away because his appearance was degrading and the owner thought this downcast of society would affect his business. Lack of respect is not good for customer relations.

This poor man turned away and walked toward the park bench where he had slept so many times. It was very unlikely that he would live through the night, as a cold, winter wind was blowing. He was also starving for lack of food.

As the store clerk watched the man disappear out of sight and perhaps for the last time, an overwhelming since of guilt gripped at the clerk's heart. Sometimes a conscience will help us do the right thing and lives will be affected eternally.

He found the homeless man shivering beneath a box. This would have been his shelter on this freezing, cold night. Soon both men were back at the store, enjoying a hot meal together. This was a time of rejoicing because the poor man's family was found and soon he would be living with them. Sentimental emotions have a way of bonding us together.

The Bible gives us a very good remedy for the inconsiderate feelings we may have for the less fortunate. "Do unto others as we would have them do unto us."

Father, we may not ever have an experience like the homeless, but we ask you to implant in our hearts, compassion that overflows with love for all of humanity, regardless of their situation. In Jesus' name, amen.

To Stay or Go
January 17

Death will come for a visit. This is a time in our lives that we do not want this visitor to come to our homes. When he comes, we do not have a choice whether we go with him or stay with the family. Resistance will not help us in any way.

His coming will be unannounced, no doorbells ringing, he will not stand outside our homes and wait patiently for the doors to open. When he comes, all of our security devices will not keep him away from us.

Locks on the doors will only stop those of the physical nature and robbers with evil intent. There is not an alarm system that will give us a warning of deaths approaching hour. High security will not protect us.

It is very important that we make a decision for Christ while we are living. When we die, there will not be any more chances to make things right with God. There are many choices we make in life, but death is not one of them. I am speaking of natural death not controlled by any human affects. Life eternal is just one choice and that is to accept Jesus.

I would say that all of us have had someone in our families that have had to go through the valley of death, maybe a father or mother, brother or sister, or even a child. The list covers a multitude of people that have departed this life. None of them had the choice of staying with the family. Graveyards would be empty if death could be denied.

Father, there are many choices we have in life. All of us will have to go through the valley of the shadow of death. We do not decide if we continue life's journey. The choice is not ours, whether to stay or go. When it is our time to go and if Christ is our Savior, we will follow Him to the hills of glory. Help us to realize we cannot choose our death hour, but we can choose life eternal in Christ. In Jesus' name, amen.

Clock on the Wall
January 18

Jesus is soon coming in the clouds of glory. Through the years of countless ages, the faithful followers of Christ have been looking to the sky for His return. The expectation of meeting Jesus in the clouds of glory is our present hope.

When Jesus ascended into heaven, two messengers of God said to the people, "Why stand ye gazing into heaven? This same Jesus, which is taken up from you into heaven, shall so come in like manner" (Acts 1:11). Sorrowful hearts rejoice at the thought of seeing Jesus again.

The coming of the Lord is at an unknown hour. This information is not even given to the angels. Before we can meet Jesus in the sky, we must repent of our sins. Unrepentant hearts will be a time of great sorrow.

If the thief had known when the family would be out of town, He would patiently watch the clock on the wall until it was the right time to break-in to the residence and then he would steal the valuable assets.

Suppose the family members came home earlier than expected and found a burglar in their home. Policemen would be called and the person arrested for his crimes.

If he were on death row, the clock on the wall would be a dreadful thing. Every hour that passed meant that the criminal had one less hour to live. Without a pardon, he would die.

We do not have to approach the death hour with fear, or dread the time, as Jesus, your Son has already made a way of escape. A pardon is available for all of us if we will just accept it, but we have to repent. Father, help us to see the clock on the wall as a time of great rejoicing and of everlasting life. Jesus is soon coming in the clouds of heaven for the forgiven. Thank you, Jesus, for the pardon of our sins, amen.

The Train is Leaving
January 19

We think about our journey to heaven and we want to make sure all of our travel arrangements are made in advance. Christ paid for the flight-fare with His precious blood. Accept Him now for salvation's transaction to be complete.

There are times in life when we could miss a train, bus, or some other transportation method. It would really be a terrible time to be left behind. If this were our final opportunity, the effect on our lives would be devastating, a traumatic experience indeed because of negligence.

We know that Jesus is coming in the clouds of glory. He will be returning for those who are saved by grace. Our flight to glory is leaving pretty soon. If we are not ready, we will be left behind and we will have to forfeit our inheritance in Heaven. Eternal life will be denied.

Some people will say, "I didn't know He was coming today. Why didn't someone tell me so I could be ready?" Travel with me a short distance back in time and we will remember the sermons at church and our family members pleading with us to make things right with God.

Father, we pray that you will send down a few reminders to help those who have forgotten the many opportunities they had to make peace with you. Also, we would like for you to give them a fresh invitation to remove all doubt of any past experiences. Accept Christ today while there is a little time.

A son was trying to catch the train. Finally, his dad reached out and grasped the hand of his son and brought him safely onto the passenger train. Help us to realize that the son could have been left behind. We know that even now, you are reaching down to save our souls. Please help us to take hold of your hand before our flight to glory has come and gone. In Jesus' name, amen.

Our Journey's End
January 20

There are certain times in our lives when we come to the end of our journey. The people on a wagon train had to cross over mountains and rugged terrain to get to their destination. Along the way there would be many days of distressful times, but it would be worth it all to cross that last river.

Those that started on this journey knew that there would be a strong possibility that all of them would not make it to their new homes. The vision of life motivates us to press onward.

Sadness and sorrow was a grief that some of them would have to endure, as their loved ones would be buried along the way. Little children and adults left behind with cross-markers as their final respects.

This was a journey that would bring the hope of a new life. Amid the hardships there would be many days of happiness where the travelers celebrate a rough river crossing, or getting over a rugged mountain. The joy would fill each person's heart as they drew closer to their new homes. Anticipation arises in our hearts of crossing that last mountain.

There will come a time when we come to the end of our journey. None of us know when our days on earth will end. Our length of stay is unknown. Today may be our last.

Father, help us to realize that on this journey there will be days of hardship, disappointment, discouragement, and even days of sorrow. These are the mountains and rivers that we must overcome; faith will prevail.

We also are on a journey that as we follow Jesus, soon we will be in our new homes in heaven. Some of the mountains will be just as difficult to climb and the rivers even more treacherous than those in the pioneer days, but it won't be long and we will cross that last river. Keep pressing on! In Jesus' name, amen.

Solid Rock Foundation
January 21

We need to be aware that an expensive foundation is not necessarily the best one. When building a foundation, the only one that will keep us safe in all of life's situations is the one where Christ lives in our hearts.

The story is told of two couples that had to choose a mansion that was built with the best materials or a home that had a solid rock foundation. The first couple chose the mansion; this was no surprise as the grandeur and splendor of this home would give anyone bragging rights.

There was only one other choice, but for the second couple, they would have chosen the foundation home as their first choice. Both couples were exceedingly happy with their new homes. However, some of the people wanted to know why the less expensive home was a better deal.

Before they could answer, storm clouds burst and the rain drenched the earth. The expensive, beautiful home fell and great was the fall of it. This was a happy ending for one couple, but a terrible one for the other.

Each of us has a choice in life. The foundation we choose will determine where we spend eternity. A house built on the sand of sinful living will fall. A house that is built by faith on a rock foundation will withstand all the storms of life. There is only one foundation that will keep us safe in the storm and that is Jesus Christ, God's only Son.

Father, when we are asked, why Jesus? The answer is quickly given, as the storm clouds rise and our dependence on any other will collapse into the tidal wave of sin. We know that the weak foundation of sin will fall while grace abounds to all generations. Help us to realize that our lives built on the Rock of Ages will still be standing when the storm is over. Choose Christ for eternal benefits in heaven. In Jesus' name, amen.

Born Again
January 22

We know about a natural birth when a child is born. Most newborn infants are born in a hospital. Life comes into existence at birth. Duration of life varies from one person to the next.

Somewhere along the pathway of life that person needs to be born again. A spiritual birth will occur when our hearts are made right with God. This happens when our sins are confessed and we believe on the Lord Jesus. The requirement time for us to be saved is before death.

He forgives us and from that day forward, each of us has a new life in Christ. We are born of the Spirit and the precious blood of Christ washes our sins away. No candles will be on a cake for this celebration.

The beginning of life is when a little baby takes its first breath. Our earthly birth reveals that we were born of the flesh. Natural birth happens only one time in life. Being born again is when we are born of the Spirit. This happens later in life as a second birth when we repent and Jesus saves us. Re-birth certificates are not required for anyone.

Children and adults have experienced this wonderful time in their lives when Jesus came into their hearts. Jesus told Nicodemus, "Ye must be born again." "Nicodemus saith unto him, "How can a man be born when he is old? Can he enter the second time into his mother's womb, and be born?"

Father, when we are born again, we then have the blessed hope of going to Heaven. "Old things are passed away and behold all things are become new." This birth gives us a new birthright of being adopted children, heirs of God, and joint heirs with Jesus Christ. God our Father welcomes us with a holy embrace into the family. Help us now to live godly, holy lives. In Jesus' name, amen.

The Last Amen
January 23

There will come a time in our lives when the final words will be spoken. We think about all the people who have departed this life. Daily reading from a loved ones Bible is no longer heard. A personal Bible is closed and the holy pages will not bee turned as in the past. It is so hard to say goodbye.

His precious words that guided us along the pathway will remain silent, as our journey on earth has ended. Family members will remember how much joy we received in reading God's Holy Bible.

The words that Jesus spoke was always a comfort to our hearts, but the words in red will not be heard by family members. Surely our lives were blessed to know Jesus as our personal Savior. He is still calling, "Follow me."

Friends and neighbors will think about all the love and devotion to a loving, caring God. They will remember the kindness and gentleness of Spirit that flowed from our lives like a river overflowing the banks.

The Bible will be closed for a temporary time in memory of a faithful follower of Jesus Christ, but only for a short while, as there will be others that need the same guidance from above. They will find that the Bible is the book of life and all those who believe its sacred contents will have the blessed hope of life eternal in Christ Jesus our Lord.

Father, before the book is closed for the last time and we are about to say our last amen, help all those around us to know that life ends on earth with amen. But glory, and hallelujah will be heard on the streets of glory from everlasting to everlasting. There will be rejoicing in the Kingdom of God as a born-again believer walks through heaven's gate. Let our final words be of praise, glory, and honor to our Savior. In Jesus' name, the last word is spoken, amen.

No Promise of Tomorrow
January 24

There are many things in life that we plan on doing tomorrow. Our salvation should not be considered a future event as none of us are promised another day. Calendar days are not fulfilled when death makes an unexpected visit.

We are allowed a little bit of time on this earth to make things right with God. If we are walking too slowly, and not in a hurry to accept Christ in our lives, we may find that our day of repentance has come and gone. Too many rejection notices on the door keep us out of heaven.

When Jesus speaks to our hearts and the Holy Spirit draws us, our response to Him should not be, "please, don't bother us today as there is still plenty of time." Later, a knocking at the door, death wants to enter.

The young and the old have departed this life. Accept Jesus at a later time is a false delusion with no hope of everlasting life if we keep rejecting Christ in our lives. If today ends without repentance, tomorrow morning may be a time of deep regret and extreme anguish.

Conviction may be in our lives today, but what about tomorrow? Some people have put off their salvation and they would gladly welcome another opportunity to make things right with God. How many have said tomorrow when today was their last? Just one person is too many.

Please don't wait too long as the sun is beginning to set. We may need to walk a little faster. No decisions will be made from the grave. Things we could do tomorrow may be a costly mistake. Call upon Him and He will make hast to deliver. It is a blessed time in our lives to hear the call of the Master, "Come unto me." Our response is urgently needed, as the days of our lives are coming to an end. Accept Christ while there is still a little time. In Jesus' name, amen.

Fading Clouds
January 25

We are thankful that God has given us another day to enjoy the sunshine. Our thoughts today are about the clouds of how they are seen for a little while and then they are gone.

They are the forecasters of all the weather conditions. Help us to be aware that sometimes they make a special appearance to help us in all types of situations. These airborne travelers are like warning detectors.

If there is a fire emergency, they might be found hovering above the flames waiting for an opportunity to release the rain. Storm burst has saved many a forest or homes from being burnt to the ground.

Another circumstance is in the wintertime when the clouds will not be satisfied until there is a fresh coating of snow on the ground, bringing hazardous driving conditions. We are truly blessed when the sun shines, melting the snow and bringing clear blue skies just to let us know it is safe to drive. Snow clouds invite the skiers to the mountain slopes.

Today we think about the clouds that represent our lives. They also come with a warning of how quickly our time on earth is only for a season. No one knows how long life will last. Whether we are here a few days or many years, life will come to an end, as the clouds disappear.

The time clouds follow us everywhere we go. The danger comes when they drift away. These clouds are not really harmful to us. They just represent our lives. Here for a little while and then they are gone.

Father, these fading clouds can also tell another story beyond the gloom of despair. If Jesus is our Savior, the traveling clouds remind us that it won't be long until we will be with Jesus in our new home in Heaven. Thank you, Jesus, amen.

Heaven or Hell
January 26

Sometimes, we go back down memory-lane to think about when Jesus Christ came into our hearts. This is one of those times and I want you to help me share my story so others can be rescued from the flames. A sixty second warning is given for Heaven or Hell.

My wife and I were in Sunday school class and the teacher gave a warning about the Titanic ship. She told the story in such a way that we would think about the collision with the iceberg and how the passengers and the crew could have been saved if they had turned the ship around.

The teacher said that the captain received a call several times warning them to turn around. Each time the call was rejected and the Great Titanic moved closer to the horrific accident. We learned that Jesus wants us to turn our lives around today; tomorrow may be too late.

Think about the warning and collision with the iceberg. Lives could have been saved if there were more lifejackets and boats. The reason the ship sank in the ocean was because of all the wrong decisions. When warnings are given of Heaven or Hell, we must respond immediately.

Father, we need to accept Jesus in our hearts or we will be on a collision course with hell. Normally I would attend Sunday school class but that morning my wife and I stayed for the morning worship service. An Evangelist was speaking that day; he was talking about God's love and mercy. His sermon was just about over and the service would be dismissed so we could go home. He gave us a choice of Heaven or Hell.

Jesus came into my heart and saved my soul. Many years has gone by since the Lord saved me and I am still thankful for that one-minute countdown. How can we escape if we keep walking toward the flames? Jesus is the only way, amen.

Spiritual Treasure
January 27

We will search today for a treasure that will enrich our lives beyond any earthly prosperity. Our mission is to find a spiritual treasure. A treasure map is not necessary for eternal reasons. Heaven's valuable resource is to find Jesus.

Peace, joy, happiness, these valuable treasures are found in a person's life. There are people in all walks of life that have these special gifts. We will find these treasures amongst the poor as well as the rich. The healthy and the sick have these characteristics in their lives. Treasures of moral value will be found in repentant hearts with true forgiveness.

We are not looking for gold or silver, or any of the precious metals that are found in the earth. We are looking for things that money cannot buy. Jesus said, "My peace, I give unto you," we want everyone to know that the world did not give us peace; neither can it take it away.

The palace will be a good place to search. The king talks about all of his earthly treasures. He is very selfish and speaks with an arrogance of pride that all the riches in the palace belong to him. He had no time to live and serve God. We knew the heavenly treasure would not be found here.

There is one other place we need to search. The visual diagram shows a poor beggar's home. As our group entered his little shack, we saw a poor man sitting at a table with just a morsel of bread for his dinner.

He said grace, gave thanks, and spoke of God's love and mercy as he held his worn-out Bible. There was no gold or silver, but where grace abounds, peace always prevails.

Father, help us to realize that money is not the source of our eternal wealth. The treasure we are seeking can only be found in the love of God through Christ. Blessed be the Lord, amen.

The Chief Cornerstone
January 28

We are going back in time to the beginning of civilization. There was no modern equipment for heavy construction. Bulldozers, cranes, and backhoes had not yet been invented.

When a structure was built, huge rocks were rolled up a steep incline. They were carefully designed and each one had a special place in the pyramid. A cornerstone was the main part of the structure. All of the other stones were locked together and held fast by the chief cornerstone.

Let's think about our lives in need of a cornerstone. This stone gives the foundation stability and strength. The Bible refers to Christ as being the Cornerstone. Our spiritual relationship with God depends on Him.

There is no good reason for the cornerstone to be declined. If we are building a structure that will endure all the storms of life, we will make sure the main support system is in place. Reject the stone and a home will last as long as the sun is shining and the wind is not blowing. But let a storm come and see how quickly the structure crumbles to the earth.

If Jesus is rejected, the formation of life will be incomplete and will end in a terrible ruin and we will not be able to enter into heaven. The choice is ours; it would be a terrible mistake to reject Jesus Christ.

Father, our lives are like that structure that the men were building. Isn't it time to accept Jesus as the Chief Cornerstone? God has given us a choice; we can either accept or reject Christ into our hearts. Please don't wait too long.

Our souls are deeply troubled about those who reject Christ and we pray that they will immediately seek Him as the Chief Cornerstone of their lives before the walls come crashing down. In Jesus' name, amen.

Where will He Find us
January 29

We know that Jesus Christ is coming back to earth and we understand how important it is to be in the right place when He comes to take us back to heaven. Unscheduled travel will be in effect, as Christ will be coming at an unannounced date.

Where will He find us? Now this is a question that we need to give some serious thought. If He finds us in a corruptible place, living a sinner's life, He will not be very pleased. We will be the ones that suffer. Let's help Him find us; here am I, Lord.

The place is important, but our spiritual well-being is God's main concern. He knows the condition of each heart, whether it is sinful or full of grace. This is something that may require our prompt attention. Without Christ, heaven will be denied.

Our Lord walks the dark hills and the desolate valleys in search of sinners whom He loves with all of His heart and soul. Many fine folks would say He found them in a place of disgrace. He brought them out with love and mercy. It is sad to say, but everyone has not been found.

He has gone to many places in search of the lost. His heart is very heavy with grief for those who would not repent and invite Him into their lives. When He comes back to earth, where will He find us?

I like to think in church, worshiping God, singing songs of praise, and rejoicing in the blessed hope of life eternal. Other places of interest would be at the altar praying, or at home reading the Bible with the family and talking about Jesus, His sacrificial love for us at Calvary.

Father, we are really concerned about those who have not yet invited Jesus into their hearts. Wherever, He finds us, I pray that our hearts will be right with God and that heaven's travel arrangements will be in order. In Jesus' name, amen.

Our Heart's Desire
January 30

Christ love is an everlasting love. His marvelous grace touches our lives and inspires us to use our talents with compassion to help others on the pathway of life.

We know the greatest need of our loved ones and friends is to know Jesus Christ as Lord and Savior. The depths of our hearts reveal a loving Savior who forgives sins. Blessings are given for us to share so that we can help one another.

Souls need to be saved before the midnight hour. Our desire is to walk uprightly, hold the cross high for God's glory and live in such a way that He will be pleased to call us His children, sons and daughters.

My good friends gather around the campfire with me. We will share our stories and sing songs of praise. Testimonies of God's grace will inspire us to live closer to Him. Talents used are turn-around favors. Love is passed on by our endeavors.

The words of praise continue as each person uses his or her talents to glorify God. There is one thing special about a talent; each one is specially crafted by the Master Craftsman and assigned to a certain individual, no two talents are the same. God's creative works is His signature design in us.

Father, help us to realize that when we use our talents to express our love and devotion to you, souls will be blessed and the sweet Holy Spirit will bring conviction on the unsaved and inspiration for the Christians.

Gifts from above will be like a shower from heaven with grace flowing like a river, touching all those that see and hear his marvelous works. We pray that our hearts desire will be to encourage and help others know of your great love and Jesus as Lord and Savior. Bless us as we commit our lives to service, using our talents for your glory. In Jesus' name, amen.

Expiration date
January 31

We realize that our time on earth will soon expire like a driver's license or a credit card, except this will be a permanent closure in our lives. Before the death hour comes we must find Jesus. He is the only one that can give us a new registration with our names written on the pages of eternity.

It is really easy to renew our cards through a business agency or have our identifications upgraded to a more efficient date. The normal process is for these business associates to send us a letter or notification of the time of expiration. Cards that are expired have no real value.

They also tell us the best way for us to go through this renewal process and they give us information on how we can contact them. There are usually a few choices such as, telephone, email, or even a personal letter.

Once we go through the process our personal information is restored and our lives are back on a normal routine. We can drive our cars without any danger of receiving a ticket or being arrested for driving with a canceled expiration date. No one likes to make an appearance in court with an angry judge. A remedy for this problem would have been timely renewals.

The problem of fixing this termination date can be easily resolved, but there is something far more important and that is the expiration date of our lives. It is too late if our names appear in an obituary column. Our response is urgently needed before any eternal reservations can be made in heaven.

Father, there may be some people here that are newcomers to the spiritual aspirations of heaven. They have not pre-registered for any spiritual benefits. While some backsliders are on the borderline of life. We pray that all new applications and renewals will receive an expiration date of life eternal that never expires in Jesus' name, amen.

God is Never Too Busy
February 1

Our heart's plea today is that we want to pay a little visit. Sometimes we are lonely and we just want to draw closer to you. We know that if we approach the throne room of mercy, the welcome mat will (literally) be placed outside and we will be greeted with a loving embrace.

There is never a time that we came knocking at the door and the angel said, "Come back at another time, I'm sorry, but He has more important things to do today." Sometimes angels need to be disciplined.

He is not on a journey or taking a vacation. God is on the throne, listening attentively to all the request of His adopted children. Arrangements are also made for new adoptees. While we are yet speaking, the answers to our prayers are being delivered from above.

We don't have to stand in line and wait hours for Him to hear us, as we do sometimes with the telephone system. The answering machine will put us on hold and keep us there until we get tired of waiting and then in frustration we hang up.

Our God is ever present to help in time of need. His love is great toward us and He takes the time to hear our heart-felt prayers, even while controlling the affairs of the universe with divine grace. He is not too busy for our personal lives. "Call unto me and I will answer thee."

Father, The Bible tells us to cast all of our cares upon you. The warehouse is full and ready to supply our needs. We are not left on hold and kept in a waiting room with a number to be called. Love always abounds and you take the time to hear each of our heart-felt prayers. Help us to realize that you are ever present and always ready to give a loving embrace. Whether we have a need or we just want to praise you, God is never too busy to hear our hearts pleas, amen.

Settled Last Night
February 2

Many years have passed since I read this story. I cannot remember a lot of the things that happened or the words that were written. This message from a gospel tract touched my heart. If you don't mind I would like to tell it in my own words.

A man who worked in the mines went to church one night. He was seeking something far more precious than gold. This would be his final search as there would be no more opportunities to attend a place of worship.

This man was not a Christian. He was carrying a heavy burden in his heart that only Jesus could help him. Whatever was bothering him had to be settled that night. Conviction will not always wait until tomorrow.

The minister preached his sermon. It was no doubt a message with an urgent warning to repent, as no one knows when life will end. He gave an altar call. This young man walked down the aisle to the altar. Some of the church members went with him and they prayed together for a really long time. Salvation comes when we earnestly seek forgiveness.

He prayed into the early hours of the morning and finally his faith brought peace as he believed in Jesus Christ. Earnest prayer comes with rejoicing when we make peace with God.

The next day he went to work in the mine and there was a terrible accident. A section of the mine caved in, and this young man was killed. "Thank God, it was settled last night." A decision for Christ may be too late tomorrow. Yield to the Holy Spirit, as there is no promise we will live another day.

Father, help us to realize that there are some decisions in life that cannot wait until tomorrow. Salvation is one of them. We need to be like the miner who earnestly sought God the night before his tragic death. Accept Him now, in Jesus' name, amen

Waiting for the Day
February 3

There is coming a day when Jesus is coming back to earth. When He comes, this will be a glorious time in our lives if Jesus is our Lord and Savior.

Jesus told the people that He would rise from the dead and we are His witnesses that He is alive; we know He lives because He lives in our hearts, as our Savior. Another promise is yet to be fulfilled and that is why we are patiently waiting for His return. Since Jesus came into our lives, we have an earnest expectation of being with Him in glory.

Jesus kept His promise and arose from the dead. The tomb is empty. There is only a little time left before Jesus fulfills the promise of coming again. It would be very wise for us to be waiting for His return.

Hurry up and wait, I can remember this from my Army days. Rise early in the morning and rush off to a special place. We had to be there on time or face the consequences of a mad drill sergeant. I don't believe anyone liked doing pushups.

It did not take us long to learn the basic skills of being on time. Army discipline also taught us to wait. When the time had finally arrived, we saw that waiting had some good benefits. Going home is probably the most rewarding event.

I remember waiting for my time to go home from Vietnam. The flight was on time and soon I would be with my family. Truly it was a wonderful blessing when I walked into my parent's home. Let's be ready for our next homeward journey.

Father, we have the blessed hope of going to our home in Heaven. Help us to wait a little while longer. It will be a wonderful time in our lives when we trade our cross for a crown. Being fully persuaded that we shall walk the streets of glory. Prepare to meet thy God, in Jesus' name, amen.

White as Snow
February 4

This morning we woke up to a beautiful work of art. It all started last night with the clouds moving slowly across the sky. All across the land as the people began to wake up and look outside for the first time. They were simply amazed at this beautiful winter scene. Admiration of the snow quickly fades away, as we drive to work in dangerous driving conditions.

In the dark hours of night, the snow continued to fall. The beauty of this picture could not be seen in the darkness. After a while the sun began to rise on the horizon. God gave us a beautiful snow scene to show that sins can be white as snow.

Mountains were glazed over with crystal snowflakes that glistened in the morning light. This snow was not polluted with impure substances; everything was pure white. Let's capture the beauty in a landscape portrait.

God painted a masterpiece in nature. He was not quite finished. Some of those fine folks who looked out their windows were impure and living corruptible lives. There was certainly a need for the snow-white effect.

The purification of our souls takes place at the cross. This is a good time for window-gazers to evaluate their lives to see if any impurities of sin corrupt their image. A good profile cannot be developed until sins are forgiven. Portraits of purified lives are developed by divine grace.

Father, the blood of Christ purifies and disinfects the harmful contamination of sin. If we are looking for a good portrait like the snow scene that God created, repentance will be the best snapshot taken for righteousness. Let's think for just a moment about the corruptness of our hearts. We need to have the sanctifying touch of grace to cleanse all blemishes from our lives. Help us to see the crystals of love will sparkle in our lives when Jesus is our Savior. In Jesus' name, amen.

Thaw out our Cold Hearts
February 5

The lake is frozen and the hills reveal a sparkling glaze. There is a wintry mix of snow, ice, and freezing rain. Snow keeps falling until a fresh blanket of snow is on the ground. Icicles hang on the trees causing the branches to hang low. A cold, winter breeze makes it unbearable to stay outside. The warmth of a fire will help us to survive.

Some people have got frostbite by staying too long in the bitter cold. Now we don't want anyone to lose any fingers or toes because of the bad weather conditions. We are more fearful of someone losing his or her life. Careless actions of staying outside can be hazardous to our health.

The blizzard is so bad that if anyone stays out in this horrific storm, it will be a tragic disaster as no one can survive in these freezing temperatures. This is not a good time to test our survival skills.

All of the people were warned and they were invited to come inside and warm by the fire. Many of them came out of the cold to escape the wrath of the storm. Warnings rejected can have fatal consequences.

Once they were inside this nice log home, they took off their coats and warmed by the fire. This would be a really good place to weather the storm. So, all those that came inside were thankful for this shelter. The storm continued and there was wonderful peace in each person's heart, as they stayed inside this warm home, while those outside were freezing to death.

Father, Some people continue to resist. We have to persuade them to come inside and feel the warmth of a loving, caring God. He is patiently waiting. We ask you now to please send down a warm blanket of your love to thaw out all earthly convictions. So, cold hearts will be revived and souls saved from the horrific storm of sin. In Jesus' name, amen.

When the Path Is Hard to See
February 6

An imaginary visual shows some people stranded in the desert with only a set of footprints to follow. The guide was unaware of five family members that were left behind in the windstorm. They were just a few hours away from their destination when they were separated from the group. Distress moves in very quickly with despair.

It would be very easy to get lost in the desert. Their only hope was to follow the footprints. All of the canteens were empty. It would be a terrible thing to die of thirst. Let's all remember, the place we were lost is the best place to be found.

This family continued on their survival route. They were so close to home and yet so far away. Visibility was very poor. The swirling sand from the windstorm caused the footprints to gradually fade until they were completely gone. Instead of giving up and calling it quits, this brave family pressed onward with unwavering determination. So they would be united with their group and make it safely to their home.

When there seems to be no way, God will make a way. Glimmers of light were seen in the distance and a voice was heard. A sigh of relief came over the group as the guide had returned to rescue the family.

On the pathway of life when the storms come and the path is hard to see, don't give up or quit. We are almost home. Jesus is calling, "Follow me." When Christ calls, we know that we are on the glory land way.

Father, a voice is heard through the pages of the Holy Bible. We receive instruction and guidance from the Word of God. Sometimes we cannot see the heavenly path because of our earthly vision. Faith is the best navigational compass to keep us on the right path. If the path has grown dim because of the storms of life, Jesus is still calling "Follow me." Yes, Lord.

The Pure in Heart
February 7

We are expecting a visitor from the throne room of glory. Arrangements have been made for us to have a personal encounter with God' Son, Jesus. He is not coming to condemn us of our sins. Before He leaves, conviction needs a good remedy of forgiveness.

This visit is of a friendly nature with the offering of peace and grace. Jesus would like very much for us to receive salvation. He will not force anyone to accept His love sacrifice. Forced entry denies us our free will.

A lot of chores need to be done before He comes. After several hours of hard work the house is finally clean. All of the unsanitary items are out of sight. We don't want Him to see the corruptible things in our lives.

Jesus is at the door; let's invite Him inside. There is a brief moment of hesitation and then the door is opened. This is a very special meeting. It's not every day that we have a chance to be with the Son of God. I expect all of us are probably a little nervous about the conversation; it will be personal. Private encounters with Christ have eternal benefits.

He arrives and thanks us for allowing Him to come inside of our homes. He makes a nice comment about the clean house. The talk becomes very serious as Jesus inquires about our soul's salvation of having clean and pure hearts. Friendly greetings lead to repentance.

The feeling of guilt seemed to overwhelm us. There was no hiding the unsanitary things in our lives. Finally, the heavy burden of guilt was lifted when we invited Jesus to come into our lives. Father, help us to realize if Jesus came by for a visit, would He be made welcome? We have accumulated many sins over the years. He came to purify our lives by grace. Let's not disappoint Him by retaining our sins. Forgive us, Lord, amen.

Open the Window
February 8

There comes a time in our lives when we must decide to open the window or keep it closed. I am speaking about the windows of our hearts by receiving Christ as our Lord and Savior.

An open window will be a blessed time in our lives, as sunshine from heaven will illuminate us with God's glory. We don't want to keep this window closed because without Christ in our lives, the intruders of sin will break the glass and rob us of any heavenly rewards.

Locked windows and barricaded doors with padlocks on each one will prevent us from having sweet fellowship with the Father. As long as we keep the window of our hearts closed and do not ask Jesus to forgive us, the agitators and tormentors of sin will invade our personal lives.

Let's open a new window today. This one will let the light from heaven shine upon us and we will have peace forevermore. We will receive grace that is sufficient to keep us unto life eternal. God's merciful kindness will be in abundance.

When we open the window of our hearts, sweet blessings come down from above. Jesus forgives all of our transgressions. Faith in God gives to us the blessed assurance that if Christ comes today, we will be walking the streets of glory and praising His name throughout eternity.

God's only begotten Son radiates His great love and purifies our hearts. An open window will allow heavenly sunshine with transforming grace to create in us pure, undefiled hearts, with holiness and righteousness.

Father, help us to realize that when we open the window, we will receive an abundance of grace. Today is a good time to open up our hearts, invite Jesus into our lives, and receive the blessings of heaven. In Jesus' name, amen.

Prayer Throughout the Day
February 9

We need to understand that when we begin the day in prayer, our time with you will help us to overcome any obstacles that come our way. Sweet fellowship with you gives us the assurance that we are in divine care and that grace will always abound in our lives. One prayer may not be sufficient to get us through the day. Blessings from heaven come down when we are in your presence. Prayer is the essence of daily benefits.

After a peaceful night's rest, it's time to get moving, the hours so quickly pass away. Our morning routine should be a time of prayer, seeking guidance from the Holy Spirit. Begin with prayer and have fellowship with God constantly. He will help us on the pathway of life.

Whatever our chores, the activities for the day will not wait any longer. Let's pray first and then heavenly sunshine will shine on our paths. We don't want to be running on a reserve tank. All that God has planned for us today may require a fresh refilling of being in His presence.

Lord, as we begin our daily routine to go through life with the purpose of living holy, righteous lives. We know this will be very pleasing to you. All of our endeavors in life are in direct response to our personal relationship and devout communication with God. A holy embrace binds us together and motivates us to love one another.

Living a godly life brings glory and honor to your name. It is such a wonderful blessing for us to be Christians and to know God is our Father. We come before your presence with thankful hearts for your mercy. Grace abounds throughout the day when we take the time to pray.

Father, we are so thankful that you accepted us into your family. Help us to live righteous lives so that we will live worthy of the honor of being your sons and daughters, amen.

Nothing but the Blood
February 10

We need to realize that the greatest sacrifice known to mankind was the death of your Son on a cross. He gave His life freely so our sins could be forgiven. His precious blood was spilled at Calvary. No man took His life; He gave it up freely for us.

Jesus died a horrible death by crucifixion. Blood was streaming down his cheek; His hands and feet had open wounds where the nails entered into His flesh. A crown of thorns was forced upon His brow. His death brought to Him extreme anguish as he suffered with agonizing pain.

What would a person give to save someone's life? We think about money or some worldly possession. The ultimate price was paid at Calvary when Jesus laid down His life. His love for us was far greater than any earthly treasure. He gave all that He could give when He hung on that old rugged cross.

Jesus was the only one who could die in our place as a sacrifice for us. His death on the cross was as a substitute to take our place. Think about the lashes of the whip that tore the flesh of His back, or the nails in His hands and feet, and even the crown of thorns.

My friends, we need to be aware that Jesus, God's only begotten Son took the punishment for our sins. He gave His life so we could have life eternal. Our debt of sin was paid in full.

Father, help us to realize that this sacrifice was the very best one, without spot or blemish. Jesus was referred to as the Lamb of God. He was led as a lamb to the slaughter.

His precious blood purifies our sinful lives. Without the shedding of blood there is no remission of sins. We come to you Father to accept the blood sacrifice of Christ (the Holy One of God) and receive forgiveness of sins. In Jesus' name, amen.

61

As I Have Loved You
February 11

Father, we think about your great love for us, and your Son, Jesus. If we could go back in time, we would see a baby boy had been born in a stable and laid in a manger. Oh, how everyone adored Him and brought gifts. This child would someday reign as a King.

Emotions of our hearts are deeply touched at the thought that one day your Son would bear the sins of the world. We think about your love as you look down from heaven and see this newborn infant wrapped in swaddling clothes, lying in a manger. Peace on earth is His mission.

Tears probably ran down your cheek as you thought about your Son becoming a man and dying on a cross for us. Father and Son were bound together with such a great love that nothing could separate them, not even death on a cross. Love that binds us can never be broken.

Father, we know that you love Jesus more than anyone can imagine. The love of the Son to you is equal in every way. Jesus tells us how great His love is for mankind. "As the Father hath loved me, so have I loved you." This love does not end there, "Continue ye in my love." Merciful kindness and compassion will touch many lives throughout the world.

The relationship of the Father, Son, and all of humanity is love that surpasses all understanding. This love is so great that the Universe is held in its strong grasp and there is no releasing the grip of mercy.

Father, we know that Jesus' love is great toward us, as Calvary was the place where love prevailed in obedience unto death. He wants us to love one another as the Father loved Him, so does He love us. Jesus' love for us did not end on the cross, nor was it sealed in the grave, but at the resurrection, His love in us continues down through the ages, amen.

Bread for the Homeless
February 12

The homeless among us are crying for bread. They search intently for a few morsels of food to keep from starving to death. There has been many a time when these unfortunate wanders have held up signs, begging for food. Life's struggles are to stay alive.

Policemen have found these victims of life, living in dark alleys and sleeping on park benches. The homeless live in unbearable conditions. They have to sleep in cardboard boxes and other self-made materials to escape the bitter cold. Comfortable living arrangements do not exist.

Some of these lonesome travelers have no shoes and they have to walk in the snow. Occasionally, there will be whole families that have been evicted from their homes because the rent was not paid or some other disaster came their way. The loss of everything is revived with hope.

Circumstances were beyond their control. These vagrants found themselves on the lonely streets of life because their bank account was depleted and the only thing left for them to show was empty pockets.

It would be good if we could supply all their needs and help them along the pathway of life. If a beggar happens to come our way, hungry and thirsty, please don't turn him or her away. A good meal and fresh water would be a beggar's delight. Restoration of life comes in many forms.

Father, give us a strong determination to help those in need. Our hearts desire should be to help others along the way. It should not matter if it is a homeless person, a neighbor, or anyone who is in need. We need to realize there are many souls that do not have the hope of eternal life. Salvation is needed to satisfy their poor hungry souls. Help us to share the love of God. In Jesus' name, amen.

Heaven's Gold Mine
February 13

Today is a good time for prospecting. There's not a cloud in the sky. The weather forecast is excellent. It will be sunny all day. Gold mining equipment is strictly forbidden. This treasure will not be found in the hills or deep in the earth. Picks and shovels are not required. No mules are needed to carry our valuable assets back home. Eternal riches will be found when our hearts are right with God.

We all know that earthly gold is valuable and some people will search all of their lives to find it. Many of them have labored many hours in search of this precious ore. Their final results ended in a shallow grave on a hill. Let's be careful, as earthly profit will not be heavenly gain.

Our search for heaven's treasure will not be found in a gold mine. When we seek after God's loving kindness and His mercy, our souls will be blessed throughout eternity. We definitely need to search for Jesus who is the only one that can enrich our lives with spiritual blessings from on high.

God gave each of us a measure of faith. The use of it will determine our final fate. We are not far from the true riches of heaven. When faith is in action, we will strike it rich with joy, peace, and love for eternity. Without faith, our quest for eternity is in vain like a worthless mine.

Valuable assets are taken from the earth. Silver and diamonds sparkle in the evening sun. We can be heavenly rich or earthly poor. Since we like bright, shiny objects, why not have a new star in our glory crown?

Father, when we search for you with all of our hearts, we will have joy unspeakable and full of glory. The best way to find God is to use our prospecting skills of search and find. Salvation will not be denied. Thankful hearts will rejoice when Christ is found and praise will ascend to heaven, amen.

He is Worthy of the Honor
February 14

There are many special events where people are recognized and honored for their distinct qualities of life. The military is a good place to show respect for those who are obedient in service. Those who obey orders and live honorable lives will be rewarded in the end when they leave for civilian life.

Our time in the military will end with either an honorable or dishonorable discharge. Let's think about our journey in life and we will realize that holiness brings God the glory.

Our honor today goes to one man who was obedient, even to His death on the cross. His name is Jesus, God's beloved Son. He was faithful all through life. His loving kindness still touches lives today. We all know Him by His love for us in that He would not come down from the cross, no matter how severe the pain. Faithful obedience comes with the highest honor.

He suffered and died as our substitute. The best way for each of us to honor Him is to hold up our cross high for His glory. We should love others as He loved us. We honor God in our daily lives, as we are representatives of Christ.

All of humanity is indebted to Him. He died on a cross in our place for our sins. God honors Him, "This is my beloved Son in whom I am well pleased." The Bible tells us to give praise, glory, and honor. A good way is to have thankful hearts.

If we do not repent of our sins, how can we expect to stand before a holy, righteous God? Jesus is worthy of the praise by the sacrifice He gave so that we could be saved, hallelujah.

Father, help us to realize that sinners and even people with good moral values are still on the dishonorable list if Christ is rejected. When we stand before your presence, we will be rewarded in glory according to our faithfulness, honorable, and repentant lives, in Jesus' name, amen.

Please Forgive Me
February 15

There is a time of guilt in our lives when we have hurt others, accidently or on purpose. The emotional pain we caused will not go away unless we go and tell them we are sorry. This is the healing process for them and us. An apology is offered; forgiveness is given and all individuals are healed. Acceptance of an apology is a good antidote for human relations.

When I was a teenager, I stole a soda from a family that lived about a half of a mile down the road. They had never done any wrong to me. Theft takes place for our own personal gain.

This family was highly respected in the community and they were really good neighbors. A short while later, I was walking towards home and I had to pass this family's home. There was a woman on the porch, ironing clothes. My conscience was beginning to bother me. Guilt brings stressful feelings.

As I got closer to her home, my aching heart would not let me pass up this opportunity to make things right with her. I walked over to Thelma's house and told her about the soda I had stolen. She forgave me and let me keep the money. When I walked home, there was joy in my heart. Confessions can relieve the burden and releases us from the guilt of our actions.

Father, our hearts are heavy laden with the guilt of the many things we have done wrong and we are hurting on the inside. We need a good dose of anti-inflammatory comments to prevent any further escalations so that peace will abide.

Help us to realize that there is a time of guilt in our lives when forgiveness is required to make things right with God. I remember when my sins were a heavy burden and my conscience would not let me rest until I walked down to the altar. What a wonderful day that was when I said, "Please, forgive me." We need to know a clear conscience is better than an aching heart and not as painful. In Jesus' name, amen.

The Old Sinful Town
February 16

We are going back in time to an old town where we lived for many years. This is a place where the world held our interest, earthly commitments, and sin was the controlling agent in our lives. A return visit to past sins will open wounds that are healed. When we revisit our sinful activities, we are crucifying Christ all over again. Guess who will be driving the nails?

All of us will be held accountable for our own sins. No one else is responsible for our indulgence by willful consent. I don't know everyone's story about voluntary involvement as sin affected us in many different ways. Lives yielded to sin will separate us from God and will void the adoption process.

Let's go a little deeper and find out that being in this captive environment caused us to live unholy, without righteousness, or godliness. Our vision of imprisonment would have us with unbreakable chains, no way to escape. Without God's grace, we are still in captivity. Taking a trip back in time revives old sins that should stay buried. Looking back brings deep regrets.

We said that if we ever got out of this town, we would never go back into this horrific, terrible place. Short memories need a longer life span so that we can receive a crown of glory.

Finally, we found there was a way of escape and we did not have to be bound by the shackles of sin any longer. We heard about one man who was crucified on a cross. Jesus left His home in heaven to come down to this vile sinful world. Please don't turn Him away. Resist the devil and draw nigh to God.

Father, help us to realize that the old sinful town will bring torment in our lives. Jesus arose from the dead and He (literally) broke the chains, opened the steel traps, and gave us our freedom. Help us to never leave our peaceful retreat. Cancel all return visits to sin and let the voice of praise be heard throughout the land. Blessed be the Lord, amen.

Bridge of Faith, Detour
February 17

Since we started on our heavenly journey, we have found that there are many detours that will lead us astray. Our commitment is to walk the straight and narrow way, which leads to life eternal. We know that if we follow Jesus then someday soon we will be with Him in heaven. It is very important to follow Him all through life.

All detours or return exits back into a life of sin are absolutely forbidden. When we look back at previous sins, sometimes they lure us into the gutters of corruption. A look can be fatal when we turn from the straight and narrow path. Avoid the pitfalls of distraction by following Jesus. Sins alluring temptations turn us away from grace.

Detours that take us back into sin city will also alienate us from God's love and mercy. If we are glory-land bound, help us to not take any unnecessary exits or we will find that we are traveling on the road of destruction. When the road is dark and drear, it is best we stay clear.

Occasionally a detour will appear that will have us to change course and still keep us on Heaven's highway. There will be times when our faith bridges need some repair. We know that without faith it is impossible to please God. If we patiently wait for this structure to receive the repair, it won't be long before we can crossover into eternity.

Father, there are many types of detours and some of them we desperately need to avoid. But there are others, like the weak faithless bridges that just need some strong braces of God's unwavering love to reinforce our weak frail bodies.

Once our belief system has been restored, the detour signs are taken down so that we can continue our heavenly journey. It is always a blessing when the bridge is safe and secure. Personal detours are acceptable, as long as Christ is in view, amen.

Run with the Son
February 18

All of us have shadows and they are faithful followers. Wherever we go, they will follow; sometimes they lead the way. Occasionally they will quietly warn us of impending danger.

They don't cause any trouble. If we happen to step on them, no one would ever know if there was any pain because they do not utter a sound. Please be aware that shadows are very good security guards.

Shadows can be fearful at times because their owners have hostile intent. There is no need to worry as the ones under our feet have been identified as personal attachments. These images lie on the ground and sometimes they hide under the table, waiting to alert us of any offender.

Please be aware of this silent warning system. When the sun comes out, the shadows will appear, but don't be surprised if they are a little bit shy on a cloudy day and disappear quickly in the early hours of night.

Father, I am talking about shadows because they can always win races when the sun is in the correct position. This is certainly something important for us to know because we are running in a race that we have to win. Let's not rely on shadows because they linger behind when dark clouds abide.

It is very hard to catch up with a shadow, especially if the sun is its teammate. Occasionally I have been able to out run my shadow. The time of day determines whether we win or lose. Let's begin the race.

Father, We cannot depend on earthly shadows to help us on our spiritual journey. Help us to realize that if we run with your Son in the right position of our hearts, we will be guaranteed to win and claim the prize. Run with the Son (Jesus) and heaven will be our reward. In Jesus' name, amen.

Talents, Overflowing Grace
February 19

We think about the many blessings that are so abundant in our lives when we use our talents. If we hide these special gifts, we are depriving a vast number of people the pleasure of worship. Lifeless talents will produce no evidence that God has entrusted us with a special ability to touch lives.

There are so many people who need a little inspiration to revive and restore their faith. Hidden talents do not profit anyone. We are leaving a void in people's hearts where there could have been praise, honor, and glory. Anointing is given in full measure, but the return is half empty.

Let the singers sing the songs of love, grace and mercy for the entire world to hear. Worship Him with the songs of praise. Preachers and Sunday school teachers bring forth the precious words that you place in our hearts to help us live holy, righteous lives. Activity is faith in action.

Many talents given, they are not all the same. Each one has been specially crafted and engraved with each of our names. Whatever the talent, use it to lift up and magnify the name of Jesus; all will be blessed.

I expect there are many people, like myself, that have been called and anointed to write inspirational words that are sent down from heaven above. Father, we are so thankful that you have given us this gift and we pray that our written words will inspire complete devotion to a loving, caring God. Writing is the base from which other talents meet together.

Father, help us to realize that when we use our talents, an overflowing of grace flows like a mighty river, touching all those who are in its path and consuming us with a love that expands the universe. Talents used for your glory will always leave a lasting impression. But the one we want to leave is praise, glory, and honor. In Jesus' name, amen.

I Can't Do It
February 20

The endeavors of life will find us too weak to stand. No matter how hard we try, the burdens of our hearts keep holding us down. Let's not give up; we are already promised the victory. There are no burdens so heavy that cannot be lifted by grace.

Challenges of life bring a certain amount of doubt that discourages us from claiming the prize. A lack of confidence will keep us out of the race. Even before the event takes place we have already convinced ourselves that we can't do it.

Let's think about a future event and visualize ourselves in a situation where we are terrified of public speaking. We are talking about a live broadcast in front of thousands of people. This is just a vision; there is no reason to be so nervous.

The day was approaching for the big interview. It seemed as though courage was hard to find. Oh, for more confidence, stronger faith to stand, and I needed just a little more assurance or this TV program would be canceled.

God touched me in His own kind of way when I saw these words on the Internet, "I can't do it, but God can do it through me." This is the confidence we have today and in the future. An interview was not scheduled but divine grace was available.

There are some things that are hard to do in life. Fear can hold us back, no victory to claim. We need to know that we can do all things through Christ, which strengthens us.

Father, earthly events can be overcome when we know that Jesus is standing right there beside us. When we are lacking in confidence and feel like we cannot accomplish the task, Let's remember "We can't do it, but God can do it through us." If fear is the overpowering force, there is no reason to accept defeat. Jesus said that He would go with us all the way. More grace is given when confidence is needed to overcome, amen.

Driving Without Lights
February 21

Let's think about the many times we had to travel at night in all types of situations. This was a requirement if we wanted to keep our jobs. Our normal routine would have us starting the vehicles and letting them warm up before driving them to work. It is very important to have the lights working properly.

There was one procedure that we could never do without. The lights in our vehicles had to be turned on, giving us a clear vision. If we pulled out of the driveway without lights, it was a very strong possibility that we would be involved in a terrible accident somewhere along the way.

Today's car industry has done a lot of things to help us drive in a safer manner. The headlights on my truck come on automatically and I always wonder if my taillights come on at the same time. Automatic features are like bad habits; we continue the same routine unaware of the dangerous effects.

There are a lot of cars that still have manual lights. This feature is completely controlled by the driver of the vehicle. Deception comes when we are driving at night and realize we took the manual vehicle. We failed to turn the lights on.

Manuel vehicles have other disadvantages. Let's suppose our headlights were not on and we pulled out into the traffic. The parking lot we just left had parking lights all around us. It was easy for us to be deceived as we had clear vision when we left the secure parking area.

Father, help us to realize that without Jesus in our lives, we are walking the dark path of sin. We think everything is ok just like our vehicles without lights. But we will soon learn that we are headed towards a terrible disaster. Let's be aware that deception of sin is like driving in total darkness. It is only a matter of time before there is a fatality. Christ in our lives is a bright light shining to keep us on the glory land road, amen.

When Jesus Comes Again
February 22

We have a hope that one-day soon Jesus will come to take us home. This brings back memories, as family reunions were a time of sweet fellowship; we would meet together, to laugh and to enjoy each other's company. We were always glad to see one another.

Many years from home fills our hearts with joy when we are with the family again. It will be a wonderful time when all of God's adopted children gather around the throne and we are made welcome by a loving embrace. Distance never separates us from His love and care.

This is a good time for us to think about the life of Christ and what it will be like when Jesus comes back to earth. The first time Jesus came to earth, angels sang: "Glory to God in the Highest." He was born in a stable and laid in a manger. There was no room for Him in the Inn.

Shepherds came and worshiped Him. Mary and Joseph were very proud of their newborn baby. In the early stages of Jesus' life, the king wanted Him dead. Earthly wishes are not made for eternal profit.

When Jesus was a young boy, the doctors listened to Him for He spoke as one with knowledge and great wisdom about God. He became a young man with a heart full of compassion. The blind received their sight and the sick were healed. Those who had leprosy were cleansed. His life touched the multitudes with kindness, goodness, and unwavering love.

Father, the first time Jesus came, He received honor as He rode a donkey through the crowd. They waved palm branches and gave Him the praise and honor. First time believers can be lifetime achievers. Later in life Jesus was crucified. He came as a humble servant obedient to the will of God. The next time He comes will be as King of kings, and Lord of lords, amen.

73

The Trumpet Sound
February 23

Many years ago, when battles were fought with foot soldiers and riders on horses, trumpets were used to signal an attack or retreat. Let's visit an imaginary battlefield. We will just watch from a distance fully removed from any action. I would say the man who sounded the brass instrument was always close to the officer in charge. Let's be as the solder with a commitment to obey orders, but from the Commander in Chief of Glory.

A soldier does not have the privilege of blowing the trumpet anytime he wants too. If he did the soldiers would be so confused that they would not know whether they should fight or run. The uncertainty of a misinterpreted signal could leave the men lying on a battlefield in blood.

The commander gives the order to charge, immediately the vibrating sound of the trumpet is heard and the fighting men run to fight for victory. These brave men would also retreat at the trumpet sound if they were being defeated in battle. A good retreat means that the fight will continue another day.

When do we retreat? Many battles have been fought and won because of decisions to escape enemy fire. Sometimes the opposing force would ambush the unsuspecting soldiers and many lives would be lost if the retreat command was disobeyed. A new plan brings defeat into triumph.

When we are out-numbered in the battles of life; we will be defeated unless we fall back to the command base. Let's obey Jesus; we will win the victory. We can be victorious in life if we heed the Master's call and follow Jesus all the way.

Father, we are aware that very soon the trumpet will sound. All of our earthly battles will be over and Jesus will take us home. This will not be a retreat for the war has been won. Our celebrating in heaven will be far greater than on earth. The voice of praise will be heard throughout eternity, amen.

Great Expectations
February 24

The mountain climbers have great expectations in that they will make it safely to the top of the mountain. Even though there are many hardships along the way, extremely cold temperatures, and strong swirling winds that would bring fear into anyone's life. Those with determination will prevail.

Somewhere along the pathway of life these brave adventures started on a journey that would bring them to the highest mountain in the land. They check all the equipment and make sure everything is just right before they begin climbing the steep incline. Safety precautions are in effect to save lives.

Their preparation will help them to stay alive, even though there will be accidents that will cause some of them to lose their lives. We have to believe that expectations of climbing a mountain are not expecting to die but to live. Overcoming obstacles along the way helps us on our journey in life.

These climbers have a rope and they use it for a lifeline. If this rope accidently breaks, hopefully, the other climbers will have the rope securely anchored to prevent someone from falling to his or her death. Lives can be saved when we help each other.

Suppose the group had climbed to a certain place on the mountain and strong winds prevented them from climbing any higher or even going back down to the camp below. Having a never give us attitude helps us to accomplish our goals.

It looked like they would all freeze to death, as there was no way a rescue team could get to them because the weather was too bad and rocky terrain was extremely dangerous.

Father, we are so thankful that when Jesus came into our lives, He gave us the blessed assurance of life eternal and He also placed in our hearts a great expectation of making it to our home in glory. Keep pressing on. In Jesus' name, amen.

No Painkillers
February 25

There is coming a day when we will be leaving this earth to go on a new and exciting journey. Travel arrangements are made in advance. We will not need any vaccinations because there are no deadly diseases or any types of bacterial infections to harm us. Physical ailments will never bother us again.

The Universal Association of Spiritual Health is an imaginary organization. They have informed us to leave all pills behind in medicine cabinets, as there is not any use for them in the city of God. Health benefits will be useless for lack of pain.

Forget about those doctor's prescriptions, painkillers, blood pressure pills, and any other thing that promotes healing in our bodies. There will not be any complaints in heaven because these life-saving remedies are taken away.

Once we enter heaven's gate, there will be no reason for us to have any type of medication. There is no need to hold onto earthly remedies when aches and body elements no longer exist. The love of God will be an antidote for our souls.

Please don't expect any hospitals or emergency care units to come up with a cure for any sick ailments. This city does not have any medical health facilities. There is no need to fix a problem when everyone is in perfect health.

Some people hold onto their medical issues while lying on the operating table. We need to tell these patients that there will be no sickness, pain or even death in Heaven. Doctors will not have a medical practice.

Father, it would be a terrible thing to be lying on the operating table, waiting for surgery when all Christian doctors and all those of the Christian faith have left the building. Let me give a word of comfort, as the Rapture has not yet taken place. We can rest peacefully when our hearts are right with God, amen.

A City in the Sky
February 26

In the very near future a big event will take place; we are going to a city that is far beyond the sky. This is not a vacation resort where tourists stay a week or two and then depart. Heaven's resort is where we live for eternity in our new home.

All of us know that when we go on a trip, the cost of airfare is extremely high. A round trip ticket always cost more because of the time and distance. This flight is a one-way trip to glory where we'll spend our time, praising God for His grace.

We need to think about our journey to Heaven and how much it cost the Son of God (Jesus) to make these travel arrangements. The purchase price for our redemption was paid at Calvary when Jesus died on the cross. Our sins cost Christ His life with horrific pain and suffering.

Payment was made in full, but there is one very important thing we must do before we are eligible to catch the glory land flight to the city in the sky. We must repent; tell Jesus that we are sorry for our sins.

This flight will be leaving soon and those of us who have made the preparations will depart immediately as soon as Jesus comes back to earth. While there is still a little time, repent.

What is the best way for us to reach this city in the sky? A slow-moving train is not a good choice for we will be airborne. Forget about high-flying airplanes for we are going higher than we have ever been before.

Father, help us to realize our flight will not be by any earthly transportation systems. In order to make this flight, we need to make travel arrangements so that all sin confessions will be accepted before it is too late. Unrepentant hearts will find it is too late for the ride. Our ascension to heaven will take place if our sins have been forgiven. Accept Christ, now, amen.

Welcome Home, Prodigals
February 27

A prodigal son and daughter lived in a time of contentment. They gave up the good-life to waste their inheritance. While at home they had the best of everything, but these drifters were not content with family life. The love was overwhelming but the glitter of worldly affairs and sins attracted them to a more pleasurable time. Sins luring temptations have ruined lives.

I suppose there were times as they walked the dark corridors of life that they thought about their families and wished they were with them. Distress abounds in the valley of despair.

This journey into a faraway land was a good opportunity to make new friends. But these two teenagers soon found out that when there is no more money, there will be a lonely road ahead. Friends that stay around just for earthly profit, walk away rapidly when there are no benefits.

Pretenders go by the name of friends, but who knows their evil intent. These abusers of friendship leave the unfortunate victims wallowing in the despair of grief and in the barnyard of mire. Friends will return quickly when they see the money.

What a terrible place for these teenagers to find food. Cornhusks with a little bit of corn were not nutritious meals for two starving teens. Poor conditions compel us to go home.

Memories of loved ones were constantly on their minds. The glitter of worldly fame and sinful pleasures had eluded them because of insufficient funds. Gone astray but not for long.

Father, this young couple had all the essentials of life before they became vagrants. Help us to realize it is a blessed day when prodigals return home. If we live in the miry clay of sin, this is hazardous to our spiritual relationship with God our Father. All backsliders and prodigals are encouraged to come home where love and peace abounds. In Jesus' name, amen.

A Riotous Son
February 28

Let us follow the life of a prodigal son. He is one that will carelessly waste his money and is very reckless with his life. The Bible tells us about a young man who lived in his father's house. However, he was not satisfied with the good-life and was determined to leave home and spend his inheritance. Big spenders have many friends, but some of them are deceitful.

Riotous living, there is a long list of things that would fit in this category. It gives me the impression of a person that could live in such a way as to cause harm to those around him. Some riots have included physical violence. Riotous living is not a peaceful endeavor. Riots can be hazardous to a person's health. Evil deeds corrupt Good intentions.

The prodigal's friends began to disappear as the money supply dwindled away. Soon there was nothing but empty pockets and broken dreams. He could certainly use a friend, but there were none to be found. This young man found himself in a very desolate condition.

He even ate the food that was given to the swine. Starvation is a terrible way to die. I would say that this prodigal son was thinking about his family relations and his life of content.

As time went by, he sank deeper into the mire and thoughts of home were constantly on his mind. One day he realized that he had it better in his father's house and he decided to go home. When this prodigal was at a great distance, his father ran to his son and welcomed him back into the family. Times of regret still bring us home to a loving embrace.

Father, perhaps there is a prodigal son or daughter in our families that has gone astray and it has been years since we saw them. Keep praying and someday, we may notice they are in a big hurry, please don't worry! I believe they are coming home. Receive them with loving-kindness, amen.

Glorious Trumpet Sound
March 1

We need to be aware that Christ will soon appear in the clouds of heaven and a trumpet will sound. The dead and the living shall rise. It will be a wonderful time when we stand before God and He says, "Well done thou good and faithful servant, enter into the glories of the Lord."

It is very important that we are aware of the sounds around us as one of these days heaven's trumpet will sound and it will be heard across the land. This will be our signal that the battle is over and we will gather around the throne to receive our victory crown and life everlasting.

Think about a jet flying in the sky; it will break the sound barrier. There has been many a time when I would try to locate these extremely fast-moving objects.

If I were in my home, I would run outside as quickly as possible to get a glimpse of the supersonic jets. Usually two or three jets fly together.

When jets fly over, I try to locate them by the sound. If there were no noise, I would have never saw any movement at all in the sky. Sound gives us the signal that if we want to see the approaching aircraft, we should look up because in a matter of seconds the sound will be gone and also the jets.

There is a sound we want to hear. We are aware that many people are intently waiting for the sound of the trumpet. When we hear that glorious sound, we know that in a moment, in the twinkling of an eye we shall be changed. Glory, Hallelujah.

Father, the evening sun of our lives may set today. But if we rise to see the morning light, we can be thankful if we have not yet invited Jesus into our hearts that God has given us more time to repent. Help us to realize we may miss heaven's flight if our sins are not forgiven. In Jesus' name, amen.

Restore to Life Eternal
March 2

Today we will go back in time to use our imaginary thoughts of restoring a 55 Chevy car. This is a good time to own one of the old classics because it can be rebuilt on the property of dreamland. We will escape the reality of life for a short time.

My vision of hope and dreams goes back many years to reveal this beautiful car on display in the year of 1955. The color was a bright red with a black interior. It truly was beautiful and it would make anyone proud to own this fine vehicle.

These car salesmen talked about this car in such a way that I had to buy this car, no matter how much it costs. They gave me the keys and I became the owner of a 55 Chevy. Since this car was built on dreamland, I never had any problems of keeping this vehicle in the best running condition. The life of a dream dies when the image fades in the light.

However, with all dreams, the garage doors of reality opened up to reveal the fresh paint had faded and the car no longer had the luster and shine when it was on display.

A real car in bad weather will lose its shine because these temporary things of earth will not last forever. After years of being out in the weather, rust and corrosion eroded the metal and now the car needed to be restored.

There is still hope for this classic car of the past. It is going to take a lot of hard work that includes sanding, replacing fenders, and repainting this old vehicle. When the work is finally done, my 55 Chevy will be in showroom condition.

Father, a field of dreams is good to restore classic cars, but the reality of life is when our spiritual relationship with you is eroded by sin, a soul cleansing is needed to purify our sinful hearts. We need a fresh supply of grace to bring back the luster of love in our lives. Restore us, in Jesus' name, amen.

A Safe Passageway
March 3

We want to visualize a dark, stormy night; the ship is in danger of colliding with the huge rocks. It looks like the crew will perish at sea. The mighty vessel with the men on board moves closer to their impending doom.

The ship sways back and forth in the turbulent waters. It seems as though there is no escape for these weary sailors. They fought the storm for days and now there is very little hope of making it safely to land.

After hitting a jagged rock, a huge hole was ripped in the side of the ship. More water rushes into the large boat and the men who are already tired and wore out from the storm continue to bail the water.

These brave men draw on their last bit of energy to keep the vessel a float and to save their lives. The ship is gradually sinking and a watery grave will claim the crew. There is no way we can safely maneuver a ship in the darkest of night without some type of light to show the jagged rocks. Let's say these huge boulders represent our sins and without a safe passageway, we are headed for disaster.

When all seems to be lost, a glimmer of light begins to shine. It is weak at first and then in a matter of seconds, a high beam shines far out to sea. The captain and men change the course of the ship and follow the light towards the lighthouse. Christ provides a safe passageway for journeymen and all of us on our life's voyage to heaven's eternal shore.

Father, as we travel through life on an uncharted sea, lost and without hope, slowly approaching death's final horizon. We will perish in our sins unless we repent. Help us to realize that if we try to navigate through sin-infested waters, without Jesus, we will never see the lights of home. We pray for guidance in Jesus' name, amen.

Open the Gates
March 4

We know that Jesus is the only way we can enter into heaven, but there are some people that will try other ways to enter this sacred place.

Help us to realize that in order for us to enter through the pearly gates, we must have our sinful lives purified by the precious blood of Christ. Heaven's security system requires us to have profiles that identify us with Jesus. Everyone does not have access to heaven, as the gate will be closed for those who deny Christ and open to those who accept Him.

Let's see how the security system works on earth. The gate is locked to keep out intruders, robbers, and anyone that does not have permission to enter the premises. There are times when criminal activity takes place because of a security breach.

This particular resident makes sure his family will be kept safe by adding extra security to his property. A special identification system is built into the gate. Entrance is completely controlled by the home dwellers.

If a visitor appears at the gate and wants to talk with someone in the family, a profile of the person will be transferred to the owner. If the person is accepted, the gate automatically unlocks and admission is granted for the waiting individual.

I don't know how the pearly gates are set up in heaven. But entrance will only be granted if we know Jesus personally. Suppose there is a time when we stand before heaven's gate. Everyone will not be allowed to enter this sacred place, only those who know Jesus as Lord and Savior.

Father, if there is a blood relationship between God and us, we will be accepted into heaven. Adopted children will not be denied. We pray for the lost children (sinners) of this sinful world who need a home in Heaven. In Jesus' name, amen.

Passing Through
March 5

Time on earth is just a temporary thing with only a short while for us to stay. Sometimes our travels will take us to a small town in a rural area with fine stores and good campsites. This is a wonderful place to visit. We will walk at the park and take pictures of the beautiful scenery and share them with our family and friends.

Everyone is reminded to enjoy their stay and enjoy the activities of the town. This is just a temporary place in our travel expedition. We will be leaving soon for we are just passing through. There is no time to waste.

This trip comes to an end and another one will begin. All of the travelers are encouraged to pack their belongings and be ready to leave in the morning.

Let's get moving to our new destination. There is so much to do and see; we can hardly wait to get to our next location. No one knew this would be our last day of worldly travels. Life always ends somewhere.

There comes a time in our lives when our journey will end. Death or the Rapture will take place and no one knows the day or hour of our departure. Whenever the time, we need to be ready to meet our God.

Our days and years upon this earth are only for a short season. Help us to realize that soon life will be over. "All the good we can do, let us do it now; we will not pass this way again." One life to live is all we have on this earth.

Father, there may be only a few days left on the calendar of life. The people we meet along the way will be influenced by our lives. We are leaving a trail. Will there be memories of faithful service to a kind, loving God? We can leave behind a trail of righteousness that will be easy to follow, amen.

Christ, No Salvation in any other
March 6

The floodwaters continue to rise as the rain falls from the sky. No one knows when this terrible weather will end. The hours slowly pass as the torrents of rain descend upon the earth.

A strong and mighty wind sweeps across the land. Flash floods overflow the banks and we have to go to a safe place on the mountain. We cannot stay in the low valleys, as they will be death traps. If we cannot make it to higher ground, we must hold onto anything that will save us.

The mighty river moves swiftly across the land, destroying everything in its path. Cars are completely emerged and homes are washed away. A huge tree uprooted by the storm is carried swiftly down-stream to stop suddenly in the rough waters. First responders were called to make a rescue.

Two small children are seen holding onto the branches to keep from drowning in the strong, river current. These kids are clinging to the tree for their lives. Their strength is dwindling away, but if they can hold on a little while longer, these two struggling children will be saved.

The parents wait anxiously for the rescue team to arrive. I hope they will be in time. These little ones cannot hold on much longer. Some men in a rescue boat risked their lives to save the exhausted children. Everyone rejoiced on shore as the parents held the kids in their arms with thankfulness in their hearts.

Father, Help us to realize that to be saved in a natural disaster, we can hold on to anything. Salvation of our souls is different then the flood victims. If we trust in anyone besides Jesus, the rescue attempt will be in vain. There are times when we are caught in the strong currents of sin, drifting aimlessly down the river of life. Jesus who gave His life is the only one who can save us. Now is a good time to reach up to the nail-scarred hand and hold onto it. Save us, Lord, amen.

Weak Branches and Heaven's Grip
March 7

We need to realize that small branches will help us for a while. But at the first opportunity we should release our grip and take hold of a stronger branch.

When the weak limb gives way and there is nothing to hold onto, it is a strong possibility that we will drown. A turbulent current will cause us to loosen our grip and we will be overwhelmed by the surging water.

If we are the ones in sins strong current, don't give up just realize salvation is possible. We have to turn loose of the weak branches, take Christ's hand and hold on tight for his grip will hold us throughout eternity. Without Jesus holding onto us, there is no way we can be rescued.

There are many people who are trying to get to heaven by holding onto the small branches and will not turn loose for fear of death. If we are the ones in the raging river, being dragged alone in the strong current. It would be wise to reach out to any limb that might help us stay alive.

Father, small branches are needed to help us on our spiritual journey. Church attendance is good, but there is more required of us to make it to heaven. Please don't stop going to the place of worship, as this may be the place where God deals with our hearts and we grasp a stronger limb.

Having a good moral conscience is certainly commendable and we don't want to stop caring for people or showing kindness. We may realize there is a larger branch of God's love and mercy when Jesus hung on a cross.

Whatever branch we are holding onto, let's make sure our final grip is in the Savior's hands. If we never try Jesus, then we will perish in our sins. In order to be saved, let's turn loose of the small limbs of sin and grasp the Savior's hand, amen.

Calendar of Regret
March 8

There is a time in life when we decide to wait another day; there is still plenty of time. We cannot choose the day of salvation. God will not be satisfied with our self-appointed day. If Christ comes today, what good is tomorrow's salvation?

It is not like an appointment when a certain date is scheduled and everyone is in agreement. We can mark off the days on a calendar. The last one marked fulfills all of our obligations.

I believe we need to take an imagination shortcut into the future. A group of people was confronted about their soul's salvation. The Holy Spirit had brought conviction upon all of them. The altar call was given and some of the individuals accepted Christ into their lives as Savior.

One young man decided he was too young. He thought it would be better if he waited many years to make things right with God. Time passed and he enjoyed the sinful pleasures of the world until old age.

The day that was chosen is finally here. He dressed up in a nice suit and tie so he would look good on his salvation day. This elderly man could hardly wait to get to church and invite Jesus into his heart. It was time to make peace with God.

Father, This was the big day for this senior citizen to repent. As the man drove into the parking lot at church, there was a sign on the church door. "It's too late! The Rapture took place." This is the calendar of regret.

Help us to realize we will make bad decisions in life, as well as good ones. The calendar of regrets reminds us of the things that we wanted to do, but we never had the time. Salvation was on our minds and Jesus was dealing with our hearts. We can eliminate the calendar of regrets by accepting Christ into our hearts today, in Jesus' name, amen.

Memories of the Past
March 9

We are traveling down an old country road with thoughts of family and friends. There are special memories of the old home place. No one lives there now and the home is in really poor condition. We like to travel the imagination roads of the past. Today is one of those days and we will be visiting some of our favorite places.

The sun is shining. Let's go for a walk at the park. Remember all the good times we had there. This is where we had some of our best picnics. We walked down the trail by the river and watched the colorful leaves fall to the ground.

It is getting late. There is still a little time to go fishing at our favorite spot. We won't stay long as there are other places of interest. This activity was really enjoyable and it was peaceful at the lake, no fish to clean for supper.

While we are still visiting the precious memories of the past, our memory lane trip will not be complete unless we visit the church. Let's all go together with a little imagination.

The preacher delivers a wonderful sermon and the Holy Spirit touches us. The altar call is given and the minister has a countdown for Christ. My memory of the past brings back thoughts of when I knelt at the altar. Jesus came into my life when Heaven or Hell was my final option.

Hold onto the memories of the years gone by. Cherish the thought of deliverance at the cross. Remember why He died, a spear pierced His side. They took Him down from the cross.
.

Father, these precious memories of the past reveal God's prevailing love that never fails or falters. As we go back down memory lane, we recall the blessings of lives transformed. It is always good to remember how we escaped the terrible consequence of sin by faith in Christ. Thank you, Jesus, amen.

Patiently Wait
March 10

There are special times when we patiently wait for a certain event. All of us have experienced something in our lives where we had to wait a very long time before it would occur. Disappointment occurs when we don't wait long enough.

When we graduated from high school or college, applications were filled out in an employment office and mailed to the employers for certain jobs.

We also visited manufacturing companies and other places of interest. The only thing we can do now is wait. The days slowly pass and no contacts are made with any of the personnel.

All of a sudden, the phone rings and our anticipation rise as we hear the employers name in the conversation. This call is from the personnel office and they have a report of our job status, hired for employment.

Our hearts seem to beat a little faster, especially when we realize we have been selected for a special position and they would like for us to report to work on a certain day.

We are overjoyed at the thought of finding a job. I have heard that good things come to those who wait. It certainly seems to be true. As we go through life our highest expectations will be met when we wait.

It is very important for us to know that Jesus is coming back to earth. None of us know when that special day will take place. Heaven will be our reward if we are expecting Him.

Father, if our patience grows thin and we get tired of waiting; it's only a matter of time before the corruptible things of this world will steal our salvation. We will be unprepared to stand before the throne when Jesus comes in the clouds. Still waiting will have us on the flight to glory, in Jesus' name, amen.

Run to Win
March 11

We want to enter a race where the winner will be rewarded with the crown of life. This is not an ordinary race. First, we must talk it over with God's Son. One of the main requirements is that we must be saved by grace. There is no need to worry, as Jesus will be here to make the blood transition from sinners to born-again believers.

The race is about to begin. There will be contestants from all walks of life. There is no age limit, as children and adults will be running for the grand prize of eternal life.

Winners will be chosen according to their endurance, steadfastness, and faithfulness. This will not be a race for the weak in heart or for those who rely only on speed. The objective in this race is to live holy, righteous lives, to lift up and magnify Jesus Christ with love and devotion to God. Life changing behavior by grace will help us claim the prize.

Awards will be given at different stages when the participants have completed all the requirements of the race. Let's say a crown will be given to those with good sportsmanship, kindness, and good deeds shown along the way. Some people will finish the race earlier than others in life.

Holy, righteous, and faithful contestants will receive a crown of life that fades not away. The duration of this race is not a one-day event, but it covers many years of each of our lives.

Some of the entrants are not qualified to run because of sinful conditions. However, they will not be disqualified if they repent, even if they only have one day of salvation.

Father, help us to realize we must repent before we can go to heaven. All faithful entrants who have run with all their hearts will be awarded the grand prize and a bonus of eternal life. Sins are forgiven, ready set, go! Let's run to win, amen.

Permanent Peace
March 12

Thoughts of a new home occupy our minds, as we get out the chainsaw and start cutting the trees. We found a good place where this home will be built.

The land is cleared of the brush and trees. This is a beautiful site with a river close to the property. Trees need to be debarked. Early the next morning, the sound of "Timber" is heard as trees fall to the ground. Mules are used to transport these logs to the work area.

Winter is coming soon and we don't have any time to waste. Many of the families have children, which if they do not have the proper shelter will freeze in the cold temperatures. There is no way anyone will survive without a good shelter.

A father and his two sons work extremely hard to cut and shape the wood beams. The mother is also busy preparing meals, carrying water for her family. This strenuous work continues for a couple of months.

Activities around the homes increase for the weather is getting colder and a few snowflakes are seen in the air. Finally, the roof is finished and this family moves into their new log home, where they all live peacefully all the days of their lives.

Father, I wish I could say this home visualization was true, we all know that storms will come our way. Our gardens will experience droughts and occasionally locust will invade our property. We may experience a house fire and lose all of our belongings. No one is exempt from hard times.

Earthly disasters will keep us from having permanent contentment. When Christ is our Lord and Savior, we have peace that will last throughout eternity. The tranquility we have in our lives surpasses all worldly effects because our source of peace in in Jesus. Blessed be the Lord, amen.

Christ our Best Friend
March 13

I would just like for everyone to know Jesus is my best friend. All those who know Him as Lord and Savior will say the same. We know our lives are blessed when Jesus calls us His friends.

The other day I saw a good friend of mine in a supermarket. It has been several years since I saw him. We talked for a few minutes and then we shook hands and parted company, grateful he is my friend.

All through life we make friends and they stay with us for a while and then they are gone. That does not mean the end of a great friendship. The reality of life is that we will be separated for various reasons.

Some of the people we meet along the way will be our friends for life. We have to go through a healing process when our friends are no longer with us and we wait on our hearts to mend, as we are left all alone.

A good, faithful friend helps us along the pathway of life with encouraging words, kindness, and loyalty to give us strength when we are weak. When we are cast down and forsaken, a true friend will always give us a helping hand and will lift us up in times of sorrow.

Father, our best friend, Jesus, there is nothing that will cause Him to depart. We may walk away from Him and separate ourselves from the love of God, but Jesus will never leave or forsake us. If we walk away, we are the ones who break the friendship. His faithfulness is not temporary.

Jesus calls us friends and He is closer than a brother. There may be thoughts that no one cares, then we haven't met Jesus. If there is anyone here that is alone and looking for a friend? Jesus on the cross with His arms spread wide, this is how much He loves us. Seek Him for an everlasting friendship, amen.

The Life of Christ
March 14

Thoughts for today reveal the life of Christ. He left His home in heaven to come to earth and walk among us. The purpose of His coming was to deliver the people from their sins and to help them know of God's great love. His mission was accomplished.

This same Jesus still has compassion for the lost and we can testify to the fact that He is still forgiving sins. When we kneel at the altar and ask Him to forgive us, immediately we receive the salvation of our souls.

Our lives are truly blessed; we can know of God's wonderful love through His Son, Jesus. Down through the ages of time, His love has brought multitudes to the throne room of grace. Had it not been for His love and mercy where would we be today? We would have no fellowship with God and still living in our sins with no hope of heaven.

Many wonderful things happened along time ago. His compassion touched many lives. He performed miracles with the sick being healed. Parents brought to Him their children and He touched them. This same Jesus is still healing the sick, setting the captives free, and the bounty of His love never ends. The whole world has felt His marvelous grace.

Remember when He turned the water into wine, fed five thousand people with a few pieces of fish. Multitudes of people have been touched by His unwavering love. His love is an everlasting love and it continues down through the ages. Lives are constantly blessed by His presence.

Father, we think about Jesus dying on a cross and our hearts are filled with remorse as He is laid in the grave. The crucifixion was a horrible way for Him to die. When He arose from the dead, all heaven rejoiced. Our faith is in vain if Jesus did not rise from the dead. He is risen; praise the Lord.

Stranded on a Highway
March 15

We need to be aware that as we travel to our home in heaven, we will find obstacles in the road that hinders our journey. These barriers of life, we can overcome. When there is no way, God will make a way.

Many of us have found ourselves stranded on a highway in a snowstorm. Icy conditions stopped all traffic. An accident was reported that twenty-four people had lost their lives because of the severe weather. Tragedies in life prevent us from going to our homes.

Tractor-trailers had jackknifed and some of them had turned over, blocking the road and causing more accidents. The roads were not safe to drive on. As travelers on the blocked highway of life, we cannot get through unless we depend on God. He will make a way when there is active faith to clear the road.

Walking on the slippery ice was also very dangerous. It was reported that someone backing·up with snow moving equipment killed a pregnant woman in a parking lot. The baby survived and was in the hospital for critical treatment. Because of hazardous roads, kids were left at school and had to stay overnight. Hundreds of people were stranded on the highway with no food or warm blankets for survival.

Some of the travelers walked to gas stations, pharmacies, grocery stores, and other places for shelter and to sleep for the night. This was a really terrible time in their lives. No way to get home. Finally, the roads were cleared and the people returned to their safe places of refuge.

Father, as we travel on state highways, obstacles in the road will keep us from going home. We will encounter huge rocks or a car pile-up from bad weather conditions. These are natural occurrences that interfere with our earthly journey. Stranded on a highway does not prevent our ascent to heaven, amen.

Ready or Not
March 16

We know that Jesus is coming in the clouds of heaven. His appearing will be a lot more serious than a game we used to play as kids. One person would close his or her eyes and count to a certain number and then say aloud, "Ready-or-not, here I come."

This was only a game, but it had consequences for those who did not have a good hiding place or if they were the first ones found. There are many situations in life where we need to be ready for certain events. Being unprepared to meet Christ will be the worst mistake of our lives.

Sometimes things happen to us whether we are ready or not. A plane will leave if we are unprepared for the scheduled trip. There is no turning back for late passengers once the airplane has left the ground.

Airports have a schedule when the planes will leave the airport. It is our responsibility to purchase the tickets and be ready to leave at the appointed time. Heaven's scheduled flight is a ready-or-not event.

An announcement is made in advance for all the passengers to board the plane. We already know that if we are late arriving at the airport, an excuse will not help us this time. Our fate is by our own neglect.

Father, the warning has gone throughout the land that Jesus is coming. This is not a time for us to run and hide. Where could we go if we have not accepted the sacrificial payment of Christ for our flight to glory?

Being ready or not is our choice; no other person can make this decision for us. People can be praying for us throughout the land. But we are responsible to catch our own flight to glory. He will find us if we call out to Him. "Jesus, Jesus!"

No Default Contract
March 17

Earthly contracts require us to fulfill certain obligations. Our signatures on the document make the agreement complete. Once our names are signed, the written statements are binding by law. Spoken words bind us with our commitments to our heavenly Father.

In our relationship with God, we are bound by the Holy Spirit to live according to His will. The acceptance of Christ in our hearts and His precious blood applied to our lives is the final proof of divine grace.

The signing of a contract is a commitment to fulfill all obligations. I have to admit this is a nerve-racking process as we decide to accept or reject the contract.

It does seem to be easier to decline a contract proposal because no future endeavors will be required. However, this also means that we might not have that brand-new car in the driveway or eternal life.

Finally, a decision is made to buy the car. A payment schedule is set up on a monthly basis. This agreement is final and both parties will be subject to the rules and regulations of the document.

Once our names are placed on the dotted line, whether it is for good or bad, joy or sadness, it will be too late to void the transaction.

Father, we do not have a written contract with you, but our commitment is binding and we will be held responsible for any negligence, disobedience, or unholy loss of character. Help us to realize that heaven will be denied if there is a breach of contract and we return to our old sinful ways. Let's not worry about heaven's contract being in default, as the blood of your own Son confirms the transaction. Thank you, Jesus, amen.

A Gentle Shower
March 18

Father, we pray that you will send down a refreshing shower. Open the windows of heaven; a spiritual downpour will revive our faltering spirits. These blessings are needed to keep us from withering away to a place of deep regret. Godly requests are not denied.

This is a time that we want to draw closer to you. Send down a gentle shower so that we will rejoice in your presence and give you the praise, glory, and honor. Our lives are truly blessed to know of your great love.

We come before your holy presence because you are a holy and righteous God. This is a time we stand before the throne room of grace as your adopted children and we give reference to you as, "Our Father and our God." Sons and daughters have a new relationship with God.

When we are going through the dry valley of despair and grief, joy will fill our souls when the rain comes down from above. Sorrowful hearts need a fresh supply of grace and peace. We need a heartfelt blessing and a holy arm embracing so that love will prevail in our lives for eternity.

Rain from heaven is what our hearts desire. This may be a gentle touch of the Master's hand. He will never leave or forsake us. We know our lives are blessed when Jesus walks among us. A gentle shower from heaven can be a time when we touch the hem of His garment and receive our healing. These are the precious moments of fulfillment.

Father, let the rain of your glory descend, saturating our lives with peace from heaven so that your grace will abound, calming the storms of life. When Jesus gives us peace, the world cannot take it away. This rain refreshes our souls and we lift up and magnify Jesus Christ our Lord. This is a time to rejoice as our hearts are filled with your love, amen.

A Refreshing Rain
March 19

There are times in our lives when we need a spiritual rain from above. A fresh shower will bring forth blessings of praise for your mercy. Praise is a return favor for us to honor God.

We lift our hands to glorify you and rejoice in the spirit of your compassion that flows like a river. Overflowing the banks with love to transform us by the power of grace. All of heaven declares your glory.

Send down a refreshing rain today, as the dry earth cannot survive without a fresh supply of water to bring the dead leaves back to life. Help us to realize we are in the same condition as a drought on the land. It is impossible for us to thrive without a touch from your holy hand.

The outpouring of your love comes down like a gentle rain. Let's consider the drought for just a moment. Grass has faded and ponds are nearly empty. We need a fresh out-pouring of rain to revive the earth and to bless us spiritually.

Nature is a lifeless place without a fresh shower from above. Look at the trees, dying leaves are thirsty for a little bit of moisture to revive and restore life to a more vibrant effect. A dry spell on the earth makes the forest highly flammable.

Tomatoes in the garden hang low on the vine. The deterioration has spread to the corn, beans, and all the vegetables are in decline. None of them has the strength to rise another day. All of nature is affected by this drought. Families will perish without a good drenching rain.

Father, our famishing souls in worship is affected by lack of prayer. We closed the floodgates of praise; it is no wonder our spiritual health is in decline. Help us to realize if we are experiencing a drought, it is not God's fault for our lack of devotion. Pray, the rain will come. In Jesus' name, amen.

A Stranger in the Camp
March 20

This is a good time to realize how short our life span is on earth. We are traveling through a world where death will come at any time. All of us will pass through the valley of the shadow of death.

There will not be any announcements to prepare us for this terrible event. Whether we are here for many years, a few months, or a limited number of minutes in a day, our time will expire with the last heartbeat.

Let's take a look and see how quickly and without warning death will sneak into the camp. It will cast a shadow of remorse in those still left alive. If we are in a camp or a well-guarded area, we are still at risk.

A campfire was built and we gathered around the fire. The fishermen were laughing and joking with one another. This conversation became more serious as we talked about life and death. The thought of living for many years brought joy to our hearts. Each of us held onto the joyful expectations of living a very long time. Life on earth is only for a little while.

When death was mentioned, an odd feeling came over us. It appeared as though a stranger had entered our camp. The campfire went out, and we went to bed for the night. Early the next morning, one of our friends had died in his sleep. All of his hopes and dreams of having a long life was cut short by death.

Father, life comes to an end, as death claims another victim. If Christ is our Savior, we still have the blessed hope of living again. The resurrection hour will be a time that we will take up residence in our new home. Death is a temporary stay, as all of our hopes and dreams come true when we meet Jesus in the air. Help us to be aware there is no need to fear death when Christ is our life. In Jesus' name, amen.

No Grapes on the Vines
March 21

We need to realize that our labor of love to help others know Jesus Christ as Lord and Savior is not in vain. The fruit of our labors will have no reward if we are standing idle in the harvest field. There is no profit if the harvest tools are leaning against the tree.

This looks like it is going to be a bad year for the harvest of grapes in the slumber-fields. At first the laborers were very productive in planting the seeds, pruning vines, and taking good care of the vineyard.

Time went by and these hard workers could not be seen laboring in the fields. A closer inspection would show a more comfortable environment of sleeping beneath shade trees, dreaming about a prosperous crop.

They didn't bother to work the fields. Grapevines were unattended, but now it is time for the harvest; the slumber workers will be paid according to the amount of grapes taken from the vines. It sure is a lot of workers disappointed in this group. No Grapes on the vines equal zero profits if the hands are still in the pockets. Neglected vines shatter all the dreams.

Workers in another field were quite different, diligent in the harvest fields. These men and women took a lot of pride in their labor skills and they continued working in the fields. They began in the morning and worked all day until late in the evening. The toil of their blistered hands brought forth an abundance of grapes. A day's labor results in profits.

Father, help us to realize that if we are on the slumber-team, our labor will be in vain. We must all work together in order to have a good harvest. Let us think about our spiritual obligations. People we meet along the way need to know about God's saving grace. Time spent in the harvest field will be rewarding if we share the love of God. Help us, Lord, amen.

High Calling of God
March 22

Every one of us has been called out for a purpose, whether to fight in a war or stay at home and raise the family. Whatever the task, we should be faithful in our commitment to serve with devotion and obedience.

My call came by mail from the government to serve in the military. Summons for service comes in many different ways. Our best response is to be available when we are called.

The most important call any of us can receive is to serve God. There will be no regrets as we commit our lives to Him. When this call comes, please don't neglect it, or run and hide.

It is a great honor for us to be called into the service of our country. Men and women of all nationalities have received a greater calling. Even little children are not neglected from serving and living for God. We have not chosen Him, but He has chosen us.

I am so glad to know that the high calling of God is not reserved for the rich or celebrities. The poorest of the poor are called for service. Little children to adults have the privilege of answering heaven's call.

Father, there is a calling beyond all earthly expectations and it comes from the throne room of mercy. This is no ordinary call for earthly employment, but it is the highest call of the land to live and serve God. When the call comes it will not be a telemarketing service with special incentives to buy or sale items.

This is a call that will bring us into the family of a holy, righteous God. He wants us to serve Him with a full commitment of unwavering love. The call from heaven is for each of us to take up our cross and follow Jesus. Let's respond while He is speaking to our hearts. In Jesus' name, amen.

Gold in the Hills
March 23

Earthly prosperity will not help us in our quest for heaven. There is no amount of money that can pay the entrance fee. The wealth of the world is vain without any eternal profits.

Let's think about discovering gold or searching all of our lives to find this valuable ore. If we are able to stake a claim, the gold will be ours and all of its delusion will have us in a fantasy world of material wealth.

The glamor of worldly things will occupy our minds and we think this will supply all of our earthly needs. It would be a terrible thing to have everything we want for our physical existence and absolutely no wealth in heaven. There will be no withdrawals without any spiritual deposits.

I believe it is possible to be earthly rich and heavenly poor. Let's think about a poor beggar with only breadcrumbs to eat and ragged clothes to wear. He can have eternal riches in heaven by grace.

Gold is discovered in the hills. Earthly riches destroy many lives. The hopes and dreams of a prosperous life come to an end when the gold is gone. Earthly wealth disintegrates while our riches in heaven escalate if Jesus is our Savior.

What does it profit a person who is in search of gold or earthly riches to lose his life and family in the end? It is always good to prosper for a better life, but if it costs our souls, what have we gained? "This day thy soul is required of thee." Earthly wealth does not give us access to heaven.

Father, we need to realize the value of gold will not last; it is an earthly treasure that will expire if it is spent too fast. Sadness comes when the pockets are empty. We can have all the riches of the world. But our lives are poor without God's amazing grace. Peace abides when Christ is Lord, amen.

Carry the Torch
March 24

Athletes train all over the world to compete in the Olympics. A flaming fire is ignited in a cauldron to mark the beginning of this special event.

The runner selected for this position was usually a celebrity or another famous person. One year for this spectacular event, Muhammad Ali, a famous boxer received this honor.

A torch would be lit and the person carrying it would hand it to another runner. This torchbearer continued down the course until the last man or woman entered the main area and lit the cauldron, a large kettle.

I saw the cauldron lit one time after the runners had completed the course; a bow and arrow was used to ignite the flame. It was really an amazing sight to see as the flaming arrow landed in this receptacle.

We could go into the Olympics area and watch the athletes compete for the various metals. People from all parts of the world attend these sporting events. The flaming arrow still has our undivided attention.

When we look at the spiritual side of these games, we realize that God is also looking for those who will carry the cross and hold it up high for His glory. Those selected will not win any earthly metals, but those faithful in service will receive a crown of life. Volunteers are now being accepted.

Father, help us to realize the difference between the Olympian torchbearer and us is that we are to carry the cross all through life. Once we take up the cross it is not a one-day event like the torchbearer. Our commitment is for a lifetime. We have a burden to help others know of your great love. The cross may be heavy at times but God will bless all of our endeavors. Light the torch of our hearts, amen.

Break Up the Fallow Ground
March 25

It was only a short while ago that snow was covering the ground and driveways were being cleared with snowplows. Now that winter is over, it is time to plow the field for the first time. This cultivating the land requires a lot of work.

Spring has arrived with fresh flowers and budding trees. All of us enjoy the beautiful landscapes. As much as we would like to stay and enjoy God's creation, we must plow the garden, break up the fallow ground. We will be rewarded for our labors when the harvest is ripe.

We have made plans today to break up the fallow-ground. According to the Bible, this is a place where the fertile ground has never been plowed. The first thing we will do is to remove the stumps and rocks so the plow will cut deep into the earth.

Stump removal is not an easy task, as we have to dig around the stump to where the roots are exposed. An axe or a chainsaw is used to cut the roots so a tractor or a horse can pull the stumps out of the ground.

We are just about ready to start plowing, but there are many rocks in the field that needs to be removed before the horses can break up the fallow-ground. Finally, the ground is ready for the plowing to begin.

After working several hours, clearing the rocks and stumps, horses will now be used to pull plows that will turn over the topsoil. Seeds planted on top of the ground will not grow. See how quickly sprouts rise when seeds are in the earth.

Father, It is time to break up the fallow-ground in our lives. This could be the fertile place in our hearts where the deep-rooted sins need a plowing of grace. Sin removal is in process. The end result will be transformed lives bringing forth the fruit of holiness, godly living, and righteousness, amen.

Build a Bigger Barn
March 26

A bigger barn was built because the other one was too small to keep all of the produce. A large storage area seemed to be a good idea.

However, the laborers were paid at a very low scale. They had to live in unsanitary conditions while the owner lived in a lavish home on a hill. The owner was satisfied as long as there was plenty of money in the bank and he didn't have to be concerned about anyone else's needs.

These workers were underpaid, they were not able to afford very much food and their families had poor health. It was good that a new barn was built, but not at the cost of keeping the employees in poverty.

Laborers that are not paid enough will find other places to work. If there were no work in the field, the bank account would also dwindle away until only a new barn was left.

The unseen danger of a small, growing farm had a drastic effect on the owner. Many years had gone by since this structure was built. An increase in the sale of livestock and produce added money to the bank.

With all of these growing pains, it was quite evident a new barn had to be built. Immediately the work began as the old barn was torn down. Soon there was a tremendous loss of corn. The cattle sales also dropped and his workers quit for lack of funds. It was certainly hard to recuperate from this tradeoff, an old full barn for a new empty one.

Father, help us to realize if we have an abundance of wealth or we do not have enough money to build a barn, we can still have an inheritance in heaven. Our spiritual destiny does not depend on wealth. What have we gained if we die in our sins? There is no profit if we die without Christ in our lives.

Wrong Side of the Fence
March 27

This has been a year of extreme drought. Farmers in the community have had to sell their livestock because the grain is too expensive.

Rivers and lakes are at an all-time low. I heard the weather report the other day and the forecast was favorable, at least for a little while. Snow was predicted, but this would not be enough to replenish the dry earth. Our souls are also in need of a good water supply to refresh our spirits.

Many of the families that live in the country depend on creeks, wells, and other resources for their survival. The drought is so bad that some of the inhabitants may have to sell their homes, land, and move away to a place where the grass is greener and the rivers flow continuously.

Water supply is scarce this year, as the storm clouds carried little rain. Some of the farmers built barricades to keep other landowners from stealing their water.

I have not heard of any range wars of fences being cut or anyone hurt because of the water shortage. We know this could happen with some aggressive owners who have property and water rights to their land.

On one side of the fence the livestock have enough water for a while. The other side is quite different, no water and the animals are dying. When it comes to survival, we will do whatever it takes to stay alive. The extremely dry conditions result in fights and even death.

Father, help us to realize that if sin separates us from God, we are on the wrong side of the fence. Let's cut the wire by repentance. There is an abundance of grace that is ever flowing, always a refreshing source of life. Let's go to Jesus where there is no drought of mercy. In Jesus' name, amen.

Switch the Rails
March 28

This is a good time to travel on the imagination railway. Passenger trains move down the rails toward certain locations in the country. A trackman is responsible for changing the tracks.

Once we get on the train and it is moving down the rails, the trackman is the only one who can keep the train on the right track. Sometimes there has to be a mechanical switchover from one track to another.

All of us have a special connection to the switchman, as no tracks will be changed unless we contact the conductor. He will then relay the message to the transfer station. This method of communication will help us to change directions so that we can go to a new destination.

While traveling on this train we realize that there is a huge fire up ahead. Everyone on the train was warned of the impending danger. We were given an opportunity to have the rails switched so that we could be saved from this awful disaster. Some of us decided to escape the fire by having the rails switched. While others continue on their journey.

The message is relayed to the switchman and he responds immediately to change the tracks. Lives were saved because of distressful cries from the passengers to change course. However, all the travelers would not make this life-saving choice.

Father, we think about a real life situation of changing directions from hell to heaven. Some people will say, "We've got plenty of time; there is no need to hurry." The warning is given so that we can avoid the fire, but sinful desires keep some of the people on the rails of ungodly living. We are all responsible for the decisions we make in life. Jesus is waiting to switch the rails if we will ask Him. Save us, Lord, amen.

A Rainbow in the Sky
March 29

We know that our lives are blessed as we walk the pathway of life with Jesus. There comes a time when the raging storms are over and peace reigns in our hearts.

A rainbow may appear with bright colors in the sky. This beautiful creation stays for a while and then leaves as there are more people that would gladly trade their frowns for a time of radiant smiles. Glad hearts will sing when the turmoil of life is over and the angels sing in a joyous melody to the King of kings. Sinners were lost but now they are found.

All of this is a reminder of your great love that never fades away. They say there is a treasure at the end of the rainbow, but we already know we are blessed beyond measure. Your supply house is full with grace in abundance. Supplying our needs is your good pleasure.

There is no need to search in faraway places for an earthly treasure that does not exist. We do not need to chase a rainbow across the hills and through the valleys when your goodness and mercy follows us all through life. Love will prevail when we seek Jesus as Lord and Savior.

When the dark clouds of gloom hover above, it is not hard for us to realize that beyond the stormy weather, a rainbow is set in the sky. This is a good sign that we are still in God's favor. The best place for us to be is in the arms of a loving God, in the ever-flowing stream of His love.

Father, The pathway of life may be filled with loneliness as we walk through troublesome times. Our blessings abound even more when your Son, Jesus meets with us along the way. He has promised that He will never leave or forsake us. We do not need to have sorrowful hearts. Just a quick look into heaven at the rainbow in the sky, we will realize the storm is over and peace with God forever abides, amen.

A Rescue from the Miry Clay
March 30

We all know the story of how Jesus came to earth. Angels announced the birth of Christ. He came to do the will of His Father. The purpose of His coming was for us to have fellowship with God, to have peace, and freedom from our sins by divine grace.

This was no small task, seeing how corrupt the world had become and how far away we were from God. Just knowing how deep we were in sin would discourage anyone from coming to earth except for Jesus.

Let's think about a time in our lives when we were sinking in the miry clay. We were unable to escape, and sinking deeper every day. This was our condition in life as sin was the heavy weight dragging us down.

I suppose it would be good if we had a visual to help us understand that our rescue efforts are in vain if there is no one else to save us. All means of getting us out alive will prove disastrous because there is no earthly way to remove the heavy weight of sin. Let's not forget about divine intervention.

No responders will come to help, helicopters will not be hovering over us with a safety basket and there is no one on the bank to throw us a rope. It seems as though we will die in our sins unless Jesus helps us.

Even if the whole world came to our rescue, we have to realize that any mechanical devices, operating equipment, or the best surgeons would not be able to have a successful operation. Only Christ can deliver us from sins evil intent.

Father, a rescue is possible but we are going to go to your own Son who specializes in delivering people from the miry clay. Christ came to save us from our sins. He is the only one who can accomplish such a tremendous task, amen.

The Shadow of Death
March 31

Our journey today will take us through the valley of the shadow of death. This will not be a tour of observing gravestones and memorials, but as we travel, we will notice these markers along the way. Please don't be alarmed if we see the name of a loved one or friend.

We can go back into history and find that everyone who lived and died had to go through the valley. When death comes for a visit, the choice of victims is not according to our positions in life, age, wealthy or poor.

"The Valley of the Shadow of Death" is not a movie title or a book promotion. This is a real-life situation where actors and book characters are not needed to fulfill the plot. All of humanity will know this is a true story and we will have to go through the valley to get to heaven's shore.

Presidents and kings will have their special places and some of them will be buried with their valuable assets or royal crowns. These memorials that we pass along the way will have the names of children and adults. None of us are excluded from the grave requisition list.

This expedition is open to the public. I cannot give a time when this journey will end or how long it will last. No one knows when the death shadows will cross our paths. This is our destiny in life; all of us have to pass through the valley, no shortcuts, fly-over, or detour will be allowed.

Father, help us to not fear death as we see more tombstones along the way. "Though I walk through the valley of death, I will fear no evil: for thou art with me." Our hope is not in the grave, but in a living Savior. We do not have to go alone. Jesus will walk beside us all the way through. There is no need to fear the shadows for the graves will open to life eternal if Jesus is our Savior. He will be our Lord if we repent, amen.

The Agony of Christ
April 1

Let's think about the severe punishment that Jesus had to endure before any of us could be saved. It appears to me that His crucifixion on the cross was arranged in such a way so that His pain was prolonged to make His suffering last longer.

On a hill far away, Jesus was nailed to a wooden cross. His visage (face) was marred more than any man. The punishment started with a beating, lashing with a whip. He was beaten thirty-nine times save one.

If there were more than the law allowed, the one who did the beating would also be punished. Many of the victims died from the beating alone. Jesus was taken to Calvary where He gave His life as a sacrifice.

The crown placed on His head was made of vines with many thorns. I believe these sharp pieces of wood were about one or two inches in length; they were forced onto His brow. Blood was streaming down the side of His face. Jesus was wounded and died for our transgressions.

Oh, this was a horrible way to die with Jesus in so much agony. He gave His life so we could have life. Without the shedding of blood there would be no remission of our sins. His blood sacrifice is a constant flowing of grace and mercy.

Spikes were driven into His hands and feet. This torture was excruciating, but He would not come down from the cross. He endured the pain for our sakes so we could have the blessed hope of life eternal.

Father, we need to think about Christ hanging on a cross; enduring the pain that was meant for us. He could have called the heavenly host to set Him free. If He came down from the cross, our sins would remain. Our hope of heaven would be in vain. Jesus said, "Not my will, but thy will be done." Amen.

111

Finding Jesus
April 2

Many years ago, people searched for Jesus, just as they do today. We would like to think about some interesting places where He was found. This journey to find Christ will take us into the past and we will continue our search to the present and even beyond.

Let's begin our search at the place where Jesus was born. When the wise men followed a star, they were able to find Him. A stable was where the Savior was born.

He was laid in a manger because there was no baby crib for this tiny infant to rest. Who would have ever thought a stable would be the birthplace of the King of kings and Lord of lords?

Later in life when Jesus was a youth, the doctors had no trouble finding Him for He was in their midst. Those that needed healing felt a touch of His hand and immediately miracles were performed.

Father, we have deep concerns for those in our families that they will find Christ before the midnight hour. The condition of our hearts in need of a Savior determines whether we will find Him or be lost forever.

I believe the cross is the place where most of us who know Him as our Savior would say this is where we met Him. When we realized His suffering and death was for us and that He was dying in our place, conviction brought us to our knees. Praise ascended to the throne above.

Finding Jesus does not have to be a life-long search that takes us into a faraway country. Help us to realize that He is not hiding from us and trying His best to keep us from finding Him. He didn't die on a wooden cross so we could play hide and seek. Let's search for Him with all our hearts, amen.

Walk on
April 3

Today we will be going for a walk and gather a little inspiration along the way. When we feel like quitting or we just don't think we can make it to the other side, our souls are inspired by two words, "Walk on." Let's be persistent with unwavering love. Each step brings us closer to heaven.

The best way for us to have the victory in life when our troubles and sorrows are dragging us down is to keep walking. No looking back or returning to the ways of the world. Active faith has no room for defeat.

"Walk on" I heard those inspirational words one day and I was inspired to hold up my cross a little higher, to live my life in such a way that God will be pleased when He looks down from his throne in glory.

Along the pathway of life, we find many days where the mountains are hard to climb. A prevailing storm hinders us on our heavenly journey. We walk through perilous times of trouble and strife. Our commitment is to keep going. The sorrows of life seem to overpower us, but we keep walking. A little while longer and we will wear the victory crown.

Father, the motivation of these two words inspires us to press onward, never turning back. Sometimes in life it is hard to take the next step, to gather enough strength to finish the race. Grief stricken hearts receive an abundance of grace when the mountains are too hard to climb.

Our struggles in life are not so bad when we know that Jesus is walking beside us. We may stumble along the way, but that does not stop us. The cross may be heavy at times but one day soon we will exchange it for a crown. We rise with a stronger determination to make it to heaven. Help us to realize the only way to win the prize is to, "Walk on!" Our journey will end with rejoicing as we walk through the gate, amen.

No Time to Wait
April 4

There are times in life when we have to make quick decisions. There is no time to call anyone on the phone or to wait for first responders to arrive on the scene. We must take immediate action, as there is no one else around to help us, no time to waste.

An emergency vehicle goes down the highway. Lights are flashing and sirens giving the warning signal. We have seen these vehicles many times in our earthly journey.

When these alarms are sounding, it is very important that we give the ambulance the right of way. Time is the deciding factor of life and death. A quick response time will save lives.

There was a dramatic scene unfolding, as there was no time to wait for a rescue unit. A woman was driving down the highway with a little baby in the car. All of a sudden, this small infant stopped breathing and its face had turned blue. This was a life or death situation with no time to react. The aunt gave resuscitation to the child.

The baby stopped breathing again and the rescue workers stayed with the baby and kept it alive. This precious child was taken to the hospital and was in stable condition.

In a tragic event there is no time to spare. Every minute counts. A short delay will have devastating results. When there is no immediate danger, we are less responsive and will wait much longer before any action is taken.

Father, we are living in a spiritual situation where life comes to an end without warning. The last breath is our final response to life. Help us to realize that emergency task force or other life-saving units cannot help us this time. We need to realize a personal decision to accept Christ in our lives is needed today for our salvation. In Jesus' name, amen.

114

Crucify All Over Again
April 5

We need to realize that if we go back into sin, we have to return to the cross where Jesus was crucified and we have to repent again. There is no other way for us to make things right with God.

Spikes will not be driven into His hands and feet or the crown of thorns forced upon His brow. He already went through the suffering. He died once and that was sufficient. How could He be crucified again?

Let's understand that by our sins we crucify Him afresh. There is no second death with Jesus being buried in the sepulcher we are crucifying Him again by our sinful deeds.

No spikes or a crown, but our sins pierce his flesh as if it were the nails, and ungodly living brings back the cross. If Jesus is crucified again, then this is a personal thing between Christ and us because of our sins.

We remember when we came to Jesus and asked Him to forgive us. It was His sacrificial death on the cross and His love that brought us to the place of repentance. Our hearts are broken because we betrayed Him.

Sins payment was paid at Calvary with Jesus hanging on a cross. He proved how much He loved us by giving His life so we could live. This was a time when we were truly sorry for our sins. Years of love and devotion are cast aside; we still hear the words of Jesus, "Follow me."

Father, we told Him that we would follow Him all through life. Our commitment was with love to never go back into sin. How could we sin, seeing how much He loved us? But that awful day came when we were no longer carrying our cross. Oh, how our hearts did rejoice when Jesus held us once again in His arms, love and mercy will prevail if we repent, amen.

Guidance from Above
April 6

We all need divine guidance, whether we are going through the valley of sorrow or by the peaceful rivers of overflowing joy. Jesus will guide us in all types of situations.

There was a time when a star was used to guide wise men to Christ. This was a long journey, but finally they found the Messiah. It is a blessed day in our lives when we find the Savior and invite Him into our hearts.

There are many types of guidance systems that help us to navigate the interstate and major highways. If we travel country roads where there is not much traffic and service stations are along ways apart, it is hard to get directions. These rural places can still help us on our journey.

Ever so often we have to stop and get the car filled up with gas. This is a good time to talk with the service attendant and get directions to a certain place. It is really a terrible thing for us to be lost at nighttime.

When we walk into a station and the attendant asks if we have a pencil and paper. The thought of writing his instructions is demoralizing and frustrating, but at least we will be able to get out of this lost condition.

Years have gone by and the navigation of the roads is made easier by satellites that circle the earth. We now have GPS (Global Positioning System) that uses these satellites to impose a visionary road map.

Father, we see how these technical devices help us to find our earthly locations, but right now we are more concerned about making it safely to heaven. There is no reason for us to have any frustration or anxiety, as Jesus your own Son will show us the right path. If we follow Him there is no way we can be lost. One day soon God will welcome us home, amen.

He Didn't Send an Angel
April 7

We think about our salvation of how that your Son died on a cross to save us. His death brings us into a family type relationship with Father and Son. We are blood relatives in Christ.

It is hard for us to identify with angels because most of us have never seen any of them. Jesus lived and walked among us. He was flesh and blood just like us. Our identity with Christ is established by grace.

Let's take a closer look at the angels. Each one has their own qualifications to perform certain activities for God. We are all familiar with guardian angels. They are vigilant to watch over the inhabitants of earth and to give us divine protection to keep us safe on the path of life.

We go to the cross where Christ was hanging between heaven and earth. Jesus could have called for the angels to set Him free, but He didn't do it. He stayed on the cross even though His pain was unbearable. He was fulfilling God's plan of salvation even to His death.

God has many supernatural angels, surely, He could have used one of them to accomplish His will and spare His Son. There have been many occasions in life where God sent an angel to perform certain duties, but not this time. None of them were qualified to become our substitutes.

Father, the salvation of mankind was so important that all of your sacred angels with all their super natural powers could not accomplish your will. None of them could forgive sin. Regardless of what we think about the angels, Jesus was the one chosen to bear our sins. He was the only one who could bring us into a personal relationship with God. Help us to realize the sacrifice of Jesus on an old rugged cross is our gateway to heaven. In Jesus' name, amen.

He Didn't Come Down
April 8

Let's think about Jesus dying on a cross and what He had to endure before we could be set free from a multitude of sins. Salvation for us cost Jesus His life. The payment, which was exceedingly enormous, was made in full.

We owed a debt that we could never pay. Payment for our sins required a blood sacrifice. Jesus was the only one who could fulfill our obligations. There is no salvation in any other person. He paid with His own life's blood the debt we owed.

The suffering of Christ was in many different forms, embarrassment, ridicule; He was spit upon which is a very despicable way of showing disrespect and hate. His suffering was more than anyone could bear.

A crowd of people cried out in anger, "Crucify him, crucify him." The executioners forced a crown of thorns upon His brow as to mock Him as a king. Blood dripped from His nail-scarred wounds to the ground.

His love for us kept Him on the cross. He didn't come down when His tortured body was experiencing excruciating pain. Jesus was wounded for our transgressions and bruised for our iniquities. On a cross He suffered, bled, and died for ungodly sinners who needed divine grace.

He was just like us with all our human qualities, except He was God's Son, the Holy One. He didn't come down from the cross and now He is counting on us to endure. Count it an honor to suffer for Christ's sake.

Father, help us to realize that if Jesus came down from the cross, His torment would be over, but our sins would remain. All Christian benefits would be cast aside with no hope of the resurrection or eternal life. None of us could sing, "Amazing grace that saved a wretch like me." Let's all praise Him, amen.

Heaven's Trip is not canceled
April 9

We are going on a travel adventure, perhaps the greatest one in our lives. We will not be going very far, but we want everyone to be aware, we are going to a place that has life-changing effects. If we are not fully persuaded, sin and unbelief will keep us from going home.

If we do not respond with faith, flights to glory will be null and void. Please observe the evidence before making any commitments. It would be terrible to find out the real truth and then rebel against it.

Those selected for this journey will be a variety of people with some faith enthusiasts, non-believers, and even those who are not sure what to believe. This group will not be complete unless we add the faithless.

There is no need to purchase an airplane ticket. We will make better time if we travel the waves of thought. Our return trip back home may be a different story, as faith will be needed to make the return trip.

I must remind everyone that the evidence we uncover will determine if heaven is our home. The truth will set us free if we believe and accept it.

We are going to a grave to see if Jesus is inside. If He is, all faith trips will be canceled and any reservations to glory will be non-existent. Faithless keeps Jesus in the grave while He is coming in the sky.

Father, we have entered into a fact-finding mission that will prepare us for the flight to glory. We want everyone to be aware that if the grave is empty, Jesus arose from the dead. This means that we must make travel arrangements immediately if we have not already confessed our sins. Jesus is alive; heaven's trip will not be canceled, amen.

Jesus Never Lies
April 10

We have found that as we commit our lives to Jesus, we are trusting in the one person who will never lie to us. All through the Bible we find the sacred pages are filled with promises He made to the people.

Jesus promised on the third day He would rise from the dead. His persecutors took Him down from the cross and laid Him in a sepulcher. He was not in a coma or unconscious as some people might suppose.

There should be no doubt in anyone's mind; He was dead. Jesus was buried in a borrowed grave. This deathbed was not going to be His permanent place with the deceased. Soon He would be leaving; He had no intentions to stay.

There is no reason to think that Jesus had told a lie about rising from the dead. "On the third day, I will rise again." So many times, we are impatient and count the days when belief and faith is quite sufficient.

One day passed and then two, surely, He is not coming back to life. But on the third day, Jesus kept His promise and arose from the dead. He was alive, alive forevermore.

Help us to realize this is a very important time in our lives because Jesus said that He is coming back to earth. All of His promises came true. When He comes in the clouds of glory, if our souls are not right, it will be too late to believe in Him.

Father, Jesus always spoke the truth and whatever He said, always came to pass. Wherever He went, lives were transformed by His truthful words. Christ said there is no salvation in any other. When we put our trust in Him we know that He is able to keep us unto life eternal because He has all power in heaven and earth. When the roll is called up yonder, we'll be glad we believed in Jesus, amen.

Flowers of Gratitude
April 11

We know that when a person dies, flower shops are busy preparing flower baskets. A lot of time goes into sorting and placing the vibrant colors in a beautiful display.

Loved ones call in the orders and sometimes they will have sentimental words attached to cards to reveal their love for the one who passed away. Precious memories revive the bonds of love and friendship.

This is really an emotional time for family members and loved ones. The flower shop takes the calls and share in the grief. Grieving hearts need words of consolation to help in the emotional healing process.

If the deceased is well known with a multitude of friends, flower shops may hire extra help to fulfill all the orders. Sometimes the workload has to be shared with other memorial shops.

We know that when loved ones pass away, the flowers on the graves will be reminders of the glorious times in life. Peaceful thoughts will occupy our minds, as the Lord assures us that everything will be all right. One touch of His hand will disperse the emotional pain. Sentimental thoughts flow from our hearts, and we are so thankful for the time spent together.

Father, It is always good to pay our respects to those who have died. Flowers have always been a wonderful way to express our gratitude. This is a sad time when life on earth comes to an end. Meditation of loved ones gone before us brings us back together in harmony of love and Spirit.

Their lives are remembered by the love and kindness they left behind. We are thankful to have had such a wonderful relationship with those departing souls. Help us to live holy today and righteousness will prevail throughout life, amen.

Battery Full Charge
April 12

Faith plays a very important role in our ability to accomplish things. We are going to use all kinds of mechanical devices to illustrate the power and source of active faith. Idle or dead faith will be ineffective in all applications.

The idle faith is similar to electricity that is running on too low of a voltage. One day my power supply was reduced to half and I did not know what was causing this problem.

My lights were not very bright and the stove did not have enough electricity to operate correctly. I discovered that one of the fuses was blown. After the fuse was replaced, my major electrical problems were solved.

Let's consider another item that has kept many of us from getting to our jobs on time; this is also idle faith. It can be really frustrating in the wintertime to try and start the car with a battery that is not fully charged.

When the motor will not start, more than likely, it is time to get a new battery. It appears to me that a battery with low charge is idle faith; only a little bit of power is transmitted to the motor. Dead faith is like the battery that is void of energy.

There is one very important thing that we have not mentioned and that is active faith. We don't have to worry about the heating elements on the stove because the full current is running through the line. If the lights are turned on, they will make any dark shadows run and hide.

Father, help us to realize that in our spiritual relationship with you, idle faith keeps our beliefs too low for any action. Dead faith is more severe as we cannot accomplish anything. Please send down a little more voltage of your grace so our lives will be restored and that the current of your love will be full charge in our lives. In Jesus' name, amen.

Obey the Speed Limit
April 13

As we travel on life's highway, we find there are many troopers on the roadside that are hidden in special locations to catch the drivers that are driving too fast, or breaking the law some other way.

Many people have died on the highway because of high speed. We find that driving too fast has serious consequences. If we are aware of the danger, we will take precautions to prevent an accident. Let's obey the safety rules; life depends on it.

Breaking the speed limit, It does not take us long to realize that we have broken the law, especially when a car with blue flashing lights pulls us over. This can be a terrifying experience.

The trooper walks up to the car and asks to see our driver's license and registration. We already have an idea why he pulled us over. As soon as we saw those lights, our car instantly slowed down to the normal speed limit.

Cars don't automatically slow down, as the driver was emotionally involved. His right foot that controlled the gas moved quickly to the brake pedal. Personal involvement is in complete control of our lives.

A good confession and using all the courtesy manners to influence the trooper can have good results. When the trooper lets us go without a ticket, we are thankful and give him our best regards. We are very careful not to speed-shift, pop the clutch, or squall the tires as we leave.

Father, when lawbreakers or sin offenders or caught in the act, punishment is required. It is always good when we are released from offences. Traffic or sin confessions get excellent results. Help us to obey the speed limit and above all, apply the brakes to all sin. In Jesus' name, amen.

Help is a Returnable Favor
April 14

As we walk down the pathway of life, we will meet people who need a helping hand. We remember the story of the Good Samaritan. A man was beaten, robbed, and left to die. Compassion was shown to this suffering individual.

When we meet someone along the way that is carrying a heavy burden, lets offer assistance to carry the load. A good deed is a returnable favor. Those people we help today may be the same ones that help us tomorrow.

We remember those in Texas that were affected by the hurricane, Harvey. Our hearts are overflowing with emotions as we see homes decimated and livelihoods completely shattered by the storm.

There are many places in life where we can help others who are in troublesome times. If we walk away without offering to help or giving assistance, families will starve including little children. Is it possible for us to see those who have lost their homes and have no compassion to help them in some way? Sensitive hearts bear the world's many needs.

I saw one person had returned to the rubble of her home and she found an American flag, which was a memorial of her late husband. She lost her home, but deep gratitude was expressed as she held the flag.

Help came from many states. Volunteers waded in water that was dangerous to their health, as it contained chemicals and other bacterial substances. I was deeply impressed with all the people working together to help those in need.

Father, give us compassion to help in any way, no matter what the situation. Let's offer a bandage for healing or a flag for comfort. Our lives will be blessed beyond measure. Help is a returnable favor. In Jesus' name, amen.

Beehives of Sin
April 15

Beehives of sin have a special attraction that will cause torment in the end. My thoughts today are taken from "Little House on the Prairie" in a type of paraphrase.

I saw on this TV show where a person was told the best time to get the honey out of an old log. These kids were playing a prank on a lady who was very arrogant.

This woman was always criticizing others and intimidating them. The cost of this honey would be a good way to connive her trustworthy customers out of their hard-earned money.

The young boy told her that when the sun is the hottest, the bees would be sleeping and that would be the best time of day to collect the honey. This woman and her daughter waited until the sun was scorching hot and then proceeded to take this delicious item from the tree trunk.

Within minutes a swarm of bees had gathered around the mother and daughter. These two scheming beehive robbers were last seen in a wagon pulled by a horse at full gallop towards the town. I doubt if any honey was sold that day, but bee sting ointment was in high demand.

A better way of collecting honey would be a uniform that seals all open areas. Hoods with screens would be good protection for the face. If we need to know the best time of day to collect honey from a beehive, maybe we should contact a specialized bee consultant.

Father, help us to realize that Godly living requires us to stay away from the beehives of sin. Otherwise we need a good supply of healing balm to take care of any stings caused by sleeping bees. Sin has no conceivable time to stir up trouble and strife. There is a remedy for aches and pains caused by sin. Send us the antidote of a fresh supply of grace, amen.

"We are Va. Tech." Let's Go Hokies"
April 16

Today we are going to travel back in time to the Virginia Tech campus. A terrible tragedy had taken place on April 16, 2007. Thirty-two people were killed, seventeen wounded, and six of the injured escaped through windows. The person responsible for this tragedy committed suicide.

This was a time of extreme sorrow and grief for the families and for the entire nation. Even though we did not know the classmates and staff personally, we still felt the emotional pain in our hearts. The dark shadow of death had crossed the path of these precious individuals.

We can still remember the words of inspiration that touched our lives in the memorial service. "We will prevail!" These are thoughtful words that inspire us to keep going, no matter how deep the sorrow or how great the pain.

Keep holding on to the memories for in them are the lives of loved ones. Our hopes and dreams are fulfilled in the love that never dies. Inspiration of life never wavers or accepts defeat.

We all became a part of this tragedy, as we were joined even closer together when the final words were given at this sacred assembly. A sweet, sweet Spirit was touching lives that day.

When the student body arose to offer their final farewells, an abundance of grace was present in solemn sincerity with peace. "We are Va. Tech." "Let's Go Hokies."

Father, precious memories leave a trail of loving-kindness. The voice of Virginia Tech was heard that day. It was the sound of triumph and victory that allows love to conquer in all situations. Let us hold fast the precious memories by holding one another and sharing in each other's sorrows. Please send down a loving embrace as we wait for the time we will meet again. In Jesus' name, amen.

Paid in Full
April 17

We have a long list of the many sins that we have committed. The price of each one is on our account. Payment of repentance is required or we will have to suffer the consequences.

Since we cannot pay in cash, money orders are forbidden, and debit or credit cards is worthless when it is time to pay off our debt. Some people would say, "I have never heard of such a thing, a debt that cannot be paid with any earthly finances."

There is no use to bring any gold or silver, as these valuable assets will not remove one sin from our list of regrettable things. Please don't be discouraged as we are quickly moving to the place where our debt of sin can be paid. Let's take our sins to Jesus; He will not hesitate to forgive.

Bear with me a little while longer as there is a certain amount of faith required to pay the debt. We must remember that each of us has our own personal account. This is not like a bank where a friend or someone with our consent can walk up to the bank employee and make the final payment.

The cashier gives us a smile and we walk away knowing that our financial obligations have been met, no more payments. It feels really good to have the heavy burden lifted from our lives.

Earthly debt is usually set up in installments. Payments are made at a specific time. If we are late, a penalty will be added to the balance. There are times when more forceful actions are taken to receive the payment. The law has a special way of handling delinquent accounts.

Father, we have created a huge debt by the sins we have committed. This is not payable by money. A blood sacrifice is acceptable for our sins. Christ is the only one who can pay this debt, as He was crucified on a cross. Sin's financial statement is available with our sins forgiven. We are debt free, amen.

Stay Away from the Honey
April 18

A special warning is given to never take up residence in a place where the honey is sweet and bees swarm with an intent to cause pain. The sweet lure of sin can have devastating results that will not be cured with bee ointment.

Perhaps it would be good to know how nature takes care of this problem. We are going into the mountains and observe a bear den where two bear cubs and its mother are waking up with hunger pains.

The cold hard winter is over and the flowers have already bloomed. Bear cubs are seen playing and rolling around on the hillside. The mother of this small family is climbing over the rocky terrain in search of food.

She did not have to go very far because a colony of honeybees had created a private honeycomb in an old log. There were no posted signs to warn the hungry recipients. But there were quite a number of bees that were armed with sting type weapons. It did not take the bears long to feel the pain.

A log of honey was real close to the bear's den. This wild animal desires the honey so much that it will not let anything stop her from devouring this delicious food.

Father, we need to think about the comforts of home, a mother bear with two small cubs. The location of their den was close to a river where there would be a good water supply and large salmon was plentiful.

It seems as though we are like the bears. Everything is going well for us until we indulge in sin. This is the honeycomb that we need to avoid. We may encounter small sins that are harmful. Soon these little sins will disrupt our lives and have us move out of the family residence. Help us to be aware the sting of sins is painful. In Jesus' name, amen.

Meet Jesus at the Crossroads
April 19

We are coming to the crossroads and this is where we have to make a very important decision. The road we choose will take us to heaven or to a place of torment. Time is not in our favor.

Lets see how long it takes to make things right with God. After considerable thought, an age indicator will give us the best results. This would probably be a birth certificate. A death certificate would not be necessary because we are just going to the crossroads; we are not going to the end of life. Accept Christ today and remove all doubt of any time effects.

The reason we are using a time schedule is to help people understand that each of us arrive at the crossroads at different times in our lives. There is not a set age limit like getting a driver's license, or being able to vote. The age indicator shows that we meet Jesus various times in life.

Time is a factor in our decision. If we wait too long our opportunity will be past. We have to let everyone know there will not be any decisions made in the grave. The crossroad to heaven does not have any extensions after death. Today is the best time to choose life eternal.

Father, some people are curious about choosing the wrong road. They want to know if there is another chance somewhere else on the highway of life. There can be many chances but none of us know which one is the last. Death has canceled many opportunities and the victims failed to get on the right road. A wrong decision can be corrected, turnaround.

Let's get a better understanding of the crossroads. This is the place where we either accept Jesus into our hearts as Lord and Savior or we reject Him. The time is right when the Holy Spirit is drawing us and with remorseful hearts we tell Jesus that we are sorry for our sins. No age limit required but death will end all possibilities. Christ rejected is heaven denied, amen.

Life in Christ
April 20

Many years have elapsed since Jesus was crucified on a cross and was laid in a temporary grave. He arose from the dead and ascended to heaven. The angels proclaim, "He is alive."

What does that mean for those of us who are living today? It means that Christ was brought back to life. He was raised from the dead and those of us who believe Christ is the Savior will have everlasting life.

Jesus' body was buried in a sepulcher. He stayed there until the third day and then He arose. The grave could not hold Him. He has power over death, the grave, and hell. We also shall rise by resurrection power.

When we repent, Jesus forgives us. Our old sinful nature dies and we receive a new life in Him. Normally there is a funeral when a person dies. However, we will not be going to the cemetery or have any flowers on our caskets. Tears of joy will replace the sadness because we live.

There will be no memorial for sins, but it will be a time of rejoicing to know that "Old things have passed away, and behold, all things are become new." Death to sin is the gateway to heaven by Christ Jesus.

We are not dead physically and they will not place us in the ground for burial. Our names will not appear in the obituary column. We are alive in Christ. Natural death is coming without any regards for life.

Father, there is remorse when a person dies, grieving hearts are aching because of the loss of a loved one. Tears of sorrow overwhelm us. Help us to realize when sin dies we are set free from the burden of guilt. Death to sin is life in Christ. There is no remorse; our hearts are overflowing with joy because we are alive. In Jesus' name, amen.

Security Breach
April 21

We have security devices that protect our earthly assets. Theft of personal identification is one of the most severe security risks. The best security agencies cannot protect us all the time.

Debit cards connect us to many types of benefits. We can withdraw money from the bank or buy something on-line. If this information gets in the wrong hands, lives can be ruined and identities can be sold to the highest bidder. Purchases can be made without the owner's consent.

A Notice has gone out to the public of a severe security breach. Computers were hacked and private information was stolen. High technology thieves affected thousands of people by stealing ID'S. Recently, there were one hundred forty-three million identities stolen.

I believe one security breach has been corrected and new cards have been reissued to the victims. Once identities have been stolen, it is very hard to clear one's name. One breach is fixed, while another is broken.

We all use security methods to protect our families and make sure they are kept safe. Our doors in each of our homes have locks on them to keep out intruders. Thieves break into our homes by cutting the locks.

We live in a time when security is our number one priority. No matter how hard we try to protect ourselves, thieves always seem to find a way to steal our valuables. If the most secure facilities are disrupted by crime, how can we be safe?

Father, we have something very important that we want to keep safe throughout eternity. This is not material wealth. Our souls are in need of divine protection. If we commit our souls to Jesus, He is able to keep them unto everlasting life. While we are in His care there will never be a security breach, amen.

It is finished
April 22

When our life long goals are complete and we have done our very best to accomplish the task, we rejoice in the finished work. Just like athletes who have trained for many years to compete in the Olympics, they eventually come to the end of their life experience and hopefully they will be rewarded for their achievements.

We all have certain expectations of fulfilling an ambition in life. The dreams of going to college and becoming a doctor or nurse is finally realized when we have finished the college requirements and have received our diplomas. A new life begins when the old one ends.

There was one person who lived His life for the sake of others. I am speaking of Jesus whose love and compassion is known throughout the world. By His obedience to God our lives have been changed forever. His mission in life was to bring us into a right relationship with God.

When Jesus was crucified, His last words on the cross were: "It is finished." He gave His life so we could have life. God's will or plan was accomplished. Jesus stayed on the cross because He loves us and wants us to go to heaven.

Father, your Son, Jesus had to finish the salvation plan. If the mission of the cross-had failed, we would still be in our sins. The ruin of the nation would have collapsed with no hope of salvation. Help us to think about Christ last words, "It is finished."

No more suffering, the excruciating pain would be gone, and most of all, punishment for our sins was finished. The final payment of our debt was made at Calvary. Help us now to know the cross is where Jesus' earthly life ended and it is where life begins for us. It will be a glorious time in our lives when we trade the cross for a crown. "It is finished." Amen.

Constantly Alert
April 23

We do not know what kind of dangers we will face in life. If we were in the mountains and hungry wolves were all around us, we would take all kinds of precautions to prevent a deadly attack.

Let' go to the mountains on a survival tour. We are going to a place where wolves run wild and other types of animals have raided campsites causing considerable damage.

Since we are going into dangerous territory, it is essential that we have the type of equipment that will help save our lives. A good shelter will protect us from the storms and it will also be a place where we can rest after hiking in the forest.

The camping gear is loaded onto the four-wheel drive vehicle. An inventory checklist is gone over before we begin the journey. We have high-powered rifles, ammunition, a good supply of food, and many other things to make sure we get back home. Preparation saves lives.

Our survival skills will be severely tested. The first night the tent will be set up in an area where wolves recently attacked and killed two campers.

We can hear the howling wolves as they are moving closer to the camp. A large campfire is the only thing that can save our lives. All of us decide to stay alert and keep the fire burning. Vigilance is a lifesaver.

Father, help us to realize that our survival training to make heaven our home, we need to be diligent and alert. We need to be careful where we pitch our tents of godly living. It would also be a good idea to keep the glory light burning. Satan's deceitful wolves may sneak in unaware with sinful intent to cause us harm. Being constantly alert keeps us safe on our journey to heaven. Watch and pray is our best defense, amen.

Locked Outside
April 24

We had a peaceful rest last night and woke up to a beautiful day. The first thing we saw when we looked outside the window was a colorful display of flowers, birds singing in the trees, and baby rabbits scurrying across the field.

However, this wonderful day would soon bring turmoil and anxiety. Stressful days rob us of the peace and fill our hearts with dismay. How could such a glorious day turn so quickly into disappointment? Days of distress will appear suddenly without warning.

This was the first day of a new job, as we were unemployed for several months. Our survival was a day-by-day process with neighbors helping out with groceries, paying utility bills, and other necessities of life.

I am sure everyone would like to know what caused all of this grief. The sorrows of our hearts begin when our keys are locked inside the house. We are on the outside, searching pockets and looking everywhere for the entrance key.

First day of turning our lives around is drastically affected by the loss of our keys. A door that is securely locked will keep us in a distressful mood until we get inside the house.

The dilemma of our situation becomes worse when we realize the cell phone is also missing. There is no way to enter or call for assistance. Our only opportunity for employment is downgraded, leaving us with bare cupboards, empty pockets, and neighbor's good intentions.

Father, earthly situations will interfere with our future endeavors. There are times when we are locked on the outside. Let's think about the spiritual aspect of a lockout. Help us to remember a call can be made to the throne room of mercy. The faith key of repentance opens the door of our hearts, amen.

Faith to See Christ
April 25

There are certain events that took place in the life of Christ. None of us in the 21st century was living when Jesus walked on the earth. We were not eyewitnesses of the healing miracles, walking on water, or when He fed five thousand people with a few pieces of fish, as it is recorded in the Bible.

We did not see any of those things. It is only natural to think if we had only been there our faith would be so much stronger. However, many witnesses saw him, but for lack of faith and unbelief it was no profit. When we see and do not repent; sins will remain. How can we see when faith is lacking? Hearing the Word creates faith and sight is restored.

It is really remarkable for millions of people around the world who never saw Jesus, any of His miracles, or at the cross to see His crucifixion. We were not there when He was buried and rose again and ascended into heaven.

He suffered on the cross. Our faith is not in vain because we did not experience the excruciating pain. Faith does not depend on us seeing or feeling extreme agony from His nail scarred wounds.

Our salvation experience is not by sight, but according to the belief in our hearts. "Blessed are they that have not seen, and yet believe." (John 20:29) "Faith comes by hearing and by hearing the Word of God." We didn't have to see with our eyes to be in His presence. Faith reveals a living Savior. Active faith will cause us to see Him walking among us.

Father, our faith is not determined by our earthly vision, but we know Jesus is alive because He lives in our hearts. If we have to see everything in this world before we can believe it, this would be a miserable place to live. Christ has risen from the dead; believe it. Soon we will see Him. Help us to be ready when He comes back to earth. In Jesus' name, amen.

Faith Never Gives Up
April 26

Sometimes, we need an encouraging word to help us on the pathway of life. If we are discouraged by a fall or an injury before we get to the top of the mountain, we are more likely to give up and go back to the valley. We cannot let the trials keep us down.

The thoughts may arise in our minds, why don't we just quit; the mountain is too hard to climb. Maybe we need to be reminded that our cross will be heavy to carry at times, but we are promised the victory if we will keep the faith.

A made-up mind and determination will allow us the power to overcome any obstacles in the way. A made-up mind is half the battle; active faith is the other half.

The fulfillment of life is our determination to keep going. No matter how tired or regardless of the pain, don't give up. Keep holding the nail-scarred hand of Jesus.

Soon we will wear the victory crown. Jesus never called it quits even when His cross was heavy to bear. Think about what He had to endure and how high the mountain was for Him to climb in order to set us free.

Spikes were driven into His hands, a crown of thorns forced upon His brow, and He had to endure excruciating pain. If He yielded to the overpowering force of sin and came down from the cross (His mountain), we would be forever in the valley of remorseful sins. If He quit, how could we be triumphant? Victory without Christ is impossible.

Father, help us on life's journey when we need strength to climb the mountains of discouragement. When we are weak from a fall and feel like giving up, hold on a little longer. One touch of Jesus' hand and a quick look at how He suffered on the cross will help us to be victorious in life. Amen.

He Died for an Enemy
April 27

There are times in life when we have had to fight in major battles. Soldiers have laid down their lives for one another. Thoughts today are about the sacrifices we make for our friends, family, and loved ones. Would we give our lives to save an enemy?

The opposing force in war is the enemy and battles are raging today across the land. It is not very hard to spot an aggressor that will do anything to harm or hurt us. The strategy of war is to fight until the enemy surrenders or until one side of the conflict is victorious in battle.

Let's give this question a lot of thought. Military opponents are considered to be our enemies. We have brave men and women in the armed forces, fighting for our freedom.

These brave soldiers are at risk of losing their lives and some of them have given the ultimate sacrifice of life for their country. War takes many lives, who is willing to give life?

The war continues overseas with soldiers on both sides inflicting severe wounds and death on the battlefield. I have heard of soldiers sacrificing themselves to save one of their own. Loyalty is honor that defies death.

It really takes a courageous person to die for a friend or a perfect stranger. But if it is the enemy, is there anyone in this country who would die for them? Some of us would dare to die for a friend, who would die for an enemy? The answer is plain to see with Jesus hanging on a cross, dying in our place.

Father, your Son, Jesus died for us while we were your enemies. He was beaten and suffered excruciating pain. Spikes were driven into His hands and feet. A crown of thorns was forced upon His brow. The death of Jesus releases us from the enemy status when we repent. He now calls us friends, amen.

If in This Life Only
April 28

We think about our lives and what life would be like without the resurrection of Jesus. Sin would be like a tidal wave overflowing the earth. The floodwaters of sin would saturate our lives.

Evil would prevail with corruption engulfing us with ungodly living. Unrighteousness would be as a wild fire spreading mass destruction with devastation. Anger flare-ups would cause intense brutal hostility.

All of Christianity would decline into a death spiral. Things of faith disappear right before our eyes. If Jesus is in the grave, those who claim Him as Lord and Savior are living a lie. All hopes of going to heaven are false illusions.

We need a Holy Ghost anointed scripture to restore our faith, hope, and love. "If in this life only we have hope in Christ, we are of all men most miserable" (I Cor. 15:19). Sin in our lives still remains if there is no resurrection from the dead. Let's all rejoice, the stone was rolled away and Jesus came back to life.

All previous closings, false announcements, lies, and cancelations of faith are hereby reverted back to their normal truthful conditions. All believers still have the blessed hope of going to heaven.

This story began in a death spiral, what happened to change it? Jesus arose! Help us to realize Christ is alive and our faith is not in vain.

Father, help us now to take a closer look at the gravesite of Jesus. The sepulcher was empty; Angels sent from heaven made an announcement that would turn back the tidal wave, quench the fire of devastation, and restore godly living. Listen very closely, my friend, as the angels announce, "He is not here, He is risen!" Christianity is alive and well, amen.

Jesus Answers All Distress Calls
April 29

First responders are constantly putting their lives in danger to save those who are in perilous situations. These lifesavers leave their homes at a moment's notice and travel many miles to help those who are struggling to stay alive.

Recently there was a hurricane in Texas and surrounding areas. Some of the rescue attempts included people in low valleys, on top of houses, even in attics where there was no way to escape the rising waters.

The TV programs did offer some good information for those who sought refuge in the attic. It was suggested that an axe or some type of cutting instrument should be stored in the attic for any type of emergency, especially for floods. Advice is beneficial in all situations.

Before the storm arrived with hurricane force winds, the residents were outside, boarding their homes and places of business. Some boats were securely attached to the pier and held fast by immovable objects.

The winds were expected to be about 135 mph. This was really a horrific storm that could cause a considerable amount of damage and even the loss of life. A surge from the floodwaters was expected to be about fifteen feet. Swift moving storms require immediate action.

Warnings of hurricane Harvey were announced several days in advance. When the storm got closer to land, high alerts were issued for certain counties to evacuate immediately. However, there were some places that never received the warning.

Father, help us to realize that all earthly attempts to save lives will not be successful. Emergency crews can have the best training, but all of the cries for help will not be answered. Jesus responds quickly to all cries for mercy, amen.

Prescription is on Order
April 30

There are special times in our lives when we have to make a call to a physician to have our prescriptions filled. A staff member normally receives this message and then it is transferred to the attending doctor where he uses the computer to verify the information.

A good clear conversation is essential in obtaining the right medicine or the treatment that is needed for good health. It would truly be a terrible thing if the wrong social security number was given or it was written down in the wrong way.

After a short while the pharmacy receives the data. Special attention is given to the order so the patient will receive the correct medicine. The patient also has a lot of responsibility to check the medicines for properly labeled items.

If the prescription is filled incorrectly the results could have devastating effects for the patient and for those who filled the order. Patients could lose their lives if the wrong pills were taken. Doctors, pharmacist, and all those involved could have lawsuits against them.

We go to the pharmacy to pick up prescription drugs. These are medicines that the doctor prescribed. The instructions vary on each container.

We have strict orders by the attending physician to take these pills at a specific time. When we call the Doctor's office for appointments or pharmacy renewals, our private information is verified for security and safety reasons. This process helps to eliminate errors and keep us alive.

Father, concerning our sins, we do not discuss these elements of unrighteousness with doctors or pharmacist because we know their expertise is only with physical problems. I am sure a referral is in order. Jesus is highly recommended, amen.

Come from Behind
May 1

The race of champions will begin in just a few minutes. We will call them by their real names, Faith, Good Deeds, and Love. These three runners form a team that will help us to cross the finish line. If these faithful contestants work together, the final results will be a victory crown.

Before the race begins, let's take a quick look at the qualifications of each runner. Faith is able to move mountains. I am sure that would be a good choice. Good deeds have inspired people around the world with kindness to help one another. Love is the navigational point of God's mercy.

All three of these runners are scheduled for the event; the third qualifier has arrived. It seems like Love has been denied access to the racetrack. Amid all this confusion the two other runners have already lined up at the gate.

The gun is fired and they are off and running. Faith and Good Deeds immediately fall behind. They cannot win the race without Love. Everyone in the crowd stands in amazement; Love has entered the race and caught up with its two teammates. Our efforts will not be in vain if there is unity.

Suddenly the three favorites are once again running as a team. They cross the finish line and receive the crown. The victory can be won as long as our heart's desire is to glorify God.

Father, if we are contestants in a race, we would like for our team players to be loyal to their spiritual abilities. It is very important for us to win this race. Eternity will be the final result. It is truly an honor to run with the champions. Divide the team and we will forfeit the prize.

Help us to realize we can win the crown of life, but in order to cross the finish line, we must have a team effort With Love, Good Deeds, and Faith. "All for one and one for all," amen.

Dust on the Bible
May 2

A Bible stashed away somewhere will not benefit us in any way if we never read its sacred contents. Pages never turned is a good sign that God is far away, and if that is so, guess who moved? I believe we already know the answer.

Before the distance gap between God and us becomes even wider, search all through the house, the attic, basement, and the closets are good places to check. Try to remember the last time it was read. I know that is a real scary thought, but it may help us to find this sacred book.

Please don't give up until this holy book is found because our relationship with God depends on these words to restore our spiritual health. Our poor aching bodies could use an antidote of forgiveness to help us recuperate from the many years of neglecting our salvation.

Over the years there has been a steady decline in moral values of spiritual things. Without the Word in our lives there is no nourishment for our souls and no guidance from heaven above. Fellowship is lacking with God because we are not attentive to His Word. Neglect results in regret.

We had best make this search as quickly as possible because time is of the essence. If we take too long to get back on the path of righteousness, the light of His glory will fade out of sight as we are nearing the final sunset. There will be no reading in the dark confinements of death.

Father, this book was created for daily living and devotion. It was not made to be a relic of the past. God's inspired Word is a book of life for all who will believe and read its sacred pages. When there is too much dust on the Bible, there is not enough time with God. Help us now to hide the Word in our hearts, not in the garage, on a shelf, or in a desolate place. Easy access has eternal benefits, amen.

The Choice is mine
May 3

All of us have to make choices as we journey through life. Some of these decisions can be made as partners of a company. We may not always agree, but we accept the results.

Follow with me on an imaginary journey where we go back in time. We will be traveling with the pioneers to our new homes out west. The Federal Government is looking for some brave individuals to deliver the mail by pony express.

Please be aware there will be risk and it is a possibility that some of us will not be returning to the homeland. I feel it is my responsibility to give these warnings because I signed the government contract for all of us to be pony express riders. Bad decisions have terrible consequences.

I hope there are no hard feelings. Just one more thing, the federal agency will prosecute anyone that fails to deliver the mail. Indians is the least of my worries. Signature fraud is a criminal offence with jail time.

It is not very wise to sign anyone on a contract without his or her permission. There seems to be a lot of angry friends who have circled around me for some unknown reason.

I am so glad that our commitment to God is a personal one, including accepting Christ as Lord and Savior. Salvation is granted on an individual basis.

Each of us is responsible for our own decisions in life. All of my angry friends agreed: "The choice is mine." I can still hear those angry words from inside the dark jail cell.

Father, all of us have choices that we make in life. A decision to accept or reject Christ into our hearts is a personal decision. All of us can pray that Jesus will save souls. However, each person may respond by saying, " The choice is mine," amen.

Sins Erased
May 4

Our thoughts today will have us using two writing components. One of them is a pencil. This is not a test, so number two lead is not required. We want to make sure we have a really good eraser because of the multitude of sins we have created.

It is our desire to erase as many sins as possible in order to have a clean, pure life. The pencil is used to write down all the activities of our lives. We have many pages filled with good things, as well as sins that are in abundance. Erasing sins will not cleanse or purify our hearts.

I cannot emphasize enough the importance of having an extra-large eraser. This will be an all-day assignment for the removal of sin. We just received word from the sin correction agency as they have been monitoring the vast number of sins that are quickly accumulating on each classmate's paper. These sins are far more than anyone realized.

The pencil sharpener is working overtime, trying to keep up with the vast number of sins that each person writes down. An industrial supply company has been called in to help with the pencil demand and the paper shortage.

It has been decided that one-day is not sufficient to complete the sin removal and the time limit has been rescheduled to all week with the addition of homework.

When personal sins are erased on paper, we still have sins in our lives. This brought a complete meltdown with the staff employees and they canceled all class efforts to erase sin.

Father, we know there is only one way to eliminate sin in our lives and that is to ask Jesus to forgive all our sins. We do not have to spend days writing them on paper. It just takes a few minutes of heart felt prayer. Forgive me, Lord, amen.

Compassion of an Author
May 5

Our individual talents will express the deep sentiments of our hearts. These special gifts are crafted by God's own hand and anointed with inspiring messages from above.

However, there are a variety of these creative forms of inspiration that will bless us in many different ways. We have chosen Christian writing as the talent for today. This will be a time of lifting up the name of Jesus and glorifying God. Fellow authors, rejoice with me in reverent praise.

It is a golden opportunity to win the lost. Words that come from the depth of our souls will inspire us to love God with all of our hearts, minds, and souls. This is the fulfillment of the great commandment.

We know our lives are truly blessed when those who read our words are encouraged to live holy, righteous lives. If we can say something that will cause sinners to repent, the angels will rejoice with them in heaven.

Words of faith, hope, and love abound in the pages. When we share thoughts of inspiration, we are leaving a trail to the Glory Land. The words we write are to help others know Jesus Christ as Lord and Savior and to know of God's great love. Righteousness leads to more grace.

It is hard for us to see the compassion of an author until the words are written down. Deep devotion flows like a river as the sentences are formed. If a rip tide of conviction is created, there is no need to worry. The current of God's love will fill our hearts with praise as we walk with Christ.

Father, we pray for special guidance in the words we choose. We want to leave a lasting impression that will help people think about their salvation. It is our desire that a reaction will be to kneel in sincere repentance. In Jesus' name, amen.

A Living Savior
May 6

We would like to go on a journey back in time to the place where Christ was crucified. It will be best if we travel by the imagination route. Let's begin at the cross of Calvary and from there we will return to the future. Visionary travel brings us to the reality of life.

Now that we have arrived at the time of the crucifixion, Jesus is hanging on the cross and a crown of thorns had been forced upon His brow. He is bleeding from the wounds, as His body aches in agony.

He is taken down from the cross and buried in a borrowed grave. On the third day, He arose from the dead. Our journey continues as we are now heading home. Tearful eyes of sorrow bring about joyful hearts.

Time has gone by with a development of new towns and cities. We can visit the place, but the cross no longer stands and the sepulcher is empty. A vision from the past is hidden from view. Nothing can erase the fact that Jesus conquered death, the grave, and hell. He lives forevermore.

Father, as we travel along the back roads, we notice there are churches in the community and the residents are praising and worshiping God. All along the way, we meet people whose lives have been changed by the sacrificial death of Jesus. Oh, how marvelous is the grace of God.

A vast number of people meet with us on our journey of life that has come to know Jesus as the Lord of their lives. The world today wants to see a living Savior. Help us to not disappoint them.

When we live in God's favor, others will see Jesus in our lives. Personal images of holiness and godly living are the best ways for us to reveal a risen Savior, amen.

A Sharp Axe
May 7

Let's learn a lesson from two woodsmen. If we take the time to sharpen the axe, our labor in the forest will prove worthwhile. It is not an easy thing to cut a tree with a dull axe.

Let's go back in time and realize the elderly woodsmen worked for a few hours in his shed, making sure the axe was sharpened with a good crisp edge. Early that morning he picked up the sharpened tool and started towards the forest. This man's efforts would be successful at the end of the day.

We find that a young man thought it was a waste of time and energy to put a good edge on the axe. He did not bother to sharpen it. When we rely on our own strength to accomplish a task, self-conceit may prevail. A large woodpile and a small one should help us to understand that mighty things are accomplished when we use the best resources available.

Soon the chips began to fly and the sound of trees was heard falling to the ground. After a while the man with the sharp axe had a good supply of wood. This would probably be enough for the harsh winter ahead.

Now the other man, he was really tired. Swinging that dull axe completely wore him out and only a few trees lay on the ground. He would definitely have to return to the forest and cut more wood. The next morning, he had a sharp axe.

Father, it appears to me that the Word of God is very much like the sharp axe. They both have sharp edges that will cut deep into the core. Trees fall in the forest, as a reaction from the blade of steel.

God's Word cuts deep into our lives and tears of repentance fall when conviction grips our hearts. Help us to realize we need a sharp axe of diligent, heartfelt prayer for better results. Our labor of love will not be in vain. In Jesus' name, amen.

Flames of Faith
May 8

All through life we have the responsibility of keeping our faith alive. A good way to understand this technique of survival is to gather more wood for the fire. The electricity is out and the other source of heat is a fireplace.

Let's think about a harsh winter wind that is blowing. We need to come in from the cold and find warmth in the house. It is taking a little while longer to feel the heat of the radiant flames, as the burning embers are about to go out.

There are a few cinders still burning. If we hurry, the fire can be restored and we will live another day. Small twigs help in the burning process. One stick is laid on at a time; too many branches will smother the fire.

At last a small flame is seen flickering on a piece of wood. The anticipation of life grows stronger with each passing minute. More wood increases the intensity of the fire.

The warmth of this heating element restores our hopes of survival. Now that the fire is blazing, it will be everyone's responsibility to make sure the flames does not go out.

We know this is going to be a long night, but our survival depends on bringing in firewood to keep us from freezing to death. This is going to be an all-night endeavor with all of us gathering wood to keep the fire alive. If we falter in our obligation, none of us may live another day.

Father, if our belief system is dying, we had better hurry and add another log to the fire. Our faith flames are different than firewood. Active faith keeps the fire in our hearts alive. Spending time in prayer is a really good way to feel the warmth of God's love. We can draw near to Him and our cold hearts will be thawed by grace. Help us to gather more wood until faith is revived and alive. In Jesus' name, amen.

Detour, Life depends on it
May 9

Our thoughts would have us in a nice vacation resort, enjoying time with the family. This vacation would be spent in a camping area in the mountains. The van was loaded up with tent supplies and all of the camping gear.

Some members of the group thought it would be good to travel some of the country roads and enjoy the scenery. We all agreed and started down the highway. Soon our pleasure trip would be drastically changed.

While traveling down the road, we saw a warning on a sign that caught our attention. There was one word on the sign in really big, bold letters and it read, "Detour." This warning did not need bright flashing lights.

The road was completely blocked; no one was allowed to enter this section of the highway. Unfortunately, this was the route we had chosen to take on our sightseeing tour. If a sign appears, don't hesitate to turn.

A sign does not have to say a whole lot for us to realize there is danger ahead. One word brought a certain amount of anxiety because we had spent a lot of time, studying roadmaps, and setting the navigation on the GPS system. All of our travel plans have to be rearranged.

Father, help us to see how important it is to follow the warning signs. While traveling down the highway, we come to a detour sign. Lives can be saved if we heed the warning. Accidents are caused when people do not go by the instructions. A moment of hesitation could be disastrous.

This sign gives us directions for a new route. We follow the arrows and soon we will be at our destination. God warns us to change directions. "Repent!" Help us to know that we can live with this warning if we turn from sin. In Jesus' name, amen.

No Talents Left
May 10

We are so thankful for each talent that you have so graciously given to us. Help us now to use these special abilities to glorify your holy name and to inspire others to live holy, godly lives.

It would truly be a wonderful blessing to come to the end of our journey and find there is nothing left to give. We gave it all for His glory. Talents are given with blessings to share, if we keep them to ourselves, what does it profit us? There is no joy in unused talents.

God has many wonderful gifts of grace that He has given to each one of us. Special talents are handcrafted for our own individual needs. He has designed them with His own signature touch so blessings will abound.

His handiwork always comes with the anointing that will bless us and will be an inspiration to His people around the world. Our lives are blessed when a song is sung, a sermon is preached, a book is written, and the lists goes on for His Glory. These gifts are given so we will be a blessing and be an encouragement to those we meet along the way.

God's creative talents are designed for us and anointed by Him so everyone will be blessed. No talents left is a really good way to finish our journey here on earth.

Father, help us to think about how miserable our lives would be if we never used our talents. Sweet melodies from the choir would not ascend to heaven. Songs of praise, no arms are raised for His glory.

Sinners would have a harder time of hearing the Word if the ministers were silent. Special gifts are given so we can rejoice together in heavenly places. How can we be a blessing except we use the talents? Help us now to be faithful servants with our gifts of grace. In Jesus' name, amen.

Illegal Bass to Report
May 11

We were along ways from home. The sun had already set on the horizon. This was a camping expedition that we had planned several weeks in advance. Memories of the past still haunt us.

When our camping gear was loaded onto the vehicle, all of the supplies were checked off of the inventory list. It seemed as though the bait was the most frequently checked item. Some of the fishermen inquired about the bait two or three times. Frustration was starting to annoy us.

We gave them full assurance that we have bait and all the fishing supplies. These doubters were content for a while when they saw these items on the truck. Please be aware other items may be missing.

There was a lot of concern about the fishing gear and the bait. Last year we drove many miles to a campsite and when everything was all set up, we realized that no one had brought any bait. This is probably the fishermen's worse nightmare unless there is no license.

Well, we finally made it to this new campsite and the truck was unloaded. Several fish had been caught and even a couple of trophy Bass was added to our collection.

However, this fishing trip took a bad turn for the worse. The game warden found that two of our members did not have fishing license. Fines were imposed on the lawbreakers and then they went home. Another day ruined because of neglect.

Father, help us to be aware that no matter how much we prepare for heaven's journey, the neglect of salvation will cost us more than a fine from a federal agency. We pray that all of our heavenly credentials will be in order and no illegal Bass to report. In Jesus' name, amen.

Stop the Train
May 12

A passenger train has already left the station. Loved ones, wave good-by from the old country store. Friends and family will be traveling to a faraway destination. They will be gone for a while, as they will be spending time at a vacation resort.

The old train moves quickly down the railroad. This is an ordinary day with the sun shining and birds chirping in the trees. No one had any idea that this peaceful ride would be so drastically affected by a storm.

Since the people left the peaceful valleys and hills of home, dark storm clouds continued to hover above them. While traveling down the track, the passengers noticed that the ground was already saturated with water.

A short distance ahead, part of the bridge is completely washed away. The train conductor is unaware of the danger and the life-threatening ordeal.

Fortunately, a young girl was at the other end of the collapsed bridge. She knew that the conductor had to be warned or there would be a terrible tragedy. The train was not very far away as she could hear the train whistle. This was a life or death situation with only minutes to warn the conductor.

This teenager at the risk of her own life crossed over the broken rail-ties and twisted pieces of metal to warn the conductor. The train stopped just in time and all the passengers were saved from death.

Father, help us to realize that sinners are traveling the rails, and unless we warn them, a terrible tragedy will take place. The danger is far greater than a collapsed bridge. We need to respond immediately and tell the people about the consequences of sin. It is not too late to stop the train. Lives will be saved if they respond in time, amen.

Life or Death Decision
May 13

Recently our imaginary skills of cleaning windows helped us to get a job with a company that specializes in high-rise building maintenance. Fear of heights is a disqualifier for this type of employment.

We were told that this type of work was very dangerous and that occasionally a scaffold would break loose causing the employees to fall to their death. However, they assured us that all safety procedures would be in place to help prevent these catastrophic accidents.

Just the thought of working thousands of feet in the air with a harness as a backup safety feature was almost a good reason to decline employment with this company. After all, none of us had worked higher than a hundred feet. A job refusal is preferable over a heart attack.

This was the time of year when jobs were really scarce. The reason we were seeking employment was because our former employer had to let us go for financial problems. It is not easy taking care of a family if the bills are not paid. Situations vary for us to solve financial problem.

While we were in the CEO'S office, thinking about this dreadful job, he told us about the benefits and also our hourly wages. When he mentioned the high rate of pay, this was probably the turning point in helping us to make the decision. After a month on the job, the scaffold broke and a quick decision by the foreman saved the lives of the men.

Father, there are times in life when fear grips our hearts and we have to make really quick decisions. If our time is limited, it is very important that we make the right choice. The most important decision we can make concerning our soul's salvation is to accept Jesus in our lives as Savior. This is a personal choice with only a short time to make it, amen.

Mothers' Day
May 14

Mothers' day is the time when we travel down memory lane or make a visit to mom's house with love and appreciation. Loved ones who have departed, let's remember the wonderful times we had together. Affectionate moments have memories that never fade.

Sometimes a sentimental card is sent to relay sincere thoughts to our mothers. If we still have the opportunity to express our gratitude, let's pay a personal visit and tell them how much they are loved. While we are there let's give a loving embrace.

Think for just a few minutes on the qualities of her life. She is always caring and concerned about her children. A mother's love will lift us up when the problems of life are dragging us down. We all agree.

Her love binds the family together with an unbreakable cord. There is no one on earth who is so close and dear as a mother. Her children bless her for the goodness of always being a caring, affectionate person.

She is known by her faithfulness and unwavering love that touches her children. She has taught us the true meaning of life. Love God first and foremost, commit our souls to Him, and someday we'll be walking the streets of glory.

Her love for us is made stronger every day by her faith in Jesus Christ. She imparts that same miracle of unwavering love to all who know her. Moms loving embrace inspires us to love our children, as she loved us.

Father, this is a special day for us to honor all the mothers with love and respect. We pray that you will bless and keep your holy hand upon them. All the family and friends gather together with a single voice of praise, "We love you, mom, happy mothers' day." Love will always prevail, amen.

Need to know Jesus
May 15

It seems like 2017 will be a time to remember as one of the worst environmental crises that we have had in our lifetime. This has been a really bad year for fires and other natural disasters.

Some of the states reported wildfires with thousands of acres burned. The last report was that those out of control fires were not contained. Homes were burnt to the ground and livelihoods in complete disarray.

One major thing that was needed in those states would be a good thunderstorm with enough rain to put out the flames. A forecast of rain was not in the near future. This was a terrible time for our nation.

There were reports of other parts of the country where hurricanes, floods, and even earthquakes were demolishing everything in their path. It seemed as though there was one catastrophic event after another.

Thoughts for today are about the many things that we need for daily existence. Food is essential for life. We think about hurricane Harvey with really strong winds and a flood surge that destroyed many homes.

Fresh water was needed because chemicals had leaked into the water supply. First responders, FEMA, and other organizations brought in bottled water to help in this tragic situation.

Father, this is a time when the entire nation is in need of many material things. Homes need to be rebuilt, vehicles replaced, lives restored, but the greatest need in all of this mass destruction is not earthly resources. Help us to realize material things can be replaced. We need to know Christ as our Lord and Savior so that peace will forever abide, amen.

Labor of love
May 16

This is another day to work in the harvest field. Many souls are dying without knowing of your love. Help us to use this opportunity to spread the seed in the furrow ground. When the Word is sown in our hearts, the fruit of righteousness will come forth in due season.

We have been called to be laborers in the harvest field. Today is a good day to work together and combine our efforts in helping others know Jesus as Savior.

Thanks to all the volunteers and young converts who have entered the harvest field. Our labor force has grown but there are not nearly enough laborers to work in the field. When it is harvest time, let the faithful workers rejoice because their labor is not in vain in the Lord.

When we help others to know Christ, more souls are saved by grace. Go quickly, as the harvest is ripe for eternity. Time is wasting; let's get started. Souls saved today because of our efforts will be the fruit of our labor for eternity.

Father, you have given us a heavenly calling to go into the harvest fields and compel the people to come to Christ. Please send down an abundant supply of grace for our seeds of faith to grow. Also, we need the fertilizer of holy conviction for sinners to repent. Our work will not be in vain if we sow bountifully the Word; it will not return unto us void.

Help us to remember that we are not part-time employees. Since there are not enough workers in the field, we are going to work overtime.

Jesus will be coming for those who have accepted Him into their lives. The harvest is ripe and the laborers are few. This is not a time to be idle in the fields. God will reward our labors of love. In Jesus' name, amen.

Strawberry Pie
May 17

It is that time of year when the strawberries are ripe. There is an abundance of these berries in the field. They hide beneath the green leaves. My friends and I thought it would be a good idea to have a strawberry pie. Pleasurable thoughts can result in regret.

A word of warning is given to those who like to go barefoot in the fields. Please be aware of the vines that have three green leaves. Poison ivy has irritated many unsuspecting victims and when the poison gets on our skin, we have an irresistible urge to scratch the affected area.

This poison can be very hazardous to our health. If the affected area is close to our eyes, we may have to make a special visit to the doctor's office. Everything will probably be all right with good medical attention.

We took our buckets out to the strawberry patch and we completely ignored the ivy vines. The plants with the three shiny leaves were easy to be seen as they covered the strawberries in the forest.

This was supposed to be a very enjoyable afternoon. Well, to our hearts dismay, all of us began to experience an itching between our fingers and toes. We tried to resist scratching the infected area, but we were not very successful.

Father, there is danger in our lives if we go to the toxic fields of sin and partake of the poison. A dose of repentance may be required for the antidote. All of us would agree that the poison ivy of sin is not worth the pain.

If we are partakers, we will have to suffer the penalty of sin. The emergency room will not help us this time. Help us to heed all the warning signs and stay away from the poison. Our participation in sinful activities will have tragic results, amen,

Weeds in the Garden
May 18

This would be a good time for us to work in the garden. We do have a problem with over aggressive weeds and unless we can eliminate these earth invaders, our food supply will disappear. It will be a lot of hungry folks in the neighborhood.

The sun is shining; it's such a beautiful day. Birds are singing and we enjoy listening to them. As much as we have pleasure in God's wonderful creation, we have to save the garden from lack of oxygen. When there are too many weeds in the garden, the plants will die because they cannot breathe.

There for a while the produce was growing and this seemed like the best crop in many years, but the weeds needed a place where they could reside for the summer. Caution! These weeds are of destructive intent.

They took up residence in the green bean row, with the tomato plants, and after a while they completely took over the garden, hiding the sun's rays and cutting off the air supply. Plants will die a very slow death.

A declaration of war is given and the battle will begin immediately. The neighbors bound themselves together with a solemn pledge to fight until every last weed is eliminated.

Soon the people with specialized training in weed removal joined in the efforts to combat this earthly environment. Special forces in advanced chemical warfare of weed removal were called to report for active duty.

Father, help us to realize that the real problem we have is with sin. These are the weeds that interfere with our spiritual relationship with God. If these sins go undisturbed, our souls will suffer in the end. The declaration of war is still in effect. We can win this war from sin invaders if we repent and confess our sins. In Jesus' name, amen.

A Fresh Refilling of Faith
May 19

Our journey in life requires that we stop at service stations along the way and have our vehicles filled up with gas. This empty tank dilemma keeps us stranded on the highway.

We feel that we are really blessed when a policeman stops to see if we need any assistance. A call is made to the nearest service station. A service attendant will make the delivery.

This problem was solved, but we soon found ourselves in another bad situation. We were driving down the highway and somehow, we realized that we had taken the wrong road.

The same policeman, who we had called earlier, answered the distress call. He gave us direction and after we expressed our thanks, we continued on our journey.

There are times in life when we are unable to reach our destination. We make a wrong turn and we have run out of gas while driving down the road. Our travel adventure was about to end in a tragedy.

One more wrong turn and this one could be fatal. While driving down the road we found ourselves on a one-way street. Some of us have made these wrong turns and were spared a terrible accident. Truly we are blessed to have God's holy hand upon us and to keep us safe from harm.

It is obvious that we need a better guidance system. Help us to realize a one-way street is perfectly all right, as long as we are following Jesus because His way will take us home.

Father, if our faith, (gas gage) is running on empty, we should immediately pull into the life-saving station and get a fresh refilling of grace. There is no way we can make it to heaven with an empty fuel tank. It looks like we are ready to continue our journey, on the right path with plenty of fuel, amen.

An Idle Porch Life
May 20

We want to have a better understanding of how idleness affects our lives. An elderly man sits on the porch, watching the people drive down the road on their way to church. He always greets them with a friendly wave and the travelers return the same gesture.

Since he retired, a lot of things have changed in his life. We need to go back to the time when he was going to church. It would be hard to find a more loyal member. He was always faithful and his attendance was above average.

If anyone needed a helping hand or was sick, he would not hesitate to offer assistance. His loving kindness was known throughout the community. Somewhere along the way he walked away from God. He left the church and laid down his cross. Grief robbed him of his joy.

This retreat did not happen overnight, but gradually church services were missed and there was less time for prayer. His daily walk with the Lord declined and after a while he stopped singing "Amazing Grace." The emotional effect of grace and mercy was no longer in his heart.

According to this imaginary story the old rocker is empty. It seems as though he departed this life. The travelers who wave on Sundays want to know what happened to the man on the porch. "Did he die?" "No, he went to church with Jesus, and his beloved songs are sung once again with sincere, reverent devotion.

Father, the sunset years of life will find us sitting on the porch, watching the travelers go by. It is time for us to leave the idleness of life and return to church with a song in our hearts. I am sure the people will understand if there are no friendly greetings on their way to worship. A man who once was idle is busy in church, praising and glorifying God, amen.

Silver and Gold
May 21

Silver and gold will buy the necessities of life. These precious metals are recovered from mines and they are melted into molds. These metals are used to make watches, rings, bracelets, and many other items. Does anyone here have a silver dollar, gold coin, or just empty pockets?

One person many years ago found out about the things money couldn't buy. He was in need of food and other physical things for his livelihood.   Peter and John were walking by this man who needed healing; He was unable to walk. This poor man was begging for money to keep from starving.

Christ disciple (Peter) told him, "Silver and gold have I none; but such as I have, give I thee: In the name of Jesus Christ of Nazareth rise up and walk" (Acts 3:6).

Immediately the man was healed and walked. One touch of the Master's hand is of more value than all the gold and silver in the world. Arise to a new life in Christ. We can only give what we have received.

No silver or gold was offered to the man. His need was far greater than the value of these precious metals. The name of Jesus brought healing to his body. Our greatest need in life is for us to believe in Jesus Christ.

The most valuable things in life are not gold and silver nuggets. These shiny gems will increase our earthly wealth. They do not bring us any closer to God. True spiritual riches are found at the cross with Jesus.

Father, help us to think about what we have to offer to help those around us who are in need. Money can help in a lot of ways in earthly situations. But the people we meet on the pathway of life need to know Jesus as their Savior. An introduction to Him comes with grace and God's favor, amen.

Allegiance to God
May 22

We the believers in Christ do hereby make an allegiance to God, to surrender our lives completely to Him. We make this promise to faithfully yield to His service in complete obedience to His (Will) plan. Our sincere resolution is to stand with the right hand over the heart in reverence of His holiness.

It is our solemn resolution to commit our hearts, minds, and souls, to love Him all the days of our lives without any restrictions or constraints. We truthfully and without reserve will proclaim to the world that Jesus is the Christ; the Savior of the world and all who believe in Him will be saved. Our oath is to say that Jesus is the only one who can forgive sins.

This faith pledge is one of belief that Jesus arose from the dead and ascended into heaven. We confirm that our lives as Christians exist in the fact that Jesus is no longer in the grave, but He is alive forevermore.

It is our moral obligation to respectively honor His name with the truth that He is the Messiah, Mighty God, Prince of Peace, and Everlasting Father. We will reveal without any compromise that Jesus is the Christ, the Son of God and that there is no other name given under heaven whereby we must be saved. Truth never yields to lies.

Our promise is given on this day to faithfully obey, serve God with loyalty, and devotion. We commit ourselves to living holy, righteous lives, and in complete reverence to God the Father, God the Son, and God the Holy Spirit. This faithfulness is for all the days of our lives.

Father, there are many types of pledges that require us to commit our lives to them. A faithful pledge is one that holds us to a promise. The Truth will be revealed when the cross is exchanged for a crown, or we hear, "Depart from me!" Amen.

Eligible for the Draft
May 23

This is a special recruiting assignment for all eligible participants. Many of us can think about the times when men and women were drafted into the military and we can remember that first draft notice we received from the Selective Service Department.

Before we were chosen to serve our country, we had to be tested to see if we were qualified for active duty. These government tests were to identify vocational abilities and to learn about our previous education.

After we finally finished all of the literary assignments, the next thing on the agenda was a physical. This was a thorough process where we were examined for any health problems. Hopefully there would be none.

These physical abilities were necessary to show if we could stand up to the rigorous challenge of fighting and defending our country. This was a long strenuous day of tests. Final results would show if we were eligible for the draft.

Father, we have a different type of enlistment for all the brave men, women, and even children who are up to heaven's challenge. There are certain qualifications that we must meet before any of us will be able to enter the combat zone.

All sinners are eligible for this combat mission; it does not matter about our education or physical abilities. We have to pass the test of repentance. Belief fulfills the obligation.

Heaven's Selective Service Unit (Christ) will accept whoever comes to Him. New converts are accepted fresh out of the ranks of sin and promoted immediately to the high ranks of Christian service. This is a time for us to be thankful, no longer sinners of disgrace. In Jesus' name, amen.

Heaven's Treasure
May 24

There are many wonderful things we search for in life, but today we are seeking for the eternal riches of heaven. We have found that those who are sincere in heart will find this wealth.

Tears are flowing from sorrowful hearts in true repentance. Remorseful souls will find that in heaven's treasure chest there is a bounty of God's love. His love always abounds in each believer's life.

This is far better than silver and gold that is found in the earth's core. These precious gems are valuable to hold and when crafted into rings, watches, and other valuable items, our hearts radiate with pride when we display these objects.

We know that the riches of earth are only for a season. These valuable assets are temporary and will soon perish. Those people who hold onto this treasure will be disappointed when corrosion has worn away its original value.

There is absolutely no guarantee that gold or silver will keep its bright lustrous shine. Today's wealth is only a temporary thing. Who knows what tomorrow will bring? We may be buried in a gold casket with diamond rings on every finger, what does it profit us if we have not made peace with God?

Father, when we search with all of our hearts for God's love and mercy, we will find that the wealth of our souls is not based on earthly treasure. The value of our lives has a much higher price, as Jesus hung on a cross, was buried in a sepulcher, and arose from the dead.

Help us now to realize that heaven's treasure is not hard to find. It just takes a few minutes of sincere heartfelt prayer to ask forgiveness. Cries for mercy get an immediate response from heaven, which includes a loving embrace, amen.

Delusional Wealth
May 25

Today's adventure will have us on the imagination trail that will take us into the gold mining country. If we have an opportunity, we will talk with the prospectors. We want to find out if these worldly treasures bring real contentment in life.

There is no need to worry for we are just going to stay a little while, just long enough to learn that the richest vein in the world will not bring peace in our lives. Gain the world and lose our souls, there is no profit.

One prospector was rich; his wealth brought him many expensive items. He had no treasure in heaven because his labor of love was in earthly things.

The second prospector we met did not have any gold. He worked his entire life to find it. This valuable ore was not found. True happiness cannot be found in delusional wealth.

Before we left this poor soul, we told him about Jesus who loved us enough to die in our place on a cross. This miner with tears in his eyes asked Jesus to come into his heart. The search is over and peace abides.

All of this man's life, he searched for an earthly treasure, but on his knees in prayer he found the greatest of all riches, peace with God. The rich and the poor have the same opportunity to make things right with God. Only those with sincere repentant hearts will be accepted. Please don't pass up the greatest treasure in life. It is still a little time to repent.

Father, cares of the world will have us disillusioned of heavenly things. Help us to be aware that gold will show us a mansion on a hill, enjoyment for a season, and a long life. Our vision betrays us, as gold is not the giver of life. A personal visit to the cross will be a prosperous journey with abounding grace for all of eternity. In Jesus' name, amen.

His Search is Endless
May 26

A search and rescue operation continues for the many lost souls of this generation. Jesus came down from heaven to search for those who need a Savior.

We will find Jesus in the valleys of despair or in the dark alleys where the homeless live. He goes to the outcast of society and He brings them home to be God's adopted children.

The love of Jesus was manifest at Calvary and extended to every day of our lives, as we are witnesses that His love never dies. Souls need to be saved; the rescue is in process.

It is not an uncommon thing to find Christ in churches where pastors convey to their congregations the love of God. He is a Father who deeply loves His children. Love always abounds in our hearts and lives. If we say that no one loves us, we have not met Jesus.

There have been many hospitals where family members and friends went into the patient's rooms. Christians would be there praying. Jesus was always in the midst, laying His holy hand upon the sick and ministering to them. It is a blessing indeed when the Savior finds us.

Wherever there is a need of salvation, a rescue operation is already in process with Jesus waiting for the distress calls for mercy. He answers all calls for forgiveness.

Father, help us to think about the time when we were in the valley of despair, or homeless with the outcast of society, or perhaps we were in none of those situations. But our need of a Savior was the same.

We need to know that the Lord has not given up on us. His search comes with conviction for us to repent. Let's make the rescue operation successful by accepting Christ, amen.

Fruit Bearing Tree
May 27

The old apple tree brings back a lot of wonderful memories. Neighbors and friends would come in the fall of the year to pick apples. Every once in a while a delicious pie would be shared with the guest. This was just a sample of the many pies that would be judged at the county fair.

We think about the old apple tree in the back yard. Many wonderful years has gone by since this tree was planted in the earth. Neighbors would come and help themselves to an apple or two. A fruit-bearing tree is a benefit to the community.

Occasionally, pies were made as an act of kindness and for good friendly relations. I have to admit an imaginary pie is not as good as a real one.

This tree was next to an old white-railed fence where we used to stop and talk about the events of the day. We noticed, as the years passed there was less fruit on the tree. Our friendship remained strong even though there were fewer apple pies.

Every year the fruit on this tree was in abundance. But now the branches are withered from a lifetime of cold winters. Neighbors no longer stop beneath the tree because the limbs are barely holding on. It is time to cut down the tree, as it is not safe for the children or anyone passing by.

Father, help us to realize that as Christians, we need to bear the fruit of righteousness, holiness, and godly living. If there comes a time we are not producing these fruitful characteristics, then we need a fresh supply of grace. A return visit to the cross would help us to get our lives back in order.

Let's be bearers of much fruit so that friends, neighbors and the people we meet along the way will see Jesus in our lives. A fruitless branch does not reveal a loving Savior. Fruit bearers will someday see Jesus coming in the sky, amen.

The Potter and the Clay
May 28

The enthusiasm runs high as the potter thinks about a new creation. It is already formed in his mind. He knows exactly what the object will look like even before the work is started.

This creative project will take many long days to complete. That is ok, because the potter is a very patient man. No matter how long the process takes, he will stay with it until it is exactly the way he wants it.

Before the work begins, the potter has invited all of us to his studio to observe the procedure and learn some important facts about shaping and molding pottery.

Once we arrived at the potter's shop, we found him hard at work, preparing his pottery wheel for a demonstration. A portion of clay is placed on the craft table or a turning wheel.

Notice the change in the clay when the potter begins the creative process. As the wheel turns, the ugly moist clay is crafted by hand. When a little bit of water is added to this pliable material, a vase begins to form.

We all gathered around to watch this skilled craftsman transform a ball of clay into a work of art. All of us were really amazed at this transformation process.

The potter continues his work and gradually the modeling material is transformed. We are drawn in a little closer to see an imperfection in the model. After the clay is reshaped, a beautiful vase is created. It is all right to start over again.

Father, We need to visualize the molding and reshaping of our lives. If sins and imperfections have entered into the molding process, we need to ask Jesus to forgive us our sins. He will create in us a vessel of honor as we yield to the touch of His hand. Let's be pliable; grace will abound, amen.

Memorial Day
May 29

Memorial Day is a federal holiday that began at the end of the Civil war. Later it was recognized as a tribute to honor all service personal that died while serving our great country.

This is a time in our lives when we remember the sacrifices of our brave men and women, those who fought and died for our freedom. There are many memorials that remind us of the battles fought. The National Anthem keeps their memories alive and revives patriotism.

When the national anthem is sung, this is a time to express our sincere gratitude for the many sacrifices that were made on our behalf. Our love for America binds us together with the blood of family members, parents, children, siblings, and friends. Those patriots gave all they could give to obtain life, liberty, and the pursuit of happiness for all.

The blood flows deep on the battlefield with grave markers on a hill. Words of deep emotional thoughts are in-graved in stone. There are so many inscriptions; each one represents a person who did not die in vain.

Please don't forget to stand for the national anthem with the right hand over the heart. This is our great country (America). It is our patriotic duty to stand beside her, fight to protect her, and die to save her.

Father, we would like to give special recognition to all military personal for their service to the United States of America. It is time for us to show our sincere gratitude. All of us with the voice of praise say, "Thank you."

Memorial Day is a time to remember with heart-felt appreciation for all those who died for our freedom. A salute is given in their honor and a pledge with a solemn promise to never forget their loyalty to country, amen.

Get Out Now
May 30

Recently there were warnings in Texas, Florida, and other parts of the country for the people to evacuate immediately because there was extreme danger of the loss of life. A couple of years earlier there were also storm warnings.

Weather forecasters announced a monster storm is coming. Severe winds and thunderstorms are predicted to come with a vengeance. This is a high alert warning for the entire eastern region of the United States. Leave immediately!

Warnings are given so the people will have a chance to survive the tremendous effects of the storm. Those who stay behind are at risk of losing their own lives. Our lives can be spared if we obey the warnings.

In just a short while the devastation of the storm will occur. There is not much time to spare. If there are family members and friends living nearby, go quickly and warn them. "Get out now! A monster storm is coming." This warning was for a quick response, no time to waste.

Dark storm clouds are already forming overhead. There was enough time to escape and most of the people in Texas and Florida made it out safely. The storm that came two years earlier had people stranded on the highways. The roads were so crowded that no one could get through. This traffic problem could have caused a lot of causalities.

Father, we have a warning that will come to pass. "Jesus is coming with power and great glory." If we are still living in our sins, the message of salvation is to repent. We can escape the effects of sin if we "Get out now," by faith in Christ.

This warning is for us to escape for our lives. We can heed the warning and our souls will be saved. Help us to leave immediately before it is too late. In Jesus' name, amen.

One Lifejacket
May 31

We need to realize there are many times in life when everything is going just right, but suddenly a storm appears in the distance and we find ourselves in troubled waters, fighting the current, trying to stay alive.

None of us know when the dark storm clouds will rise and torrents of rain saturate the earth. We may find ourselves in a life-threatening situation with only one life preserver to save us from imminent drowning.

A fishing trip is planned and we arrived at our destination. Our favorite fishing spot was along-way from shore. We noticed a few dark clouds beginning to appear, but we thought it was nothing to worry about as the weather forecast was for a slim chance of a thunderstorm.

This is one time the meteorologist was completely wrong. This is a day we wished we had stayed at home. Our problems were only beginning. Just because we expect smooth waves because the sun is shining, does not give us a guarantee that fair weather will be with us all day. A peaceful day can quickly change as lightning flashes across the sky.

While we were fishing, we kept looking up at the small clouds, as they kept getting larger. It did not take us long to realize we were in a lot of trouble and unless we could make it to shore, this fishing adventure would turn into a disaster. One Lifejacket on board was not enough to save three men.

Father, we want everyone to have the same opportunity to be saved. Our spiritual journey will have us in troublesome waters with the weight of sin dragging us down.

Help us to realize that our rescue from sin does not depend on lifejackets, but on our pleas for mercy. Christ responds immediately with salvation to impart. Thank you, Jesus, amen.

Endurance and Praise
June 1

Let's think about the many times in life where we have to endure certain situations. There may be a storm forming that will cause stress, heartache, depression, and even pain.

These things often require a great deal of patience and endurance as the body heals from the wounds. This healing process sometimes takes days, months, and years before relief is in sight. Patience is a good cure.

Deep wounds take longer to heal like the loss of a loved one; more time is needed because a lifetime of fellowship is broken. Emotional pain does not go away overnight. Keep pressing on, there will be peace at last.

The people in Texas, Florida, Mexico, and Puerto Rico will have to endure hardships for a very long time because of the devastation caused by hurricanes, tornadoes, and earthquakes. Rebuilding process takes time and endurance will have us patiently waiting for the final results.

Homes will be rebuilt and lives restored, but in the mean time we have to endure the effects of the storm and not give up hope, the sun will shine again. Shattered hopes and dreams will be revived from above.

Even as I speak, glorious rays from heaven shine upon the earth and the sound of hammers are heard in the distance, as new homes or being rebuilt. Soon families will gather together with thankful hearts for God's intensive care.

Father, church bells are ringing again; the sound of beautiful melodies fills the air as those who lost everything give God the praise. Storms will pass and endurance will prevail throughout the land. Lives are restored when worship ascends to the throne room of mercy. When God lays His holy hand upon us, we know everything will be all right. Praise Him now, amen.

Red Flag Warning
June 2

There are certain times of the year when abnormally dry conditions exist. This is a time when it is extremely dangerous to have a fire. It is also predicted that strong winds will make the hazardous conditions worse. A wildfire spreads quickly.

The weather forecaster has issued a red flag warning for some of the counties in Virginia. High alert! Please be advised that today the conditions are extremely hazardous with a possibility of strong winds.

No fires are allowed at any time of the day until it is considered safe by the officials. The weather will be monitored on a daily basis for any improvements to these dry conditions. All fires are strictly prohibited.

Now would be a good time to warn the neighbors and those who will be going on camping trips, burning brush, or any other activity to avoid all fires. The law will be strictly enforced with penalties, including jail time.

It just takes one little spark to land on the roof of someone's house and after a while the home is destroyed. Hopefully no one will lose his or her life because of the flames. Regretfully, all fires cannot be prevented.

There have been too many incidents where a family member or a friend has lost their lives in a fire. While these fire conditions persist, we must refrain from any type of burning. Lives saved may be our own.

Father, maybe there should be a red flag warning of hell; the conditions are persistent in our lives because of sins. Try waving the flag of truce to a forgiving God and see how fast we avoid the flames. Sins are like the wildfire burning out of control. Send down a fresh shower of grace so that our hearts will be saturated with love and mercy. In Jesus' name, amen.

Adopted Children Gone Astray
June 3

There are times in life when some of God's adopted children return to the ways of the world. The luring power of sin persuaded them to lay down the cross and reject His loving kindness. We need to know we can resist the temptation.

When we are away from God, we are not out of His reach. He never gives up on any of His adopted children. No matter how far we go down the sinner's path, His Son searches for us, as God is not willing that any should perish, but all should repent.

If God's adopted children are lost; sin and ungodly living has decreased their value, until nothing but the blood of Christ will restore the eternal wealth of their souls.

A Father never abandons His wayward children no matter how far they have gone into sin, but those with unrepentant hearts will still be punished. Heaven will be denied. It is time to come home and receive a loving embrace. We don't want to wait too long or we will miss the flight to the Glory Land.

Another thought comes to mind about a prodigal son who left his father's house and went into a faraway place. We remember that this young man wasted his life with riotous living. There was a time when his life had more value than when he ate the husk that was fed to the hogs.

Finally, this disillusioned young man realized he had it far better in his father's home. A decision was made to go back to his parent's house. His father received him with a loving embrace. It is a blessing when adopted children come home.

Father, help us to realize that sin will devalue our lives, but grace will restore us as sons and daughters. The father welcomed him home and gave his son more than he deserved. "This my son was dead, and is alive again." Rejoice a son's relationship with his father and family is restored, amen.

Lost and Found
June 4

All of us can think of those times in our lives when certain items were lost. This brought a lot of distress and anxiety if we lost something of great value. If we depended on these items for our livelihood like a driver's license, credit cards, and personal identification, we would be overwhelmed with worry and frustration.

Let's just say we lost a gold pocket watch; this heirloom was in the family for many generations. The value of this timepiece is very sentimental, as the deceased father owned it. This was his gift of farewell to his children. A gold watch holds the precious memory of life.

Imagine the grief and guilt we were feeling at the loss of this work of art. Sadness filled our hearts as we told our children that grandpa's watch was nowhere to be found.

Our memory of his life would end without this gold pocket watch to honor his legacy. This antique watch was engraved with his full name inside the back cover. What made this watch different than all the others was a handcrafted eagle with an American flag on the backside of the cover.

An ad was placed in the lost and found section of the newspaper. The owner of the watch had moved away. This new homeowner called with a report that a watch was found. It was the family heirloom. When the watch was returned, the family members rejoiced together, a legacy of life would live on.

Father, we need to think back to the time when we had something more valuable than a gold watch. This was our souls and we were lost without God in our lives.

All types of lost and found advertisements could not help us. Help us to realize that the Lord will find us when we call out to Him. Let the legacy of life begin. In Jesus' name, amen.

In the Miry Clay
June 5

We have a very important message to deliver and it must arrive on time in order for millions of souls to be saved. This is an emergency! Sound all alarms. There is no time to waste.

It has been reported that individuals are sinking in the miry clay. The weight of sin is dragging them down. We need as many people as possible to make a rescue attempt. This is not a time to be in idle mode.

Some of those perishing in the clay are family members, loved ones, and even friends. Strangers and enemies also need a helping hand.

If we were the ones sinking in the miry clay, would it matter who came to save us? We would not be concerned about their nationality, friend or foe. A rescue is possible if we will only yield to the one who is trying to save us.

It is not very likely that we would request an identify report before we would commit our lives to this saving process. While the responder is searching for his social security number, the clay is already up to our necks. Our cries for help override any identity problems, as we can hardly breathe.

God is calling all Christians to active duty because He knows that sinners cannot save themselves. Response is urgently needed to rescue the perishing. No ropes are needed for this life saving process, but souls will be saved if we do not hesitate. A moment of delay is a big mistake.

Father, we know that we cannot save any one, but this emergency response is to reveal Jesus Christ as the Savior of the world. Alarms are still sounding. We can extend a helping hand by giving ourselves to the rescue effort by sharing the gospel. Help us to realize that Jesus is the only one who can save us. God verifies his credentials, amen.

A Wrong Turn, Sin City
June 6

We are going to go for a ride this morning on the imagination highway. The scenery is beautiful this time of year. Leaves on the trees are already changing colors. We are going to take the camera so we will have beautiful pictures to share.

Before we left home there was concern about our navigational equipment. Our GPS was not working properly and it was making a strange type of noise. However, it only lasted for a few minutes and we decided it was just a temporary malfunction. This is one time that we should have stayed at home. Being lost in some remote area is nerve-racking.

We spent the whole day driving, stopping at tourist locations and taking pictures of the beautiful scenery. Our families would be pleased with all of the photographs. This was such a wonderful day and we had no idea that a day so pleasant could turn into our worst nightmare.

It was starting to get dark and the GPS began clicking and then all of a sudden it stopped working. We continued driving as we still had the roadmap, but after a while it was too dark to read the small print.

Somewhere along the way we took the wrong road and found ourselves in Sin City. There was corruption all around us and we didn't know if we would get out alive. This story has a happy ending as a policeman escorted us to a nice, friendly neighborhood where we spent the night.

Father, help us to realize as we journey through life, there is only one-way to heaven. Even the best and most proficient GPS system will not help us get on the right road to the glory land. Worldwide navigation is probably the most efficient way of traveling from one place to the other. Advanced technologies will not help us this time. Heaven is our destination and the only way to get there is to follow Jesus Christ, amen.

Prisoners by our own Sins
June 7

It is very important that we understand that freedom from sin cannot be bought by any amount of money. Whether we are rich or poor, it does not matter. The price of our freedom cost a whole lot more than we can afford.

If we offer money for our freedom, it will be denied. All the gold and silver in the world cannot set us free. We think about all of our sins and we are unable to escape, no matter how hard we try, our conscience will always remind us of our unrighteous, sinful ways.

The truth is that we are held captive by our own sinful deeds. This does not mean that we are holding a metal key to take the shackles of sin off of our lives. If the key is faith in Jesus, we will be released from custody.

Shackles of sin keep us in bondage with unrepentant hearts. There seems to be no way of breaking free. We cannot buy our freedom. Gold and silver is a valuable asset, but it is worthless in the redemption of our souls. These strong chains of sin keep us in the dungeons of grief and despair.

The Bible tells us that Jesus broke the chains and fetters from a man who was bound. He will do the same for us if we ask Him, the captive will stay bound as long as sin abides.

Father, chains of steel are placed on ankles and wrists to make sure the criminals do not escape. Armed guards transport the prisoners to certain locations. All safety precautions are taken to ensure a safe delivery. These heavy chains make it impossible to run away.

Sin binds us the same way as chains. Jesus came to set the captive free. Help us now to realize that Christ releases us from the bondage of sin when we use the faith key. Sins are forgiven; now is a good time to praise God for deliverance, amen.

Asleep on Guard Duty
June 8

All of us like to think our neighborhood is safe with policemen patrolling the streets in the day and also taking care of the community at night. Night watchmen stay up all night to watch for criminal activity. When these men are on guard duty, we can sleep peacefully.

Let's visit a certain neighborhood by imagination where a security breach allowed three robbers to break into a person's home and steal the priceless jewels. It was late one night; everyone had gone to bed. Now this was really a peaceful community. Neighbors were friendly and there was no reason to expect any danger.

Doors were always locked, just in case a burglar would try to break in and steal from the family. There was always someone from the citizen's patrol, walking the streets to make sure the homes were well protected.

A policeman would come by and check the businesses to make sure they were locked and secure for the night. His job was to guard the community and be alert for any night prowlers with evil intentions.

This neighborhood was so peaceful that the security personal became relaxed in their obligations. While this policeman was asleep the house was robbed. "Nothing is going to happen," this was the attitude of the officer. Instead of performing his security watch, he was sound asleep in his patrol car. No one was aware of thieves in the area.

Father, the officer that we used as an example of sleeping on guard duty could have been either one of us. Is it possible that we can become so relaxed in our Christian journey that we are unaware of sin that is invading our lives? Help us to be alert and if we happen to have slumber eyes, shake us if you must! Arouse us from sleep. In Jesus' name, amen.

Accused of being Sinners
June 9

Let's say we have to appear in court in a few days and be tried for our criminal offences. A list of them is given to the judge. This is a very unusual case. We are accused of being sinners. How could anyone think such a terrible thing? All of us have sinned.

The jurors have to be selected without any prior experience in sinful matters. I believe we all know the final verdict. No one is without sin. Is there anyone in the world that can truthfully say, "I have not sinned?" The judge is leaving the courtroom.

Notices were sent out to the residents of the community to see if they could get enough jurors that would not be partial or inclined to bear false witness. Well, we noticed that the juror section was empty.

There seems to be a lot of evidence against the offenders. We had better get the best lawyers in the country if we want to win this case. After a thorough search of the most intelligent lawyers in the world, we found that none of them were qualified to represent or to defend us.

The Federal Bureau of Investigation did a background check and found that the lawyers were equally corrupt in their sinful ways. Information was given that these representatives of the truth would incriminate themselves; the guilt of their own sins would convict them. Our search for a lawyer without any prior sin proved to be in vain.

Father, we think about the legal establishment of lawyers, judges, and even the jury was false representatives of justice. There was as much corruption in their lives as it was in ours. It certainly looks like the verdict will be guilty as no one can verify that we are not sinners. Further investigation shows that a guilty sinner can begin a new life. Once we were sinners, but in Christ the verdict is changed to not guilty. Thank you, Jesus.

He Is a Friend
June 10

We are so glad to know Jesus, as our best friend. He is the greatest friend we have ever had in life. When we are walking through the valley of the shadow of death, His presence gives us comfort with the blessed assurance that we will live again.

Our lives are richly blessed to have Him walking with us, to know that heaven is in sight. Daily living with Him is to constantly have fellowship with the Father in glory divine.

We give Him the honor and respect for He is worthy of our praise for the sacrifice He gave at Calvary. His love never wavers. It is like a mighty river flowing through the channels of our hearts. We are so thankful that He is our friend who abides with us on the pathway of life.

There is no need to ask, where is Jesus when we are confined to a hospital room. We will find Him standing at our bedside, interceding to God on our behalf. If a special touch is needed, He does not hesitate to lay His holy hand upon us. His care for us is twenty-four seven.

Some of our friends are considered temporary; they go part of the way and then disappear. They rob us of all our money. We are no longer needed, so they cast us aside, penniless, and begging on the streets.

Our journey in life will find us traveling a path where loneliness covers us like a dark cloud. But walking with the Savior opens the blue skies of God's favor. So, all of us need to realize in the loneliest times in our lives, we are never alone when we are alone with Jesus our Savior.

Father, there are many people here that are living lonely lives. I am sure you would be pleased if we introduce them to your Son, Jesus. It only takes a few minutes to get to know Him. Let's accept Christ as a friend; He will also be Lord, amen.

Be of Good Cheer, It Is I
June 11

Suppose we had to stay in the hospital for a few days. We are allowed visitors, even ones from the Bible years. Friends and family members are usually the first ones to visit us.

However, we do have some unexpected guests that had to travel thousands of miles by the Imagination Express-way. We learned about these people in church and they are very special acquaintances.

Now that all of us are aware of the situation, we can welcome the first guest. It looks like Abraham is the first one to arrive. Remember how he was going to offer his own son for a sacrifice and God provided a lamb. If we want to be in God's favor, it is best we obey His commands.

This visit was very encouraging and we learned a lot about faithfulness and obedience. We thanked him for coming and sharing with us his faith. He departed and the next person of interest comes in for a visit.

Moses just now entered the premises. Truly this was a man of God. He led the people out of Egypt and they crossed the red sea. God used him to bring us the Ten Commandments. He left us with an inspired message of how that we are required to live godly, righteous lives.

There is another group of people that just now entered the hospital. They are the Disciples of Christ. We all remember how they followed Jesus and witnessed His miracles. It is a wonderful thought to think that all of these people came for a visit with words of encouragement.

Father, we are truly blessed to have our friends from the Bible make this visit to the hospital room. However, there is one visitor that we have not mentioned and His appearance is real. Jesus speaks, "Be of good cheer, it is I." Amen.

Without Christ
June 12

All through life we depend on certain types of mechanical equipment in order to accomplish our goals. There is no way we would try to climb a mountain if our survival rope is still below with all the accessories for our life sustaining efforts.

This adventure would be a complete failure if we refused any help from our skilled mountain climbers. We think we can climb better by ourselves. Let's just see how far we can go on this treacherous mountain slope. Survival depends on our reliance and entire trust of each other.

Two men began climbing, as they thought they were up to the challenge of scaling the mountainside. After a short while of climbing, shouts of distress came from one of the men who was hanging onto a cliff. His partner who injured himself was still able to pull his friend to safety. These two men might die.

If they had only brought the survival rope, they would at least have a way to get off the ledge. It was not very likely that they would live through this ordeal. We remember that they had left all of their accessories behind, including the survival kit.

We cannot give up hope just yet, as the people below heard the cries for help and immediately they responded by forming a rescue team. These two men might freeze to death without their thermal winter coats.

If we cannot get to them in time they will most certainly die. There was no time to lose, as every minute would be either life or death. Let's never give up hope; we need to keep holding on a little while longer. This rescue was successful.

Father, we may never be on a mountain, hanging on a cliff, clinging to life, but there are some things that we cannot do without. Our survival depends not on self-reliance. We cannot go to heaven without Christ. This is a team effort, amen

The World or Jesus
June 13

We know that Jesus is always on call. He is always ready to make a rescue or just to be with us on the pathway of life. Wherever there is a need, it does not matter if it is day or night. There is no hesitation as He responds quickly in a moment's notice.

Let's just take a look at His schedule. If we are sick and need a healing touch, we will find Him in the hospitals ministering to our needs. Not only does He heal our bodies, but also, we never receive a bill of debt.

His care goes beyond all medical facilities, as He is not limited to a certain state or county. Jesus cares for each of us and He even makes house calls. No one is too far away for Him to make a personal visit. We may be in good health with no physical problems, but we just need someone who will listen.

There is no need to check a schedule because it is His good pleasure to meet with us and talk over our spiritual concerns. Occasionally we like to take a walk and share our feelings with friends. We are even more blessed when Jesus is there.

Sometimes we are walking at the park, having fellowship with friends and we cannot help but wonder why Jesus has not met with us. When we gathered for our morning walk, some of the people were in doubt if Jesus was going to show up.

Everyone was assured that He would be walking with us this morning. All of us were so energetic and we just couldn't seem to wait. All along the way we talked about worldly things and Jesus was not with us.

Father, help us to realize that Jesus had not met with us for the morning walk because we were too busy in worldly affairs. If we are too busy to meet with Him in sincere love and devotion, we may find ourselves all alone, waiting in despair. Amen.

Vision is Blurred
June 14

Let's understand that our trials are like being caught in a sandstorm on the desert. This is a good time for us to learn that we cannot always see the path ahead of us. Vision is blurred.

Footprints in the sand are hidden from view and faith is the only thing that will see us through. Total reliance and trust in the unseen hand of God will bring us through the storm when we cannot see the trail.

When our vision is blurred from the difficult times in our lives, let's not give up hope. We know we are going to make it if we keep the faith. Never falter or waver even though we cannot see the path ahead. Determination and perseverance will keep us going when there is no trail to follow.

Survival depends so many times on words of encouragement. Sometimes just a couple of well-placed words will inspire us to: "Get up!" Inspirational thoughts will give us strength and courage to rise from our stormy trials. Take one step and then another; keep pressing onward. It will not be very long now until we claim the victory crown.

Sandstorms can be so bad that a shelter is the only thing that will keep us alive. It is not a disgrace to wait for the storm to end. Waiting in a shelter has saved many lives.

The sun will shine again. If we are in the trials of life unable to see the path ahead, wait until the storm is over. Peace will prevail and we can continue our journey.

Father, we need to realize that with Christ as our Savior and guide there is no giving up or calling it quits. If we cannot see through the storm and we have fallen from the heavy weight of our trials, take hold of the unseen hand of the Savior. Keep us in the shelter while we wait for the words of encouragement. "Follow me!" In Jesus' name, amen.

Greater Is He
June 15

We are in the training process of defeating an enemy. As we travel through life our combat skills must improve on a daily basis. Our enemy (Satan) is probably preparing for an ambush.

Every day we prepare for battle because we never know when the enemy will attack. When we commit our souls to the Commander in Chief (Jesus). Victory is promised to us if we will be faithful to the end.

Young recruits are at a disadvantage because they have not learned the full military tactics of survival. There is no need to worry. Our strength is in the One who has all power in heaven and earth. It is time for us to claim the victory; "Greater is He that is in us, than He that is in the world."

Jesus was wounded and suffered excruciating agony on the cross. He never gave up or surrendered to the enemy. We can be confident that we also will win the war, as we hold the cross up high for His glory.

It is good to be well trained and combat ready, but we need to remember, the battle is not ours, it is the Lord's. We are His infantrymen, walking across the fields, carrying the gospel message of God's great love to a lost and dying world.

Our hope and desire is for the people we meet along the way, to surrender, so they can join with us in the battle for liberty, holiness, and forgiveness for one and all. We will never regret surrendering to Christ.

Father, help us to realize that Satan will try with all of his might to defeat us. He will use any resources that are available. How can we win against such a mighty foe? We yield our lives to Jesus in full assurance of the victory. Christ abiding in our hearts gives us strength t overcome. He abides, hallelujah.

Fresh Shower from Above
June 16

We find there are many instances in life where a refreshing drink of water will revitalize our lives. Actually, it will take more than one drink, but raindrops of heaven will keep us from dying of thirst. Oh, the joy that fills our hearts when dark storm clouds form overhead and soon we will have an abundance of refreshing rain.

Sometimes in life we are more concerned about our selfish needs then we are about eternal things. Our imaginary journey today will find us in a dangerous situation with some gold prospectors who struck it rich.

Mules were loaded up with heavy nuggets of gold. There was enough water for us to cross over the desert, but the extra weight of gold would cause the mules to work harder. We could have taken just a little bit of gold and come back later with wagons and plenty of fresh water.

These pack animals required more water or else they would die along the way. Soon death shadows would cross our paths. This is one journey we wished that we had stayed at home. We looked up at the sky, hoping we would see storm clouds, but we saw buzzards instead.

After walking for several miles in the blazing hot sun, two of the mules died for lack of water. This did not alter the plans of the prospectors because these disillusioned individuals had a misconception of gold. My partner and I knew that these two gold miners would force us to carry the heavy gold.

Father, help us to realize as much as we need water, there is a need of a spiritual refreshing rain from the throne room above. When our souls are withering from the heavy weight of sin, we need to cast this burden aside and get a fresh anointing of divine grace. This is a good time to receive an outpouring of love and mercy. In Jesus' name, amen.

Our Father, our God
June 17

Our unity of love is bound together by the words that Jesus prayed, "Our Father and our God." Their love combines as one. This love is equally shared with all of mankind. There is no separating the two characteristics of one divinity.

Let us take this day to show our most sincere appreciation to God for His Loving kindness. The morning hour has come and we offer up praise with holy hands raised to glorify Him. He is worthy of the honor.

This is a day of sweet communion. We are so blessed to be in God's favor. He gives a loving embrace and takes the time to hear our heartfelt pleas. Answers to our prayers are always His good pleasure.

Blessings continue to flow from the throne room of mercy. There is no end to His bountiful love. When we mention His Son, He does not hesitate to give us more grace. Angels gather around as we meditate.

If we need a special blessing, He opens another window and supplies all of our needs according to His riches in glory. Jesus intercedes on our behalf so we can be in God's holy presence.

Fellowship with God brings us closer together. Family relations grow stronger as we refer to Him as Father. Our love extends from the depth of our hearts. Sweet peace comes down as we worship Him.

Father, as adopted children, we offer sincere gratitude with love and devotion. We all know that Jesus (God's Son) prayed to you as His Father. There were many times that Jesus prayed saying, "My God." He wanted us to have the same relationship. Notice how this prayer is not focused on himself, "Our Father and our God." His choice of words was not by accident. This was intentional to bind us together with divinity. Amen.

Fathers' Day
June 18

The years of our lives slowly pass from one to the next. We would like to honor our fathers on this very special day. This will be a day of thankful hearts as we express our gratitude.

Special recognition is what they deserve. Their love is expressed in so many ways. If they are still living, let's give them a special visit and tell them how much they are loved.

This can be a time to remember the special characteristics they give to the family. Their caring ways are unrestricted for each of their children and other family members.

We thank them for daily guidance as they help us on our journey in life. There are so many times we would have gone astray if it had not been for our fathers to show us the way.

Sometimes we are separated for various reasons. Our time together has been hindered by distance. There are so many things that keep us apart. If the days and years have been broken without any fellowship for many years, it's never too late to say, "I love you," from the father and the children.

Our Father and our God, we are so thankful for our fathers whose love for us never wavers. They would do anything to help us on our journey. Keep your holy hand upon them with grace to spare. Guide them in the ways of righteousness.

Little children grow up imitating their father's example and they want to be just like him. As fathers, let us look back at the trail; little ones may be following. If we want our little boys and girls to grow up as kind-hearted citizens with deep devotion to God, we must leave a trail of godly living.

We bless our fathers and all of those who have departed. Our thankfulness goes into one voice of affection, "We love you, Dad." Let the praise be heard throughout the land, amen.

Spiritual Rain
June 19

There are times in life when we desire a fresh outpouring of grace to revive our faltering souls. This blessing is like the rain that saturates the earth. Plants are revived and brought back to life when a gentle rain comes down from the skies above.

Many of us have seen times of drought when the earth was parched and dry from a lack of rain. Crops have been planted and died in the fields.

The vegetation cannot grow if there is not a good source of water to replenish all the nutritional needs. An abundance of rain is urgently needed or we will die of starvation unless we have a fresh water supply.

Irrigation systems are working overtime to save the withering crops and the livestock. The weather forecaster announced rain for this week. Our anticipation was running high as we placed the rain barrels in convenient places. We cannot survive unless the rain comes quickly.

There is rejoicing throughout the land as dark storm clouds are beginning to form. These are little clouds that would not have enough rain to quench the thirst of a drought stricken nation, or fill one barrel.

As we watched the clouds move a little closer, our hopes and expectations of a great storm filled our hearts with joy at the thought of an abundance of rain. Little faith may have big results; keep praying.

Father, those tiny storm clouds must have had a little bit of mustard seed anointed with effectual prayer, as there is now a massive storm. Help us to realize that in a time of spiritual drought, the rain will descend when we offer up the praise. The blessings of God come down when we are sincere and the meditation of our hearts is pure. Send the rain, amen.

Neglect our Salvation
June 20

It was a peaceful night as the security guard checked the jail cells to make sure his prisoners could not get out. All of the locks were examined for safety reasons, probably more than once. Keeping prisoners safe can be a traumatic experience.

This guard must have been more nervous than usual. The security of these inmates would cost him his life if they escaped from the jail. If we were guarding the cell, we would have been terrified if the prisoners broke free from this confinement area. Let's just visit this place where the prisoners are kept so that we can experience firsthand the emotions of this jail keeper.

Our over active imagination has two other men in prison for their criminal offences. Everyone is secure in the cells and the jail keeper is taking a nap. He certainly doesn't seem to be worried, at least for now.

Suddenly he awoke from his sleep and found all the doors were open. He was going to take his own life because he thought the prisoners had escaped. They were still in jail. Paul or Silas, told the jailer to believe on the Lord Jesus Christ. This guard would be saved and his family.

Visionary prisoners did not escape either. The door was open, but they would not walk away as free men. They had the opportunity, but they did not take it. These criminals neglected their freedom.

Father, how shall we escape the punishment for our sins if we neglect our salvation? If we refuse God's love and mercy, we will have to face the consequence for our sinful lives.

Help us to realize that Jesus died to set us free. We do not have to remain as captives. A pardon is offered for our freedom. It is more blessed to receive than to die in our sins. Salvation neglected can also mean that heaven is denied, amen.

A Daily Walk with the Lord
June 21

As we walk the path that leads to glory, we find that we are always blessed when Jesus meets with us along the way. We always enjoy this relationship with God's Son, walking with Him, and having a good time of fellowship.

This walk with the Lord began many years ago, as some of us can recall. It truly has been a wonderful friendship that started on our knees at the cross. When our sins were forgiven, we received the blessed hope of going to heaven. Now, Jesus walks with us on a daily basis.

Some of Jesus' friends have not known Him as long as other faithful believers. We may have gone many miles or just a few years in our journey with the Lord, but even if this is the first day, His merciful kindness goes with us all through life.

Our companionship with Christ binds us together with a love for the Father. Jesus would be really disappointed if we did not invite sinners to join with us on the pathway of life. Walk with the Savior and have the benefit of becoming one of God's adopted children and having eternal life.

While we are walking, there are many times that we need special guidance to help us stay on the right path. Sometimes we get discouraged, but Jesus always has words of encouragement. The best ones that influence us when we are about to make a wrong turn is when Jesus says, "Follow me." These words will keep us on the right trail.

Father, this is a good day to walk the path that leads to our home in heaven. But what makes this day so special is that we will be walking with your Son, Jesus Christ. We leave the trail of sins behind with no remorse, as we are now walking a path where Jesus is our Lord. Help each of us to rise in the morning and to take a daily walk with the Lord, amen.

Jesus in our Midst
June 22

There are times in our lives when we go for walks and enjoy the scenery. Somewhere along the way, Jesus always meets with us and we have fellowship with Him.

He has given us a promise that where two or three people gather together in His name, then He will be in their midst. This encounter with God's Son revives us in spirit and rekindles the fire in our hearts.

Several years ago, while I was walking by the river at the public park, a good friend of mine met me along the way. If my memory is true, we spoke of our fathers and other family members who had passed away.

This was a good time of spiritual reflections. All of a sudden Jesus was standing beside us and we knew that we were in the presence of a loving God. Angels did not entertain us, as it was Jesus, God's only Son.

Comments were shared of how wonderful it would be to walk the streets of glory. Our conversation was not of wishful thinking, or a Disney Land adventure, neither was it a Hollywood production. It was a real-life situation where the saints of God gather around the throne.

We like to think about heaven as our home and family members together again. Heaven's greeting will be filled with laughter, praise and worship. Our heavenly Father will be waiting with a loving embrace.

Father, there are times in life when we meet friends walking by the riverside, talking about heaven and the love of God. Did not our hearts burn within us when we realized that Jesus was walking right beside us? It truly is a blessing to meet friends we haven't seen in a long time, but the blessing is greater when Jesus is in our midst with mercy to share, amen.

Touch the Lord
June 23

This is a good day to reach out and touch the Lord. We know that a blessing is on the way. Prayers ascend to heaven with urgent request for a miracle to come our way. A response is quickly given as Jesus is waiting for us to touch Him.

Reach up and touch the hem of His garment. It does not matter if thousands of people have gathered around with a variety of needs. His healing power is unrestricted and miracles of grace always abound.

However long it takes for our healing, we have no doubt that the Great Physician has our best interest at heart. Our healing process may take longer as there are special needs on earth. God sees those who are struggling, unable to conquer and rise above the present situation.

He is also aware of certain individuals who are in need of divine healing. They have strength and stamina with unwavering faith to touch the hem of His garment on behalf of those whose faith is weak. God wants them to help others.

The person that God chooses to be an inspiration to others must be brave enough to hold up the cross in times of extreme circumstances. If healing is a long time away, it is because someone else needs a bright light shining so faith can be restored and hope of life will be given.

Father, help us to realize as we journey through life, we don't always understand the obstacles we have to cross in order to make it to heaven.

All things are possible when we touch Jesus. Let's be thankful for the blessings sent down from above. Whatever our need is in life, grace will abound when we touch the Lord. There is no need to wait any longer, touch Him now, amen.

A Personal Visit
June 24

Every once in a while, Jesus will make an unannounced appearance. His visitation hours are unknown to us. Jesus' main concern for us is the welfare of our souls. We are always blessed when He comes for a visit. Let's suppose Jesus is coming by for a casual meeting.

This is a personal visit to talk over some eternal concerns. Some of us have already accepted His plan of salvation for our lives. He will keep all conversations private. Secrets will not be on the morning news.

He will speak with each of us individually. Please don't be surprised if He mentions sins. If He does, there is no need to be alarmed. His visit will not be to condemn but to help us realize sins can be forgiven when we repent.

This is not a painful process, at least not for us. But it was for Jesus when He hung on an old rugged cross and died so we could have a new life in Him. There is no need to make a payment for this visit. His offer of salvation is a free gift.

His precious blood was spilled to wash away all of our sins. Everyone who accepts Christ will have the blessed hope of life eternal. If we accept Him as our Savior, we can be really thankful for this visit. However, if we cannot come to an agreement because of sin, please be advised there will be no admittance in heaven unless Jesus is the Lord of our lives.

Father, we must also realize that life has an expiration date and we are not promised another day. The sun is already beginning to set and some of us may not see the morning light.

When Jesus comes for a visit, He is not coming with a contract to negotiate our spiritual aspirations. This will not be a game of "Let's make a deal." Accept or reject, we can only choose one. Jesus, you are welcome here, amen.

Rescue Without Christ
June 25

We have a very important assignment today, as there are responders needed for various life situations. Certain types of emergency equipment will be used to help save those who are in danger. Rescue operations will fail without proper training.

A good navigation system is required to give the correct location. Satellites in the sky have helped to save many lives. We have to realize that false information or misguided instructions can take us to the wrong place. Expressions of sorrow fill our hearts; the rescue attempt was unsuccessful.

Responders are urgently needed to save lives. Emergency skills will help us determine the most qualified people. Men and women will be considered in the selection process. Only a few rescue-training positions will be filled, as there is a limit as to how many trainees will be placed on the job-roster.

We have certainly learned from our mistakes and will take all precautions to prevent any further casualties. The loss of one life is too many. Training for all employees will immediately go into effect.

Father, help us to realize another very important rescue is in process. Many souls are dying because of sins aggressive tactics. Responders will be accepted from all walks of life. This life-saving endeavor includes children.

Most of our saving techniques will be with on-the-job training. Bible study and worship services will help us in our rescue attempt, as there is no time to spare.

We have already learned there are some things that we cannot do without when rescuing victims in disastrous situations. Concerning our soul's salvation, there has never been a successful rescue without Christ. Help us to present Him as Lord and Savior so souls will be saved, amen.

Accepting Volunteers
June 26

This is a special volunteer assignment for all eligible participants. According to the rules, we all have the same opportunity to sign up. The duration of our service will be eternal life. Little children to adults will be accepted.

Sinners are called to take up the cross and follow Jesus. When we volunteer to serve Him, if we are faithful we will receive a crown of life that fades not away. Just a reminder, this is an all-volunteer operation.

We are all eligible; without repentance, there will be no acceptance by grace. The main qualification is for us to be sinners. If there is someone here that does not fit in this classification, please step aside. Several minutes go by and not a single person can claim non-sinner status.

The military force has changed over the years. At one time, it was mandatory to recruit private citizens into service. We did not have any choices of our own. If we did not want to be in the military, we could not stay at home. Soon we would be following orders and eating army chow, or some other type of military food. It is an honor to be a volunteer.

Father, your Son, Jesus is looking for those who will serve Him faithfully in battle, stand strong against the enemy, and be victorious against all evil in war. Accept the challenge; Heaven will be the reward.

Voices are heard throughout the crowd, as Jesus patiently waits for us to choose Him as Lord and Savior. Those who come to Him must come of their own free will.

Help us to realize that each one of us has to decide, accept or reject Christ. It is our choice. If Christ is chosen, it will be the best decision we have ever made in life. Choose Jesus today and receive eternal life. In Jesus' name, amen.

Storm Chasers
June 27

We are going on an adventure to an extremely dangerous territory. The items we need for this experience are cameras and video equipment. Good pictures and live action will alert the people of the hazardous living conditions. A warning is in place, high alert!

Photography does not seem like a life-threatening event, but this is a life or death situation. We need some qualified individuals to be storm chasers. This job will be up close and personal. Please follow me to hurricane alley. There is always a lot of turbulent activity in this area. Storm chasers report the news and lives are saved because of their heroic efforts.

Hurricane winds are already destroying property and lives are in danger. This is an extremely dangerous mission that will require our complete submission to the cause. Saving lives is our number one priority. It is our responsibility to give an accurate report of the storm.

When the storm is raging, we do not have time to waste. There are things in the house that we would like to take with us. It will take just a few minutes to gather these valuable items. Worldly cares can be fatal.

Outside the floodwaters continue to rise. If we had left at the first sign of danger, we could have made it to a safe shelter, no time to waste. How long are we going to wait before we seek shelter in the Lord?

Father, the challenge for us in our daily lives is to warn the people to repent. Get out of the storm's path and seek shelter immediately. There is only one shelter that will keep us safe in the turbulent times of life and that is Jesus Christ. Help us to realize we cannot all be storm chasers, but we can sound the alarm to escape now. In Jesus' name, amen.

Come unto Me
June 28

There are certain times in life when we have special needs and Jesus is the only one who can fulfill the desires of our hearts. He calls for us and gives personal invitations to follow Him.

He gave His life so we could have life. Let's think about this personal call for us to gain our freedom. We can go through life, dragging the heavy weight of sin around and have no hope of everlasting life.

Another alternative is to repent and receive the promise of life eternal. Jesus is calling, "Come unto me." Oh, it is a blessed day in anyone's life when the decision is made to follow Christ. There will be no regrets as we walk the streets of glory and praise the name of Jesus forever.

When we go to Him, He forgives us. We may have burdens that are weighing us down. Whatever our needs in life, the call is the same, "Come unto me." These are the words of God's only begotten Son.

Listen very closely as the words echo through the mountains and valleys, "Come unto me. Wherever there are souls in need of salvation, Jesus is still speaking to hearts.

Father, "no one cares about me." We can truthfully say this person has never met Jesus. This call is not of a stranger that intends to do us harm, But of your Son. His love is so great; excruciating pain would not bring Him down from the cross.

Help us to realize that we need to respond while Christ is calling us to follow Him. The days and years will pass and we will come to the end of our journey. It will be a sad time if we have not taken up our cross and followed Jesus. There will be rejoicing in heaven if Jesus is our Lord and we follow Him throughout life. Yes, Lord, I will follow you all the way, amen.

Safe and Secure
June 29

This is an important day for us, as we need to be persuaded or convinced that our treasures are secure. Suppose we have a painting by a well-known artist. We will not leave this expensive artwork unless we are sure it will be kept safe.

Security of earthly investments is a good way to insure monetary items will not be stolen or damaged in any way. There is something far more important than gold or silver. Curiosity will have us wait to the end of this story.

We have been authorized by a higher power to commit our most prized possessions to His protective care. I assure all of my good friends of the stability we have in Him. There is no better way to protect our investment than in the care of almighty God and His Son, Jesus Christ.

Banks have been used around the world to secure our earthly treasures. However, thieves have robbed some of them. Call out the National Guard and all military personnel to provide security against all evil forces. I hate to discourage anyone, but they just do not have the capabilities to maintain a secure environment for our personal needs. Whatever we are protecting must have eternal value.

The suspense has gone on too long. Each one of us has a soul and this is our most prized possession. "I know whom I have believed, and am persuaded that he is able to keep that which I have committed unto him against that day" (Timothy 1: 12). When we commit our souls to Jesus, He will keep them safe in His care. We are safe in the vault of His love.

Father, there are some people that have not yet made an investment into the eternal affairs of life. Souls are left unguarded and the open gate of sin allows for unrighteousness, and ungodly living. Help us to lock the gate by committing our souls to Christ. In Jesus' name, amen.

Under the Radar
June 30

Radar is used extensively around the world to track airplanes and to guide aircraft safely in the sky. Recently a commercial airliner disappeared and a search began for the passengers. All efforts failed and the rescue had to be aborted or abandoned.

It has been announced that an airplane was flying under the radar and it may have crashed into the sea. There were no identifying parts of the wreckage. The search for the passengers and crew was also in vain.

Bad weather hampered the rescue operation. We all hope that everyone has survived this terrible ordeal. After several days of searching, official investigators decided to cancel this mission. This search ended without a trace of the aircraft, years later, still nothing.

Aircraft radar is a very sophisticated system that follows airplanes and keeps them from crashing into other aircraft. The enemy will fly beneath the radar system.

Let's concentrate now on the surveillance of a loving God. His watchfulness over our lives is a continual process. There is not a day that goes by without Him knowing everything about us. We can try to hide in the vast ocean of worldly cares, but sins will be a bright flare.

Father, help us to be aware that if we go back into sin by staying below the radar system, the guilt of sin will entrap us. It will be like a red flare warning as a signal of our transgressions.

Since the flare is already burning and God knows of our location, cry out to Him for mercy and put the flare out. The report we give will be sinner's lost and found. Help us now to realize if we are under the radar having never repented of our sins, God will never abort the mission. In Jesus' name, amen.

Debt is paid
July 1

Today we will look at the high price of our sins. This cannot be measured on a grocery scale or in monthly payments. The cost is way too high to even consider a large amount of money. Jesus paid the price when He gave His life on an old cross. Our debt was paid at Calvary.

Let's look at our sins and see how much it cost Jesus to clear the debt. There was a loss of blood, a beating, unbearable pain, a crown of thorns upon His brow, and three nails held Him to a cross. He gave His life to pay a debt He did not owe.

His persecutors did not use the blood of bulls, calves, or even lambs. None of those things would be sufficient to cover the price of our sins. The blood of Jesus (God's only begotten Son) was the only thing that could purify our sinful lives.

He paid with His life and now we receive forgiveness, salvation of our souls, and a home in glory. He gave His life so we could receive mercy. What He gave and what we received should cause every person to fall on their knees and say, "Thank you, Jesus." My debt is paid in full.

Father, Jesus made a payment that was worth more than any financial investment. The debt of sin requires a living sacrifice. Jesus paid the debt with His life. One life to give equals forgiveness that will last throughout eternity. This is a good time to claim a title conversion with repentance.

When we purchase a vehicle, it does not matter how many years of service we drive back and forth to work, the car does not belong to us until the bill is paid. Our salvation is not based on any type of material wealth, but only in the sacrifice of Christ. The debt of sin is paid and we immediately receive forgiveness of sins when we repent. Help us to realize our debt was paid in full with a living sacrifice. In Jesus' name, amen.

Final Review
July 2

Suppose our lives are in review and we have to give an account of our earthly journey. God is on the throne and He knows everything about us. Let's just suppose He is examining the final pages of our lives. We can make it more personal by each one of us being the one that is reviewed. A good approval rating is desired for a passing grade.

This book is open and there are special characteristics that God wants to see in each of our lives. Each page is filled with kind deeds of helping neighbors and friends. The pages are turned and there are many commendable things that are favorable for us. It shows that we lived honorable, respectable lives. Heaven's evaluation is not complete.

More pages are turned to reveal some important things that happened along the way. This book is really interesting and it shows the good qualities of life. However dark clouds abide without the sun's rays.

Each page is filled with kindness, love, and mercy. God notices a forgiving attitude has been a consistent process in this book. It looks like each of us really lived a good life. Oh, there seems to be a problem.

The final review probably brought tears to our Father's eyes. There was no mention of His Son in the book by certain individuals. A good life is commendable, but without Christ, a life is void of real peace and forgiveness that comes from above. Accept Him for a favorable report.

Father, pages of life are turned and the image we want everyone to see is Jesus. Godly living is the best way for others to see Christ in our lives. Help us to realize we can only have a passing grade if Jesus is our Lord and Savior. Final review, Jesus is on every page. In Jesus' name, amen.

Only by Permission
July 3

It is really a nice day to enjoy the comforts of home. This is the place where we like to meet with our friends and family members. We have a mat in front of the door that says "Welcome." When the doors are locked and no one can get inside, is it possible that the display sign is telling a lie? Patience reveals the truth as it waits for action to occur.

I guess our visitors could answer this question. They are the ones that have to stand outside and wait for the door to be unlocked. One thing is for sure; no one will be allowed to come in without permission. If the door remains locked, visitors will graciously leave or depart in anger.

Let's visit a house where a good friend of mine will be visiting. He waits patiently outside the door for permission to come inside. After waiting for a short while, he decides to leave. There is a possibility of a return visit tomorrow. Life has no guarantee the sun will rise in the morning.

Well to everyone's dismay, at the midnight hour, death came to claim one of the family members. Jesus is the one who was standing at the door with a decree from heaven to give life eternal, a glory crown, and a home in glory, but the heart's door was locked without a faith key.

Father, if we do not invite Jesus into our lives, He will graciously leave and we might forfeit our inheritance in heaven. Today may be our last opportunity to unlock the door. He will only come in by permission. Our greeting should be: "Jesus, you are welcome, please come into my heart."

Along the space of a lifetime, we have had many visitors to come to our homes. Some of the residents are invited inside, while others are turned away. One thing is for sure; none of them will enter without permission. Let's open the door and receive God's love and mercy. In Jesus' name, amen.

God Bless America
July 4

Let's go back in time to the signing of the Declaration of Independence. According to history, we were officially separated from Great Britain in the year of 1776.

This national holiday is known as Independence Day. We celebrate July 4th to refresh our memories of what it cost the soldiers as some of them gave the ultimate sacrifice of life for freedom. The price of liberty is the integrity of a nation.

Let us think about the every-day citizens who left their families, children, loved ones and friends to fight in a battle where the blood trail would leave fatherless children and homes without loving companions.

Men and women who were called for service paid the high cost of keeping our freedom. Some of them gave all they could give. Dying for the country we love, "America." Families torn apart by war where brothers and sisters, wives and mothers would say freedom is not free.

The blood flows deep on the battlefields with grave markers as grim reminders of hard fought battles. There are many graves with each of these brave men and women's names engraved in stone for a memorial.

America continues to fight for our freedom overseas. It seems to be a never-ending war. We are the United States, the home of the brave, land of the free, and one nation under God. Our brave men and women have answered the call to fight for this great country. Let's continue to stand beside her, fight to protect her, and die to save her. God bless America.

Father, we come before your holy presence in the name of your Son, Jesus. This is a time we celebrate our independence with thankfulness for our freedom. Keep us in your loving care all the days of our lives. In Jesus' name, amen.

The Master of the Clay
July 5

We will visit a place today where clay is shaped into a certain object. This will be an interesting adventure for us to watch and be partakers as lives are changed by the molding process. Our lives will be affected.

I am sure everyone will be impressed when we meet the Master of the clay. There is no one like Him for He labors continuously in His shop. The door of His shop is always open and He welcomes all visitors. No one is turned away. He is never too busy to hear our heart's cries.

All of us can think of times when we needed a special touch to mold and reshape our lives. God's love is the modeling tool for all imperfections. If we are in need of a spiritual remodeling, a touch of His holy hand will transform us. When our lives are shattered by the sins of the world, He picks up the broken pieces and bonds them together with merciful kindness.

The Master of the Clay does not hesitate to make a personal visit, no matter if it is day or night. He is always on call and will respond in a moment's notice, even if we come in for unexpected emergency repairs.

Sometimes the imperfections of sin will corrupt our lives and we definitely need a touch of the Master's hand. Tears of repentance restore us to godly living. Disgraceful living is not pleasing to God. He works diligently with our hearts, calling for us to repent. Vessels of praise and honor begin to form when we make peace at the cross.

Father, we are thankful for the molding process. A visit to the throne room of mercy is urgently needed. God will create vessels of honor when Jesus is the Lord of our lives. Let's take the time to visit the shop where the Master of the clay is transforming lives by His marvelous grace. Touch us now and recreate us in Christ image. In Jesus' name, amen.

Behold, the Man, Jesus
July 6

The discovery of a man's true identity is shown in the characteristics of His life. We are going to visualize the life of Christ so we will have a better understanding of His love and merciful kindness for mankind.

There are many interesting things about Jesus that we would like to know, "Who is this man?" Those of us who know Him would say, "He is the good Shepherd." Sheep that go astray find solace in His arms.

As a shepherd watches over his sheep, so does Christ keep us in His loving care. We do not need to fear any evil because we know He is always beside us and will help us to stand against the wiles of the devil.

He is a man who can calm the storms that prevail in nature. We would all agree. When the trials of life are hard to bear, Jesus never leaves or forsakes us. Christ speaks to the storms of our souls. "Peace be Still."

Please go with me to the cross. We will witness through the eyes of faith, the crucifixion and resurrection of Jesus. He is dying for our sins; the suffering is unbearable. They took Him down from the cross and laid Him in a grave. "Behold, the man, Jesus!" All of us who know Him say, "Jesus is the mighty God, Prince of peace, and Savior of the world.

Father, this is a good time to behold, the man, Jesus. He gave His life on a cross. We see Him with spikes driven into His hands and feet, a crown of thorns forced upon His brow and suffering as a man with excruciating pain.

However, we take a deeper look into the identity of Jesus and we see He is the only begotten of the Father. Help us all to realize that Jesus is the Christ, the Savior of the world and He is the only one that can forgive sins. Thank you, Jesus.

Stay Alive
July 7

It looks like it will be a good time to take a vacation. We are going to get away for a while and spend some time in the Great Smokey Mountains. This event was planned several months in advance. We will travel on this adventure by imagination.

This is not going to be a luxury vacation. All of the modern conveniences of life will be left at our homes. There will be no electricity to give us light in the evening. Forget about running water, unless there is a creek nearby. Livelihood of past generations is today's nightmare.

I should warn every one of the possible dangers of hungry bears in the area. These creatures of the wild have been known to attack people. This is an adventure that will test our survival skills. Our food supply will be fish, berries, and other natural resources. The purpose of this vacation is survival training. This is a personal endeavor to stay alive.

Let's just say for imaginary reasons that we received some bad news. One of our family members passed away early this morning. We will have to reschedule our trip to a later time. This is an unexpected tragedy of the loss of our loved one.

Our adventure was to spend one week in the wild country. We had made the plans and were well prepared to stay alive. No one knows the day or hour when death will interrupt our plans. A commitment to stay alive is unfulfilled on this earthly journey. All of us need survival skills from the Bible to stay spiritually alive. Christ in us is life forevermore.

Father, every once in a while, we go on a vacation to get away from the routine of life. We did not know the dark shadows of death would cross our paths before the day was over. Before we go on a survival mission to stay alive, the best way for us to prepare is to make peace with God by accepting Jesus into our hearts. Thank you, Jesus, for life eternal, amen.

Shelter in the Rock
July 8

We are going on an imaginary adventure into the forest where the trees will be cut and run through a sawmill. This log cutting area was in a remote part of the forest that was overgrown with dense underbrush. No one was aware of the fate of a little boy's life, as he came towards us.

This harvesting of the lumber created many jobs in the neighborhood. Several positions were posted in town and at the lumber mill. Many lumberjack positions were filled. However, there were still jobs available at this worksite. Soon the lumber company had enough employees to cut the trees. The work began early the next morning.

All week we heard the sound of chainsaws and trees falling to the ground. Lumberjacks were cutting trees and transporting them to the sawmill so they could be cut into lumber. These rough boards were then loaded onto trucks and hauled to factories for the smoothing process.

Everyone was hard at work and no one noticed a young boy had entered the danger zone. Entry into this area was strictly prohibited, no one was allowed below the tree line. The lad didn't notice the warning signs as he was trying to catch his runaway pony. This day could end in a terrible tragedy. Chainsaws grew silent as the men watched in fear.

All of a sudden, shouts from above alerted the boy to the danger; maybe it was too late. A huge tree was falling right towards him. He crawled in under a rock ledge as the branches crashed around him. This shelter saved the young boy's life.

Father, help us to realize that Jesus protects us in all kinds of situations. He is a refuge that is fortified with God's love. Let's commit our souls to Him and when life is over, we will still be abiding in Him. Today is a good time to seek shelter in the rock (Christ) before the tree falls. In Jesus' name, amen.

The Fire Escape
July 9

We think about the tragedy in the year of 2016; a city is consumed by fire. Wildfires were out of control, destroying everything. Eighty thousand people have had to evacuate. Homes completely burned to the ground. Emergency routes have been created to help the victims escape.

Modern high-rise facilities have fire escapes on the side of the building. When one of these structures begins to burn, the men, women, and even children are in danger of losing their lives. Flames reach higher as the firemen, first responders, and medical units respond to the rescue effort.

Those in the burning building are instructed to move quickly to an emergency exit. There is danger in our sinful lives of moving too slowly to escape the fire. Run from the flames. How can we escape the fire if we neglect our salvation? Jesus will provide an escape route if we take the emergency exit and receive Him, as Lord and Savior. Let's run a little faster.

Residents in the hotel are being evacuated. A fire is raging through the facility. People are running for their lives to escape the flames. Hundreds of firefighters and residents of the community have joined in the efforts to save the people trapped inside the burning building.

But a father does not realize his daughter is also safe. He goes back into the burning building to save her. My imagination cannot let this man die in the flames. Firefighters are able to save him. A rescue effort will be successful when we repent.

Father, help us to realize that if we go back into sin, there is a strong possibility that the rescue effort will be in vain. Jesus has made a way of escape by dying in our place for sins. If we are not in a hurry to invite Jesus into our lives, all of the emergency responders will not be able to help us. The fire escape of repentance saves lives. In Jesus' name, amen.

Pardon Me
July 10

Let's say we are walking at the park and someone accidently bumps into one of us. The words most commonly used are: "Excuse me or pardon me." Most of the time, the reaction is good and both parties continue on their way. If there seems to be some contention, walk away quickly before the emotion is lost in the fray and ignites into a flare-up.

Today we will be approaching the throne room of grace. There are many offenses, sins, and transgressions that follow us on the pathway of life. We know there is not enough time to express our grief for a lifetime of corruptible things. Sorrowful hearts disperse when tears of joy flow.

The few words that we choose must be strong and sincere. They must come from the depth of our hearts. A really long speech is not needed to make things right with God. However, He loves having company and He will stay with us as long as it is our hearts desire. He is a merciful God.

An apology or confession of sins is needed for us to approach the throne room of mercy. God will welcome us into His family as adopted children, sons and daughters. Love will intervene to interrupt strife.

A long prayer or a short one will be sufficient. But today, let's be brief, the honesty and remorsefulness of our hearts will get better results. Whether we use a lot of words or a few, it does not matter as long as we are truly sincere. "Jesus come into my heart, I am sorry for my sins, please pardon me." He will never walk away from a repentant heart.

Father, we have many offences and sins that need to be forgiven. It's not possible to name them all. Sins can hold us until grace sets us free. The Lord is attentive to the cries for mercy. He does not flare-up in anger, but He accepts our apology and God gives us a loving embrace. Thank you, Jesus, amen.

Stagnant Life
July 11

After several miles of traveling, we finally reached our destination. This is a popular camping site that is visited by many tourists. We were really looking forward to hiking through the woods to our favorite fishing spot. However, this return visit came with remorseful feelings.

We set up camp and enjoyed some of the recreational activities. This seemed to be the perfect time of year for meals prepared over a fire or on a grill. The next morning, we had breakfast. Fresh trout was on the menu for the evening meal.

The time had finally come for us to begin our hiking trip through the mountains. We were surprised at the amount of brush that was cluttering the trail. Our sorrowful hearts were already feeling the distress.

It looked as though no one had walked this path for years. In times past, the trail was always easy to follow. Our journey through the woods was taking a lot longer than we had planned. After battling the elements of trash and debris, untangling fishing rods caught in the shrubbery, we finally make it to our destination. We stood there frustrated, as the stagnant water was unable to move swiftly downstream.

Our hearts sank with grief when we saw the stagnant water and more garbage in the river. Our favorite fishing spot was polluted and this part of our imaginary vacation was ruined. There will be no fresh trout this year.

Father, impurities of a sinful life will not only hinder, but they will stop the flow of grace. The pathway of life is not cluttered when Jesus' precious blood cleanses our sinful hearts and makes us holy, pure within. Help us to realize you are not pleased when you look down from heaven and see the moral values of our lives are contaminated. Purify our hearts of ungodly living with a fresh flow of grace. In Jesus' name, amen

Light in Darkness
July 12

Darkness is often referred to as sinful conditions. It is a blessed day in our lives when the glory of the Lord shines in our hearts and turns the light on. When Jesus forgives our sins, we have a new life in Him. The light came on at Calvary's cross when we invited Jesus to come into our lives.

Let's see how this darkness affected our lives. Our daily routine consisted of unrighteous, ungodly living, and no prospect of heaven. We definitely did not have good directions, no one can see in the dark, but where the light abides our vision is clear. "I once was blind, but now I see."

Jesus is the only one who can dispel the darkness. We commit our souls to Him and He leads us safely home. Jesus is the light of the world. Those who follow Him will not walk in darkness but will have the light of life.

We can see that following Jesus, living holy, righteous lives, the radiance of God's glory shines upon us. This is far better than falling in the dark and having to suffer the consequence of sin, which is eternal punishment in hell.

It was a dark, dreary night when the lights went out. All across the land darkness had invaded the homes and businesses. We were all alone in this strange environment. No one knew how long these miserable conditions would last.

Father, all of us have had electrical power failures. The power goes off and does not come back on for a long time. Meanwhile we stumble in the dark and bump into hard objects. This can cause excruciating pain.

Occasionally an injury will occur that results in broken bones. Sins can cause us to waver in faith and fall from grace. People are still asking what must we do to be saved? If the power is off, turn the light on by faith in Christ, amen.

Take Hold of Jesus' Hand
July 13

A massive fire was spreading through a large living facility. Outside of the building a contractor was seen hanging onto the ledge for his life. The fire was becoming more intense and the walls were ready to collapse any moment. It seemed as though he would die in the flames.

There was not much time to save the man, a few minutes at the most. He maneuvered himself into position to hold onto the window ledge and then he swung himself to a lower unit as the upper level was ablaze.

The fire department had extended the ladder to the individual, but was it too late? This contractor was within arm's reach of the equipment, but the flames from the burning structure were reaching for him.

He climbed onto the ladder and the fire department had width-drawn the extension of the ladder about three feet from the building when a section of the structure fell to the ground, barely missing the contractor.

The construction worker was saved just in time. He was just barely saved before the building collapsed. This rescue operation was a success and we are thankful the man's life was spared. This was a true story.

One part of this rescue caught my attention. The contractor was holding onto the window ledge and then he let go when the fire was blazing all around him. How close to the fire will we get before we decide to receive Christ as Lord and Savior? Hopefully, we will decide in time; the flames are getting higher.

Father, we need to let go of sins and take hold of Jesus' hand. Holding onto sin will not help us, even for a little while. Jesus is waiting for the call of help to rescue us before the wall comes crashing down. Save us from the fire. In Jesus' name, amen.

The Stain of Sin
July 14

Volunteers are needed to help in the woodworking shop. All those interested in staining a nice piece of furniture, please come to the craftsman shop at the end of town.

The wood receives the stain and penetrates deep into the grain. A short while later shellac is applied to the surface. Light sanding between coats is always an improvement. It is time to stand back and look at the finished product.

We were admiring the beautiful finish when we noticed a dark spot right in the middle of the desk. It seemed as though all of our hard work was in vain. Small imperfections brought a few moments of sadness.

The woodcraft had to be refinished, so we took it out of the stain room and carried the desk back to the wood working area. Now that the varnish has been removed, we begin the difficult task of removing the stain. Stain is harder to remove because it is not just on the surface but it is completely saturated into the grain of the wood.

This beautiful desk was now ready for the customer. Everyone in the woodshop gave a sigh of relief as this item was refinished before the deadline and the customer was satisfied.

Father, sins of our lives penetrate deep into our souls like the stain on the wood. They are the stains that corrupt and defile us. We should go through the refinishing process and let Christ precious blood cleanse our hearts. A fresh layer of mercy combined with grace will restore our relationship with God.

Stain can be removed with sand paper, but to remove sin from our unholy nature, we need a touch from heaven. Before we can be completely restored, we must ask Jesus to forgive us of our sins and all unrighteousness. We want God to be satisfied when it is time for delivery. In Jesus' name, amen.

The Worth of a Soul
July 15

This would be a good time for an excavating project. Our search today will be for rare artifacts found in the earth. Vases have been discovered long ago that were of great value. These artifacts are very old and can easily be broken. Some of these vessels are covered in mud and need to be thoroughly cleaned. None of them were found in perfect condition.

We are sending out this information so all collectors and antique specialist will be ready to inspect these priceless objects. Digging in the earth is a very tedious operation. It can be a little boring, but we appreciate all the help we can get. Endeavors to find will be rewarding.

Several glass containers have been dug up and taken away. They need to go through a cleaning process. It is really hard to tell if the glassware is of any value while it is covered in mud unless shouts of joy arise.

Well it has been several hours now of carefully removing the dirt so as not to break any vases. Finally, some ornamental pieces are found. The value of them exceeds all expectations. What once was worthless is now of great value.

Suppose we go through a divine excavating project. The search will be more intense as it will be in the depths of our hearts. It appears to me that at one time we were all broken vessels, polluted by sin, until Jesus found us and made us whole. God was well pleased with the results.

Father, I suppose that some of the most valuable treasures in the world have been found in the miry clay. God's excavation process is to find sinners in need of a soul cleansing. He stretched out His arm and reached down His holy hand to lift us out of the mire. We were worthless just like the mud-spattered bottles that were found in the earth until Jesus purified our lives by His blood. Thank you, Jesus, amen.

Blind Spots
July 16

While I was traveling down the road one day, a car pulled right out in front of me. The driver had stopped at a stop sign to see if there was anything coming down the road. Impaired vision causes accidents or a dense fog makes terrible driving conditions. This was a beautiful day with the sun shining and blue skies hovering motionless above the earth.

I was turning left at the intersection where this woman was located. But all of a sudden, without warning, she drove right in front of me. Blood pressure and anxiety can be affected very fast in dangerous situations.

This accident was barely avoided as I slammed on the brakes just in time. Sometimes it takes a few minutes to recuperate and let the jittery nerves calm down a little bit. Anxiety departs when peace abides.

I'm sure most of us have been in the same situation. We look and know that the roads are clear, but they are not. Sometimes we cannot see because of blind spots in our mirrors.
One day when I was coming home from work unaware of the danger ahead. There were some college kids at a crosswalk. They were laughing, and texting, not really paying much attention to the traffic.

Blind spots are very dangerous and so is texting while walking across a highway. I didn't see them coming and they didn't see me either. Well, there was not an accident to report. We all made it to our destinations.

Father, as we travel down the path of life, we need to keep our eyes on Jesus. Sometimes we cannot see Him because of the blind spots, worldly cares, and sinful pleasures. This is when we are in the greatest danger. Will He see us in the Rapture? He will unless we have lost sight of Him and our vision is impaired by sin. Help us to see clearly, in Jesus' name, amen.

217

Race for Life
July 17

The media has broadcast a special event that will take place on a certain day. All competition sports are announced with a month, day, and year. We want everyone to be aware that these calendar dates do not apply to our spiritual journey.

However, there is a race that we cannot afford to lose. The news media keeps quite about this important event but we have daily briefings from heaven and from the Bible with words of encouragement to run to win.

This will be a race for a crown and a new home. All active runners will have a chance to win the prize. There will definitely be many winners. All those who cross the finish line will receive a lifetime benefit of eternal life. Just to make this race more interesting, God has included a position of permanent residence in the celestial city with no evictions.

All of these rewards will be presented when each of us finish the course. Whether we start to run as a little child or later in life as senior citizens, our chances of finishing the race is determined by grace.

Help us to understand that all of us are qualified to run in this race because of our sinner status. It is necessary for us to make peace with God. Without Christ in our lives this race would be in vain. Lingering sins have to be discarded before we can win.

We all know that we cannot finish a race with the burdens of sin, dragging us down. Just so everyone has the same opportunity to win, Jesus will take all corruptible things from our lives if we ask Him. Forgiveness will get us in the race.

Father, we are in a race for the glory crown. There is no secret about the weight of sin. None of us will be able to cross the finish line if we are carrying this heavy burden. Jesus has promised us the victory if we keep our hearts pure, amen.

Transformed Lives
July 18

When we receive Jesus into our lives, there is a transformation that takes place. Immediately our sins are forgiven. This is the result of repentance when we tell Jesus we are sorry for our sins.

It does not look like we have been changed. All of our physical features are the same. Let's go deeper into the depths of each heart where we will see our corrupt nature is purified by the precious blood of Christ.

Each of us could talk about the many sins that we had committed and how we were delivered from them by God's amazing grace. Jesus set us free. The blood of God's sacrificial lamb (His only begotten Son) cleansed the contamination of our sinful lives and made us whole.

Transformation may not be noticed at first in our lives. We used to walk by those places that held us captive and we always yielded to sins evil temptations. Resistance has us walking a godly path of holiness that glorifies God.

Since Jesus came into our hearts, the worldly desires have lost their appeal. Now we are attending church and praising God for His great love and mercy.

This change that takes place in our lives is like having an old car that is kept in the garage. The paint is faded and the fenders are rusted beyond repair. We think about the scripture, "Old things are passed away, and all things are become new." Buying a new car is different than restoring it.

Father, when Christ comes into our lives, we enter a restoring phase. We are not given a new body but our old sinful ways go through a transformation process. Our lives are so much different when we we've been touched by the Master's hand. Purified hearts reveal a loving Savior, amen.

A Decision for Life
July 19

As we travel through life, we will have to make many decisions. Let's say there are two paths in life to follow. One of them is with Jesus; the other is the sinner's path. These two paths have entirely different destinations. All of us start out on the sinner's path. The choice we need to make is to stay on this one, or take the one where Christ is leading the way.

Our corrupt sinful desires lead us down the sinner's path. This is the path that all of us have traveled and the only one that leads away from heaven. We must decide to keep walking towards the fire or turn our lives around by accepting Jesus into our hearts. The path of salvation leads us to the throne of God where love and mercy abide forever.

The decision we make in life will determine where we spend eternity. Heaven or Hell, we choose to follow Jesus or stay on the sinner's path where we will suffer the consequence of sin. Choose the path of life where sins are forgiven and Jesus is Lord. He is calling, "Follow me."

Father, our journey today will help us find the pathway that leads to heaven. There are two paths. Let's say the sinner's path is covered with thorn bushes. We know how painful these sharp briars can be when we touch them. This path will have the effects of sin. There will be no real peace and no hope of going to heaven. It should not take any of us very long to realize we are on the path that leads to hell.

The other path is also marked by pain, but Jesus is the one who suffered it. A crown of thorns was forced upon His brow. Spikes were driven into His hands and feet. He was crucified on a cross. When we follow Jesus on this path we will have peace and have the blessed hope of living with Him in heaven. Now that we know of God's great love and the sacrifice Jesus gave at Calvary, Let's walk a new path. This one leads to glory and everlasting life. In Jesus' name, amen.

Too Faraway to Focus
July 20

It's been a while since we walked at the park and enjoyed God's wonderful creation. This would be a good time for all of my photographer friends to take some snapshots of the imagination landscape. Imagine each person telling this story as a self-photographer.

I am not very familiar with cameras. Perhaps there is someone here who could show me the best way to take pictures. Someone made a comment that the evening hours would be good for cool colorful scenes.

After a while the photo images were shared among us and we commented about each one. When the photo is reviewed, we are not always satisfied with the results. They were all good, except mine. This was an embarrassing time for me, as my pictures were out of focus and I was ashamed for anyone to see them. Blurred pictures can be distressing.

My good friends understood my hurt feelings. They showed me the adjustment to control the distance of objects. We all went home with beautiful pictures and some of us carried a burden of embarrassment.

Our Father has created us in His likeness. Sometimes we get out of focus; maybe it is because we are too far away from God. Personal images will always improve when each of us gets closer to Him. Please don't be discouraged; God's creative image in us is still being developed. This is not an illusion or a dream but a real-life adjustment.

Father, all of us amateur photographers would like to know if we are the ones out of focus or is there a camera defect? More pictures are taken so we can solve the problem. Beautiful landscapes reveal the array of color is just right. The camera is in perfect working order. We have a distance problem between God and us. Let's draw nigh to God, in Jesus' name, amen.

Bread for a Beggar
July 21

Let's take a moment and imagine the life of a poor beggar. We find him standing on a street corner. He would beg for some money to buy food. His little child was taken care of by her grandparents. This poor man was unable to work and he relied totally upon the generosity of strangers.

Sometimes he stayed out all day in the cold weather. His job efforts were often in vain. He kept hoping that someday he could take care of his daughter whom he loved so much.

At the end of the day he would stop by the pantry. The owner would always greet him at the door. This place of business sold bread and other types of groceries. A clerk of the store would always get some bread and give it to the poor beggar. Generosity goes alone way to help those in need. Occasionally the beggar would seek shelter in an abandoned shack.

As he sat at the table in this little shack on the hill, he always prayed, thanking God for his daily bread. It was discovered that the beggar had a wonderful speaking voice. Soon a broadcasting company hired him. His daughter would be so happy. After he was employed, we would probably find him and his child living in a mansion on a hill.

The homeless live on streets and in dark alleys. They sleep on park benches and wherever they can find a shelter. We have seen them at Christmas time, holding their signs and begging for money to buy food.

Father, some of our spiritual needs is the same. We could not survive without a shelter, a place for us to lie down at night. Our greatest need is food for our hungry souls. Jesus is the only one who can keep us alive spiritually. There is a deep longing in our hearts for Jesus. He offers us the bread of life. Let's think about our reply; we can say, "No thank you," or accept the bread and have life eternal. In Jesus' name, amen.

All Have Sinned
July 22

Many years ago, a woman was about to be stoned for her sins. This was really a cruel punishment. We know that she didn't murder anyone. What did she do that was so bad that the men were going to stone her to death?

It appears to me that the law of justice was nowhere to be found. She did not have a trial and no lawyers to represent her. Immediately these men had gathered big rocks for her slaying,

Before we continue with this story, we want to make sure that she has a fair trial. This is a special mandatory meeting for all of us to gather around and witness the final results.

No one can stay at home this time so please come with me to the rock quarry. There is one man who will defend her. Whatever is decided on her behalf will also be our judgment.

This woman was taken in adultery, in the very act. According to Moses law she should be stoned. They tempted Jesus by asking Him, what do you say? He stooped down and wrote on the ground.

He said unto them, "He that is without sin among you, let him first cast a stone at her" (John 8:7). A mob is quick to blame someone else when they are just as guilty. If one stone is thrown, it will be the first lie that others will follow. Is there anyone here that will throw the first one? Let's go home, we have all sinned. Jesus said, "Go and sin no more."

Father, help us to realize that we have all sinned and come short of the glory of God. Jesus your Son died for all so that we would not be punished for our sins but we would have the blessed hope of going to heaven. Oh, how great is the love of Jesus to give himself as a living sacrifice so our sins could be forgiven. He made us aware of our sins so we would see our need for a Savior. Thank you, Jesus, amen.

Garden of Sin
July 23

Weeds in a garden are like sins in our lives. Sins multiply quickly as one sin leads to another and after a while the garden is full of corruption. Sinful Weeds in the garden will eliminate holiness and pureness of heart. These harmful qualities of life separate and annihilate us from God's mercy.

This would be a good time to observe the fruit of our labors. Let's take a close look at the produce. We sow in corruption and that is what we reap. Unrighteousness sowed will not produce holiness or anything worthy of God's favor.

Sin in the garden is a contamination of the weeds, which surround and choke any good deeds that might produce a crop of righteousness. There is no reason to be dismayed as God's grace always abounds over sin.

Our best resource for a productive life is to make peace with God through faith in Jesus Christ. The fruit of our labors will then be a bountiful crop that comes forth with a blessed assurance of life eternal.

We need to take care of the weeds of sin that are trying to invade and disrupt our relationship with God. Sins of disgraceful living try to crowd out the blessings from Him. Where sin abounds grace does much more abound, expect a good crop.

Some of us took the time to weed the garden by accepting Christ into our lives. It's sad to say that some of the gardens are dying for lack of grace. It is time to get rid of the weeds and keep the produce pure.

Father, when our work on earth is done, we will be so thankful that we took the time to weed the garden. If there are sins still remaining, forgiveness is a weed killer of all sinful effects. Purify our hearts in Jesus' name, amen.

One Lost Lamb
July 24

Soon it will be dark in the hill country. The shepherd is busy bringing his sheep into a more secure area for the night. Everything seems to be peaceful and calm. The shepherd knows all of his sheep by name and He calls for each of them. One small lamb is preoccupied somewhere else.

It is nowhere to be found. Occasionally a small lamb will stray from the fold and wander into some dangerous area. The shepherd will risk his own life in the rescue effort. Hopefully the lamb will be unharmed.

A search began immediately for the one that was lost. Ninety-nine sheep were left because they were safe and there was no immediate danger of wild animals while in the care of other sheepherders.

This shepherd will search the dark hills and stay as long as it takes to find the little one that is completely helpless against any type of attack.

After a while of searching, the shepherd heard the squalling of a lamb, not very far away. This man moved quickly through the underbrush and briar patches to the place of rescue. A lamb gone astray had fallen onto a ledge of a cliff. The shepherd reached down and lifted up the frail creature.

Father, there are times in life when we go astray. We have wandered too far from the fold. Sometimes we are just barely on the edge of total disaster. Jesus is the Good Shepherd and His love for us is never ending.

He will not be satisfied until we are safe and secure in our Father's arms. If we have drifted away, and no longer in the fold, Jesus is calling us by name. The best way for Him to find us is to cry out to Him from the depths of our hearts. He responds to the cries for mercy. Thank you, Jesus, amen.

No Doubt in Faith
July 25

There are special appointments that we make in life. We visit many places that will help us to improve our health. Today is an excellent time to have an eye exam. According to my schedule it is in the afternoon.

We will learn some important things about faith while we are there. Saying that we believe leaves a whole lot of room for doubt. We only believe just a fraction of what we see. While sitting in the chair and looking at the chart on the wall, some of the letters are blurred.

The Optometrists begins to rotate the alphabet scale. And he will ask which row of letters can be seen the best. After we tell him, then he wants us to choose the frame of the best focus. Vision test can be discouraging.

We come now to our faith test to see if there is any doubt. I would say most of the people in this group didn't even know there was such a thing in the exam room. The Optometrists will ask us to read the smallest line we can see. Giving an honest report will help us to have better vision.

The letters are spoken and sometimes we are not sure of the letters and we might say, "I believe it is an o, r, k, and we are just not sure." It could be something else. Doubt keeps faith from reaching full potential.

Father, I am glad our real faith is not based on an image on the wall, but in the Lord Jesus." I know whom I have believed, and am persuaded that he is able to keep that which I have committed unto him" (2Timothy 2:12).   Our faith is a full belief without any doubt. We believe and know He is Lord. Vision is restored when faith is applied. Let's be fully persuaded in our faith that Jesus is the Savior of the world. Help us to realize that doubt keeps Christ in the grave. Whereas, faith reveals He is risen. Blessed is the Lord, amen.

Runaway Train
July 26

We have waited a really long time for this vacation at one of the national parks. All of us were really anxious about this trip. This is the first time any of us has traveled by train. The big day has arrived.

Steam engines used to be a regular sight on the railroad. This would be our main transportation to and from our vacation resort. We were skeptical of riding this old train. After all it had been in a museum for half of a century. Joy abounds in this once in a lifetime opportunity.

The anticipation in our hearts was overflowing with excitement as we boarded the train. All of our fears were cast aside as the train began to roll down the track. None of us knew we were in for a life-threatening experience. It was too late to get off the train with the wheels in motion.

This old train climbed slowly up the mountain and was starting down the other side. Gradually "Old Iron Sides" picked up speed and was traveling way too fast; telephone posts looked like a picket fence.

There was a young engineer who was driving the train for the first time. Finally, he managed to use the emergency brakes and slowed the train down, but they were still traveling too fast to safely get around a sharp curve. More pressure was applied to the brakes to stop the train. Suddenly the train came to a screeching halt; many lives were saved.

Father, if we continue on the track of unrestricted sin and full steam ahead without braking leverage, we will not make it to our home in Heaven. Jesus stood between heaven and earth on a cross to stop our runaway lives. Many of us have more than a once in a lifetime opportunity to make peace with God, but who knows which is the last? Speed will keep us out of heaven if we do not stop in time to accept Christ in our lives, amen.

Highway of Holiness
July 27

Every once in a while, we hear about travelers who got lost while driving down the highway. These stories range from suspenseful terrifying events to a peaceful day where we received guidance to help us continue our journey. The days without instruction can really be distressing if we are alone and there is no one to help us find our way.

It is always a comfort when we are with someone else because there is laughter and friendly conversation. Decisions can be made to help us find the correct road. Two or more people traveling together relieve the tension of stress and replaces worrisome frowns with big smiles. One person alone carries burdens of fear that grow stronger with each mile.

Let's go back down the highway where some people made a wrong turn and ended up many miles from their appointed destination. The people in the group were not nearly as frightened as one person would have been in the same situation.

These travelers were in a strange neighborhood in the middle of the night. A policeman stops to offer assistance. When uniform officers are in the area the distressful moment ends with peace and contentment.

Now is a good time to think about our spiritual journey when we were lost and traveling sin's highway. If we were lost and traveling down one of the state roads, we would probably be looking at the signs.

We want to make it to heaven, so it is very important that we stay on the right road. An exit sign caught our attention with these words, "Sin's Highway." The name itself reveals sin. Whether we are in a crowd or all alone, we need someone to guide us on our heavenly journey. There will be rejoicing in heaven if we follow Jesus on the highway of holiness, amen.

Personal Invitation
July 28

The mailmen are faithful employees that deliver our mail. Severe weather conditions have hindered their efforts. If we only knew the hardships that these dedicated employees have to go through, we would be more grateful of their endeavors. Gratitude would be in abundance.

There have been times when road conditions were very hazardous and these postal workers would be seen stopping at mailboxes on their routes. Cars and trucks sliding into ditches and highways blocked for hours, but these brave men and women continued on their journey.

The delivery of the mail is so important that drivers and even those who walk postal routes literally risk their lives to make sure the mail is delivered. Often, we may wonder why the mail is delivered in extreme situations.

This would be a good question for those who have medical problems and need life-saving medicines on a daily basis in order to survive. Another situation is a confidential letter has to be hand carried to the customer. A signature is required as final proof of the transaction.

If this mail is not handled properly, there could be drastic results. God sends personal invitations to each of us. He wants us to accept Jesus as Lord and Savior. Hopefully each reply will be, "Yes, Lord."

Father, Invitations from heaven are not sent through the mail or by any other transportation system. God does not use the Internet. His communication is on a wireless network.

God sends personal invitations daily and He is waiting for our response. Jesus himself is calling for us to follow Him. There is not much time to accept Christ. The prayer line is open and God is accepting calls. In Jesus' name, amen.

Blind Beggar
July 29

Let's go back in time to when a blind man was begging for alms. This man sat by the wayside. This was a place where a lot of people walked down a path to the market place. He sat on a section of land that was close to the road. Alms are anything that will relieve the condition of the poor. It is doubtful if he had a sign unless someone made it for him.

There was a lot of commotion that day and the blind man wanted to know what was going on. The travelers told him that "Jesus of Nazareth passeth by." What would our response be if we heard the same thing?

Suppose it was said in a different way, "Jesus will be at church Sunday morning." This is not a false statement because Jesus said where two or three or gathered in His name, then He is in the midst. This promise has been fulfilled over and over as Jesus has never missed a worship service.

When the day arrives, church pews are empty, worldly affections distort our minds. Excuses are many as there are a multitude of activities to distract us from being in the presence of a living Savior.

Let's notice the response of the blind man; he stopped begging for alms. "And he cried, saying, Jesus, thou son of David, have mercy on me." The people "rebuked him, that he should hold his peace: but he cried so much the more, Thou son of David, have mercy on me" (Luke 18:38,39).

Father, we are blessed beyond measure when Jesus stops to greet us personally. Little children to adults have called upon Him. Even today tears flow down our cheeks, as we cry out for mercy. Let's remember the time when our aching hearts were overcome with sorrow. We heard about Jesus and we asked Him to forgive our offences. Jesus is making personal visits wherever mercy is needed. Thank you, Jesus, amen.

Lies of Deceit
July 30

We are going into a very dangerous territory today. The best way to avoid these treacherous villains is to speak the truth. Lest we are attacked while in this area, it would be to our advantage if we know the identity of these villains so that we can defend ourselves against them.

Many lives have been affected by the proper use of words. Lies is the real name with deceitful intent. These villains steal from the truth and they betray the innocence of righteous living. No one is safe from the lies perilous pursuit unless a barricade is fortified with undeniable facts. Those who live by the truth walk uprightly and have no shame to bear.

The Bible gives us good instructions about saying false words and even thinking thoughts that would affect our relationship with God. "Let the words of my mouth, and the meditation of my heart, be acceptable in thy sight, O Lord, my strength, and my redeemer" (Psalm 19:14).

Lies are the villains that steal from the truth. If they are unattended, the end results will be disastrous. These corruptible words seek out victims of all ages. Children and adults please be aware of the contamination process. One lie cast doubt on all the words spoken.

There are many fatal consequences by speaking and believing the untruthful words. False words will ruin lives and they will follow us all the way to the grave. Lies unrestrained will leave a trail of dishonor.

Father, We need to be careful what we hear and more reverent to what we speak. Lies will deceive, but the truth is as a mighty fortress with indestructible walls. All of us are not held captive to the villains of sin. The chains of our corruptible lives have been broken by the truth. Jesus is the way, the truth, and the life, no man cometh unto the Father but by Him, amen.

A Decision for Christ
July 31

There are many decisions that we have to make in life. These choices will affect us in many different ways. All of us know that travel arrangements have to be made for a vacation before we get in the car and start down the highway. Traveling on the wrong road has unpredictable situations.

A tire may blow out while we are driving and the car plunges over an embankment. This accident has caused us to receive cuts and abrasions. Some of the injuries are life threatening and there is no one around to help us. One of the passengers may die if he does not get medical care.

This story was just an illusion to help us understand how important it is for us to plan ahead of time so that we will be on the right road. Planning ahead helps us to find hospitals in times of an emergency. Choosing the correct route will save lives when time is of the essence.

Let's think about the incident that just happened and decide what methods we will use to help us arrive at a predetermined destination. When we travel down the highway, there are signs to direct us. It would be a good idea to highlight a map so we will know the correct route.

A GPS system will give us guidance to our destination. It is not entirely reliable either because construction projects have altered the landscape. We can decide which method we think is the best, a map or GPS.

Father, since we are already deciding on the best route to take in life, why not accept Jesus and follow Him on the straight path? He will not lead us astray. We will never be alone, as He will go with us all the way. If we proceed down the highway of life without deciding our eternal destination by accepting Christ, we will have to face the consequence of sin. Save us now is our plea! In Jesus' name, amen.

Left Town, No Regrets
August 1

We are held as captives of sin in the town of corruption. There seems to be no escape but some of the people are content with this environment. Living daily in these sinful conditions corrupts our minds and hardens our hearts.

A multitude of sin binds and holds us as prisoners that keep us from escaping to peace and contentment. Sin indulgence is voluntary. It will ruin our lives if we continue to yield freely to its disastrous effects.

While driving down the road, we were thinking about the old town that held us captive because of our sins. This is where we yielded to ungodly living and unrighteousness. Perhaps the old town was just an image of the sins in our personal lives. Leaving town is a symbol from sin to grace.

Our thoughts will take us back in time, just long enough to help others escape the daily routine of unrighteousness and ungodly living. The old town in each of our lives has a luring appeal with pleasures of sin.

Freedom is offered, but we cannot escape if we neglect our salvation. There will be joy unspeakable and full of glory when the shackles of sin are no longer holding us as prisoners.

Father, help us to realize that we have all sinned and come short of the glory of God. We need to leave our personal sins behind. Leave town as quickly as possible and make a commitment to follow Jesus throughout life.

Let the people be warned that the pleasure seeking towns will cause devastation. Grace in our lives is the escape route. When the Holy Spirit convicts us of sin, then it is time to leave and that is what many of us have done. We left town with Jesus and there are no regrets. Please join with us on our way to glory. Soon we will be at home in heaven, amen.

One Word Assignment
August 2

We have a writing assignment today that requires us to write the word Jesus on the paper. It is our desire to fine the best place where this one word will not vanish over time.

After this assignment is completed, please turn in the suggestions. When everyone is finished writing the name, we will decide on the most permanent place for our eternal benefit and to sustain us in life.

This assignment is for each person to write this name in a place that will leave a lasting impression in our lives. A good example would be in a book. These reading sources have been around for thousands of years. However, the name vanishes as the pages are turned and the ink fades away.

Someone wrote it could be placed on a TV or radio program. That sounds like a good place. Millions of people are attentive to these broadcast stations. After a short while the signals would fade just like pages in a book.

A pilot used his plane to write Jesus' name in the sky. Well that didn't last very long as clouds fade away. See how quickly it turns to a cloudy haze. What about on the sand? It does not take long for the waves of the sea to erase it. The sand seemed to be a good idea until giant waves of the ocean came ashore.

Father, a number of places were listed but they all had disintegrating factors. There are many temporary places, but only one that will last for eternity. Let us write His name on the glory pages of our hearts.

Some people may suggest that this is only a temporary place, as death will claim our lives. Remember the assignment was to write the name of Jesus in a place that would be for our eternal benefit. When we stand before a holy, righteous God, He will be pleased if Jesus is abiding in our hearts, amen.

Sins will find us
August 3

There are several men who have committed a variety of crimes. It is very important that we find these criminals, as they are extremely dangerous. The security patrol is seeking help from various agencies.

If anyone has a good team of bloodhounds, we could use them in tracking the fugitives. We want the law enforcement to use these canines to follow the trail. These dogs are well trained, but even the best dogs cannot follow a water trail. Neighborhoods are warned of the danger.

It is not advisable for our good friends to help search for these criminals; this mission is just too treacherous. We want everyone to be alert and notify the proper officials of any unusual activity or visual contact. A warning was given for anyone who has seen these men or suspicious characters to contact the police department immediately.

The news media has broadcast on the TV and radio that prisoners escaped late last night from a high security installation. They have been on the run for about seven hours. It has been reported that they are armed. All the evidence shows that these criminals are in the mountains.

Escaped convicts will take advantage of all-natural resources, creeks, and even a rocky terrain. Their main objective is to escape for their lives. After several hours of searching, the men were captured and returned to prison. A sigh of relief spread quickly throughout the town.

Father, let's just say we are the runners from our own personal sins. We can run and hide, but our sins will find us. Sins abound and we have many hiding places. If we repent, God will have mercy. How far in life can we go before our sins catch up to us? This could be a devastating time in our lives. Wouldn't it be better if Jesus finds us first? Amen.

Keep the Fire Burning
August 4

There have been bears sighted in some of the campgrounds. A forest ranger came around to all of the campsites. He came to warn us of a bear that had killed some livestock. The warning was for all the campers to be aware and keep the fires burning throughout the night. After each meal, place all the leftovers in a secure trash container.

Recently a young man and his wife with their two small children went on a camping trip to the mountains. He was a policeman and he had brought along his guard dog, a German shepherd. Their campsite was too far away from other campers and it was close to some thick brush.

Safety violations were ignored and these parents with two small children should have been more selective of their tent sight. The game warden gave them a warning about a bear that recently invaded this camping sight, looking for food, as this had been a terrible season for berries.

Almost everyone had gone to sleep for the night. There were a few campers staying up late to make sure their fires did not go out. It is sad to say, but these loners failed to keep their fire alive by adding branches to the dwindling flames. Their campsite was now in total darkness.

The bear came into the area next to the tent, but the German shepherd heard the rustling of the brush and he went after the bear. Parents awoke to the sound of snarls and growls as the bear was being chased away by the dog.

Father, we need to keep the fires of faith burning in our daily lives. When the flames are low and we are not very close to you, we are in danger of an attack and the wounds may be fatal to our spiritual health. Let the burning flames of faith grow higher and our devotion stronger. Draw us closer to you so that we will be kept safe from sins evil intent, amen.

Almost Persuaded
August 5

There is going to be a big race today. We have made plans to go and enjoy this special event. Now some of us have never been to a race. It certainly sounds exciting. My racecar enthusiasts have encouraged me to go. It took quite a bit of persuading but they finally convinced me.

I have noticed that some of my friends have declined to go with us. No matter how hard we tried to get them to come. They would not yield to our request. They had just as many excuses as me, if not more.

They held fast to their arguments and would not surrender. However, some of them came close to committing themselves to the racing event. We arrived at the racetrack and watched the cars cross the finish line. Everyone was thankful for the persuasion from racecar enthusiasts.

There are times in life when we are almost persuaded to participate in certain activities. The final result of the challenge is to accept or reject the request. An almost decision may leave us behind in the valley of regret.

Perhaps we can remember when our friends tried to persuade us to accept Christ. Time and time again we refused. Well I am glad my friends never gave up on me. Almost saved will keep us in our sins.

Father, if we are fully persuaded, we will receive a crown of life when our earthly race is won. There are times in our lives when almost persuaded can keep us from the kingdom of God.

Almost believing that Jesus rose from the dead will not open the gates of heaven. A partial belief will keep us in our sins. Grace abounds when we believe whole heartily. There must be no doubt in our hearts that Jesus is the Christ. We must have full assurance that He is our Lord and Savior, amen.

237

Ten Commandments
August 6

We have a very important message that God gave us from heaven. When it was first delivered to the people, it was written on a stone tablet. God wrote on it with His finger and gave the tablet to Moses.

Now these words have traveled through the ages as His guidelines for our lives and to help us live godly, righteous lives. These are His laws; we are required to live by them. They tell us how to live and obedience to these laws keeps us from doing the wrong things. "Thou shalt not."

God did not ask us if we would please live by these words. He commanded us to obey the Ten Commandments. It was so important that God did not give us a choice, but a direct command from heaven.

We see today how unlawful and disrespectable some of the people have become in our generation. They do not want God's laws or anything to do with Christ. It is a terrible time in our lives when dishonor is given to the Creator of the world and people follow their own laws. Corruption abounds by evil deeds when righteousness is forsaken.

The laws of God have been removed from libraries, courthouses, and many other facilities. This is the voice of a few and the response of a government that has forgotten God. "Take it down, get rid of it, and we don't want it." That is not true, as people around the world are consecrated to living holy, godly lives with unwavering faithfulness.

Father, "We the people" stand in unity that there is one God and He is the Father of all. "In God we trust." He has created us and we are the people who will honor and always respect the Ten Commandments. Let's obey God! Laws of the land will perish while His laws are endless. Obedience is required so that holiness will prevail with the benefit of life eternal, amen.

Come unto me
August 7

There are certain times in life when we have special needs and Jesus is the only one who can fulfill the desires of our hearts. The Master calls at certain times with personal invitations. "Come unto me," this is one of them. Our response should be to immediately follow Jesus.

Those of us who know Christ as Lord and Savior confess that our lives have not been the same since Jesus came into our hearts. His love grows stronger by the day.

Sometimes the call is for us to repent of our sins and invite Him into our lives. This is the beginning of a new life for each one of us when we answer the call. Please don't turn Him away and reject His love and mercy. Many sorrowful hearts have carried their grief to the grave.

There are times in our lives when the burdens are hard to bear and the troubles of life weigh us down. Jesus wants us to cast all our cares upon Him. Burdens are lifted when we answer the call, "Come unto me!"

When there is a longing in each of our hearts for peace. There is no reason to be dismayed, just reach up and take hold of His nailed scarred-hand. He gives us peace the world cannot take away. He is calling now "Come unto me!" What He has done for others, He will do for us.

Father, these words echo through the highest mountains and the lowest valleys. Wherever there are souls in need of salvation, Jesus is still speaking to hearts. Think about the one who is calling; He is God's Son.

Our response is needed before the sun sets on the horizon. We can have fellowship with God, a home in glory, everlasting life, and peace all through life. Jesus is calling, "Come unto me." He will never turn away a repentant heart, amen.

The Verdict
August 8

We are scheduled to be in court to answer for our offences. A lawyer and a jury have been selected to defend us. These proceedings will take a while for we have many sins.

The judge asked us to arise and to affirm that we will tell the truth. We all agreed. He reminded us, "We do not want any lies, no partial truths, or any false statements." The judge asked the first question? "How do we plead?" Our answer is with boldness as we stand before the courts.

"Your Honor, we will not dishonor the court with lies. There are many sins that we have committed and we confess to all of them. We are not denying any of the evidence that is brought against us. We have sinned, but our plea is not guilty!"

This judge was startled with our confession and could not believe we were claiming to be innocent. "Your Honor please let me finish. Jesus died for our sins and we have been forgiven. He paid for our offences with His blood. We cannot be punished for sins that no longer exist."

This Jury came forth after hours of deliberation and told the Judge, "Your Honor, we have reached a verdict." The defendant acknowledges his sinful deeds. There is no denying the actual involvement in sinful behavior.

However, because of the confession of sins, we request a not guilty verdict. The judge listened to the testimony but he could not go against the law of the land. Guilty was the verdict. Lawbreakers are punished for their crimes.

Father, Trials on earth will keep us in our sins with a guilty verdict. Christ on the cross, dying in our place sets us free. Accept Jesus now and the verdict will be not guilty. Jesus took our punishment for our sins. He suffered and died to release us from sins heavy burden; we are free. Thank you, Jesus, amen.

Temptation Trap
August 9

Recently my imagination took us to a boat dealer where we bought a boat that had been restored. The salesman assured us that it was in perfect running condition. Please be aware that all imaginations cannot be trusted and they will even deceive the owners of these thoughts.

We had a very unfortunate accident the last time we went on a camping trip. After we got the sunken boat back on land, it was hauled into the shop for repairs.

It was almost like history was repeating itself. I suppose it was like restoring an old boat that we recently bought and it sunk in the lake. The same deceitful imagination team was in the restoration business.

Friends at the lake were offered a ride but they ran away just like before. While we were fishing for bass, all of a sudden, the boat sprung a leak and we had to be rescued. It was then that we remembered buying the boat. Our last imagination encounter brought to us misery and deep regret and now the grieving process is repeated.

Father, occasionally in life we go back to the same crooked dealers. They give another sales pitch and the next day we are sinking in water again. Sin also has temptation devices to lure us back down the road.

The salesman or the deceitful man calls us back into our sinful ways and immediately we fall into temptation's trap again. My best advice is to avoid or resist the bait and sin's evil devices will not ensnare us.

Jesus delivers us from our sins and He does not want us to return to them. Remember where He brought us from and don't go back to sin. Resistance is a lifesaver that will keep us out of the temptation trap. Resist, in Jesus' name, amen.

The pathway of Life
August 10

Our adventure today will have us walking on the pathway of life. This will be a journey where we will overcome many obstacles along the way. Heaven will be our destination as we walk through troublesome times. Peace will reign in our hearts throughout this spiritual journey.

When we commit our lives to Jesus, the burdens of our hearts roll away. Heaven's journey begins at the cross and ends with us walking the streets of glory and praising the name of Jesus throughout eternity.

The cross is the starting point where sincere repentance brings us into a right relationship with our heavenly Father. Christ precious blood washes our sins away. Peace is made with God and our souls are saturated with His love.

When we meet Jesus on the pathway of life, Old sinful deeds pass away and all things are become new as we walk the straight and narrow way. A new life is given with holiness and righteousness that produces glory, honor, and praise to God.

Another important thing to know about this journey of daily walking with the Lord is that Jesus will never leave or forsake us. He will go with us all the way. When our cross is heavy to bear, He will give us strength and we will realize that we can do all things through Christ, which strengthen us. Now is a good time to cast our burdens on Him.

This pathway reveals God's love for mankind. "God so loved the world, that He gave His only begotten Son, that whosoever believeth in Him should not perish, but have everlasting life."

Father, the pathway of life is before us. This would be a good time to take up the cross and follow Jesus. A crown of glory is waiting. We cannot make it to heaven without Him. Let's make a commitment to follow Jesus wherever He leads, amen.

Bad Apples
August 11

Nice fresh apples in the marketplace will make a delicious treat. Inspect them carefully to make sure there are no decaying spots. Take them home and make a delicious apple pie. This will be a really fantastic desert for the family to enjoy and a good way to finish a great meal.

Apples were bought by the bushel. We had enough to last a while. They will be kept in the kitchen if anyone would like to have one at a later time. Throughout the week this food source began to disappear.

We were enjoying this fruit when someone noticed a bad apple in the basket. There seemed to be a certain amount of anxiety and distress that all the apples would be ruined. One bad apple will spoil all the others.

It was decided by the hungry participants to get rid of the rotten apple. Throw it away or it will destroy the entire lot. This bad fruit was removed and cast aside. The remaining apples lasted a long time.

Let's say there is a stain of sin that has developed in each of our hearts. If we leave it alone, the corruption will spread and will eventually ruin our lives. There is a way to stop the decay. Forgiveness is the best antidote for contamination.

The deterioration of our souls begins in the early stages of sin. When a small stain of sin appears, we need to remove it as quickly as possible. If purity of life and moral standards has already been affected, we need a fresh supply of grace.

Father, we must keep our lives holy, pure, and free from sin, to present our bodies a living sacrifice unto God. Sins forgiven, life is restored. When God looks down from heaven, will He see the freshness of the Spirit in our lives or will He see moral decay? Purify our hearts with sanctifying grace, amen.

Bind Us Together
August 12

One day at church a man was speaking to the congregation about unity in our lives. He had a very good illustration that I would like to share with my friends.

This image of a bundle of wood would be a good example for the members of a church congregation to unite together as one. Eleven sticks were tightly bound; one stick was by itself.

He tried to break the eleven pieces of wood and he could not do it. Finally, an attempt was made on the single piece and it was easily broken.

Another instance of weakness is shown in the Bible when Judas separated himself from Christ. He betrayed Jesus for thirty pieces of silver. Afterwards his conscience bothered him so much that he hung himself. One person alone can easily be broken, whereas a multitude bound together can rely on each other to be victorious in battle.

There was a time in this man's life when he was a lot stronger. But he separated himself from the disciples and just like the single piece of wood was easy to break. Let's bind ourselves together with cords of love that cannot be broken. Christ in our lives replaces weakness with His power and might.

The eleven disciples stayed together because of their strong bonds of love for Christ. These men were securely bound by faith in a living Savior. Suffering and pain was the wounds they had to bear, but through it all, Jesus was with them all along the way, now a crown of glory to wear.

Father, there were times when these men were not always together. They remained strong because with Christ they were not alone. Let's all remember that our journey in life is not a one-person event. If we do not know Jesus as our Savior, then we will break easily as there is no strength without Him, amen.

A New Image
August 13

We are going to take an adventure today in the art studio. Lives are being developed by God's creative design to transform us spiritually. Let's think about how an artist paints a picture.

He mixes up the paint and then applies it to the canvas. After a while the image begins to form. Many colors are used in this painting and the end result will be an image pleasing to God.

After a considerable amount of thought is given to this creative work, we finally decided on which type of visual would yield a godly image.

We have decided to paint a self-portrait, as this will be the one that will be on display. Outward appearance will be nice to show, but our main interest is the development of life through Jesus Christ our Savior.

Let's think about the time we met Jesus and surrendered our hearts to Him. Immediately sins were forgiven and the Master Artist brushed them out of our lives.

Sins no longer abide as the artist continues to paint, a new image is formed as the old one is transformed by the mighty power of God. Old sins fade as the artist brushes them away.

The picture of life has the marks of sin disappearing with each brush-stroke of righteous living. An unrighteous life is a vanishing shade. A new character begins to appear. Crimson red is no longer in sight as the color of white is added to the profile to show our sins are white as snow.

Father, old sins are gone. There is not a trace. A new image is shown. This picture reveals one of grace. The painting is finished and we want everyone to see Christ is the new image. A profile of godly living reveals a living Savior, amen.

Enticed by Sin
August 14

We have a lot of dedicated fishermen in this group, or adventure lovers of the great outdoors. There is usually plenty of action when we go camping. The survival rate would be better if everyone followed the safety procedures. Upstream the fishing is better but it is too dangerous.

Our safety procedure was to keep everyone in sight. It did not work this time. A better fishing spot enticed an elderly man who was traveling with us to a more appealing place.

We need to be aware that some things that capture our interest will cause us to leave a safe environment and put our lives in jeopardy. He would soon find himself struggling to stay alive.

While he was at this new fishing spot, a slick rock caused him to fall into the rising creek and he could not get up. His weak voice did not carry well with the sound of the rushing stream in the background. A floating object was found downstream and this led to the rescue of the elderly man.

There are times in our lives when we are enticed by the lure of sin. It is sort of like calling us back to our old sinful ways. Resist the devil and he will flee. Just to be sure he leaves, plead the blood of Jesus Christ.

Father, the cares of this world have luring temptations to draw us back into sin's territory. Once we are there, shackles of guilt hold us in a tight grip and the chains of remorse surround us.

We are guilty before God in that our sinful deeds crucified Christ all over again. The shame we bear keeps tears in our eyes. If we have wandered away and fallen from grace, a rescue is possible if the current of mercy is revived in our hearts. Christ will find us better if we call out to Him. Cries for mercy or not denied. Save us, Lord, amen.

Restore to Life
August 15

It is that time again for a fresh coat of paint on the house. This past winter has been especially hard on the board siding. There are some very bad places where the paint has cracked and withered away.

The first thing we need to do is scrape the old scaly paint from the planks. We will be working from ladders and scaffolds. All of the old residue will have to be removed before fresh paint can be applied.

This is a time-consuming job. If everything goes well, we should be finished in one week. Our time will begin early in the morning and we will finish in the late evening hours.

Now that the old finish has been removed, let's begin the painting process. We like to use the paint that already has the primer in it. This saves time and we will still have a good protective coat of paint on the home. It feels good to know that this restoration will last many years.

Sometimes we let our lives of faith degenerate to a poor condition. Our normal standard of living has been downgraded to unsatisfactory. Spiritual modification is a daily process that will last for eternity.

Father, in order to restore our relationship with you, we need to reapply the blood of Christ to our hearts. It will not hurt to confess our sins all over again. Lives will be restored when we return to our first love, Jesus Christ.

Our lives may be rundown and in need of repair. We need a protective coat of grace to rehabilitate and refresh our devotion to God. These old homes are like our souls in need of restoration. The value of our souls is an upgrade in progress when we return to Christ and plead for mercy. Restore us to godly living and we will be blessed for eternity, amen.

Peace Prevails in a Storm
August 16

It was a very stormy day at the old homestead. Lightning flashes lit up the sky with atmospheric electricity. Every once in a while, a huge tree would receive a direct hit from the electrifying current. Trees that have withstood hurricane winds and hundreds of years of destructive force are shattered by one stroke of lightning with devastating effects.

Roaring thunder could be heard for miles. This seems to be the gentle part of the storm. Trees are left standing in the forest and no damage is reported to surrounding areas. However, a lot of fear is created when this noise or loud roar is heard. Animals scamper across the field, seeking shelter. Thunder is the warning signal heard far and wide.

There seemed to be no end to the unrelenting rain. Creeks were swollen and the riverbanks overflowed with gushing water. Strong winds were breaking tree branches and strong oaks came crashing to the ground. Storms come with a vengeance and unrelenting force.

This was the worst storm we have had in years, but imaginations can create other storms as powerful and more deadly than this one. This visionary thought is dangerous enough without increasing the voltage.

There are times of severe heartaches when we go through the storms of life. Storms have a devastating effect in our lives. Some of them are more severe than other. No matter how terrible and violent the storm, if Jesus is in our hearts even the strongest lightning flashes cannot disrupt the peace we have with God. Turmoil desists and peace prevails.

Father, the best way to survive a severe storm is to take hold of the Savior's nail-scarred hand and by faith hold onto it for dear life. Storms of strife and trouble bring lightning flashes of turmoil. Peace abides even while the storm is raging, amen.

Never Give Up
August 17

While I was watching TV one day, a race was in progress. One of the runners left a very strong impression in my life. This is where having a never give up attitude gives us the strength to keep pressing onward to heaven. A positive attitude overcomes any obstacles in our lives.

There was one young girl on this competition team that had a really strong determination to win. My imagination tells me that all through life she had stamina and endurance.

She stood out among her classmates as a leader and as person who would accomplish all of her goals in life. Her fellow students looked up to her as their role model. They respected her because of her never give up attitude. When physical conditions restrain us, our ability to run may be hindered, but that does not stop us from winning the crown.

The race was in process and the runners were close to the end. This young lady was in the front position, but the miles and hills bore heavily on her physical condition.

She was utterly exhausted and only a few feet from the finish line. She fell to the ground and could barely stand by herself. Rescue workers offered help but she refused. Her legs were trembling as she struggled to cross the finish line. Persistence is a trophy winner even when resistance is in our way.

This young girl did not come in first place, but she won all of our hearts. Her attitude in life will be the same one that helps us to cross over onto the hallelujah side. "Never give up, we are almost home."

Father, it is very important that we have the right attitude. There are some people with these special characteristics. They have a never give up, never quit attitude. Their example in life helps us to claim the victory. Give them the honor, amen.

High Security
August 18

There are many important positions in life that require dedication and trustworthiness. Those who work in banks and other financial positions are responsible to the public. The money is kept in steel vaults to prevent robberies. Security is stronger with walk-ins and visual crooks.

Sometimes guards are hired to protect our investments. They are well trained and will use force if necessary. There are many security devices like cameras and burglar alarms, which are used for criminal defense.

It is good to take precautions to ensure our money is safe. All of this protective equipment is used for our benefit. We have peace when these security measures are in place. Our biggest worry is a security breach on the Internet. A robbery can take place from an unknown source. Criminals who hide mysteriously in the worldwide web are hard to find.

There are protectors of the peace and these law enforcement officials keep us safe from lawbreakers. Policemen protect our lives from those who would steal, harm, or even kill us.

Safety measures prevent thefts. Security is a very important thing in all of our lives. It is really a comforting thought to have someone guarding us day and night.

There is no absolute guarantee that our finances will remain safe. Considering the welfare of our souls, it is far more important to have security that cannot be disrupted by thieves. No one can break into heaven's vault where there is personal security with Christ.

Father, if we are not careful with the welfare of our souls, sins will creep into the vault of our hearts and steal from our treasure in heaven. We have a responsibility to be stewards of our lives. Christ is able to keep us to life eternal, amen.

Thorns and Nails
August 19

While I was looking out my window one day, a bird had landed in the top of a rosebush. After watching it for a couple of minutes, I saw a nest and it had baby birds in it. Each of the baby birds had a bright yellow breast. These birds were completely hidden from view by the beautiful red roses.

It seemed to be the perfect shelter except for the sharp thorns. This was an unusual birthplace. Green vines were spread throughout the bush like a barbed wire fence with barbs that would cause a lot of pain.

I just couldn't see the little birds getting out of the nest without those thorns piercing their small bodies. One touch of the thorns creates an automatic response that makes us withdraw quickly from the agony.

When I observed the birds another day, they were gone. None of them were entangled in the long stems of briars. This is one time that an empty nest was a welcome sight and a big relief for me.

Think about our birthplace, we are born into a world of sharp thorns of sin. Corruptible things are all around us. The sharp thorns of sin would keep us from living holy, righteous lives. How is it possible that we could survive in such a horrible place? We need an escape plan.

There is only one way for us to be delivered and that is by Jesus Christ who gave His life on a cross so we could be saved. Jesus took the thorns that were meant for us. The nails pierced His hands instead of ours. He gave His life so we could be free.

Father, our journey to the cross was not through fields of thorns. There was not even suffering from sharp splinters as we made our way to the cross. The crucifixion and the pain He bore should bring us to our knees with repentant hearts, amen.

The Wrestling Match
August 20

A wrestling match is scheduled for us in the arena of life. Our opponent is known for his deception and wicked ways. We will be wrestling a very powerful foe today. He has been around for a long time. Those who have fought with him would say that he is the cruelest of all fighters. Our enemy is known worldwide by the name of "Satan."

We have all met him somewhere along the pathway of life. His main objective is to dominate and rule with fear. This defender of evil will do anything to win, no matter how bad the opponents are hurt. Each of us will be in our own personal conflict with him. We wrestle not against flesh and blood but against principalities, the rulers of darkness.

How can we be victorious in life? The first step to wear the victory crown is to invite Jesus into our hearts and put on the whole armor of the Lord. Take up thy cross and follow Jesus. Commit our souls to Him because He has never lost a battle. We will never go into battle alone.

Satan's worst defeat was at Calvary when Jesus was taken down from the cross and laid in a sepulcher where He arose from the dead. It is true we are no match for Satan by ourselves. We are not alone because Jesus abides in our hearts and we know that God is with us.

Father, the battles we fight daily give us strength to overcome the wiles of Satan. We will be knocked down and the referee will begin the count. This battle will be lost if we stay on the ground. Although, we are bruised and our bodies ache with pain, we rise to finish the fight.

If we want to be victorious in life's battles, we must let Christ be our strength and fight for us; soon we will wear a crown. Defeat is not an option for cross-bearing Christians who abide in Christ. Lift up thy cross and claim the victory, amen.

In the Line of Duty
August 21

Tragedy strikes a community that leaves the residents with grieving hearts, as a loving father will not be coming home to his wife and children. He will never again enter the family residence to hold his wife in his arms and tell her how much she is loved. The children will have to go through life without the guidance of a father and his loving care.

A young man was in police custody at the hospital. He took the guards gun and shot him. The criminal escaped and had eluded the police for several hours.

A search continued for him throughout the night without any results. Early that morning a patrolman was walking at the park. He was probably thinking about his family. He had no idea that this family relationship would end, as he would die in the line of duty.

His job was to protect and ensure the safety of all citizens. I don't know how long he had worked on the force. The media portrayed him as a kind-hearted man who cared deeply about the people he served.

No one knew that this morning there would be a fatality at the park. What seemed to be a peaceful walk turned into a terrible tragedy. Later the criminal was recaptured.

Family members, friends, and members of the police force gave honor to him at the patrol officer's funeral. The family and all the people who knew him were deeply saddened by his tragic death.

Father, I like to think this policeman received a promotion in heaven. His badge of loyalty here on earth was traded in for a position in God's Security Force. A policeman fell in the line of duty and now a new guardian angel meets daily with his family. When life on earth ends, it can begin in heaven, amen.

Traffic problems
August 22

There are many roads in life that will take us to various locations. It is very important for us to choose the right one. Sometimes they will take us to a dead-end street.

Occasionally we will make a turn in which there is no way back; a good example is a one-way street. We can only go so far in the wrong direction as panic grips our hearts as we are facing the oncoming traffic.

Steering wheels are gripped tight and brake pedals are held to the floor. A sigh of relief is given when the car completely stops and no one is injured from this traffic ordeal.

Another traffic incident can have us going down the highway in the right direction and suddenly we miss an exit and that causes us to be on the wrong road, at least we are going in the direction of the traffic. We may have to travel many miles before we are back on the right road.

We have to face the consequences of our choices. Several years ago a bus was traveling down a major highway. There were a lot of people on this vehicle. The driver made a wrong turn and crashed, killing some of the passengers. This was a very costly mistake by the bus driver. One wrong turn and families would never make it safely to their homes.

Let's take a close look at our traffic situation and relate it to our spiritual journey in life. If we stay on the wrong road, our sins will keep us from going to our heavenly home. We need to take salvation's exit by asking Jesus to come into our hearts. Following Him will keep us from being lost.

Father, hopefully we will get on the highway that leads to the Glory Land. We realize there are many traffic problems in life. Our main concern is choosing the right way to get us safely home. Life in Christ is the only route to heaven, amen.

254

Survive the Storm
August 23

A winter storm came through last night, bringing frigid temperatures with a wind chill below zero. This was a terrible time to be outside, as snow had accumulated to about eighteen inches. The weather station had given us a warning about the danger of this monster storm.

We wanted to make sure that we were properly prepared for these terrible weather conditions. Stores were going to be closing early so everyone would be at their homes enduring the bitterness of winter. Batteries, candles, and other emergency supplies were in high demand.

Since we were warned ahead of time of this catastrophic storm, we had time to prepare. Groceries were on our list of necessities. When a storm is announced, a multitude of shoppers will invade the stores to stock up on the accessories of life. Bread and milk disappear quickly from the shelves.

Conditions on the outside were becoming life threatening. While looking out the window, we watched the snow being swirled about in the horrific winds. We lived in a valley between two mountains. Howling winds were more than disturbing as they roared through the valley, uprooting trees in its path. This small dwelling was no longer safe.

Telephone poles were ripped into pieces, which caused us to be without electricity. We did not have access to the woodpile because snow and ice kept us from opening the doors. The fire had gone out and the family would have frozen to death had it not been for a rescue.

Father, help us to realize that storms will come in our lives. We do not always have time to prepare for these disastrous events. A warning is given for us to repent of our sins. Jesus is coming in the clouds of glory. Preparation for this journey should have us earnestly seeking salvation for our souls, amen.

Instant Replay
August 24

There are many instances in life where an instant replay is used to help us in various activities make the correct call. God will be reviewing our lives and the decision made will determine if we go to heaven and have everlasting life. No mechanical devices are needed because the evidence presented will show our qualifications for heaven.

Instant replay has recorded the past and the present. Let's begin by telling the story of how we lived our lives. We have to travel back in time before any of us knew Christ. This journey will also have Jesus in our lives. The review is in process and it will reveal if we are worthy to receive the glory crown.

Some of us would probably say that we showed kindness all along the way. Helping others throughout life is also added to the list of favorable things. It looks like we have many commendable things that would surely put us in the top ranks of eligibility by all of our kind deeds.

Oh, just a reminder of all the times we went to church and stayed a while. The preacher spoke of sin and some of the people walked down the aisle to the altar and accepted Jesus as their Lord and Savior. This was a time of rejoicing as sinners wiped tears away from their cheeks.

Another thing we try to reveal in our life's story is the sermons, songs of praise, and we were always there in special events. Neighbors would speak highly of us because of our caring attitude. We could almost see God handing us the key to heaven when we spoke of compassion. Surely all of those things would qualify us for a grand entrance into heaven.

Father, we must realize that no matter how much good we do in this world; the instant replay shows that Jesus is never mentioned in our lives. Heaven is denied. "Depart from me." Jesus as our Savior makes us worthy to receive the crown.

River of God's Love
August 25

Our journey today will take us back into the mountains where we will meet at the lake for a family reunion. Some of the family members left early this morning so that a canopy could be erected over the picnic tables. There was a lot of anticipation for this special occasion.

Relatives would come from many miles to be with loved ones they had not seen since last year. An even longer time has elapsed for this family as distance and other circumstances kept us from meeting together.

Those who arrived early at the park finished their task of preparing the picnic area. Everything was in order and so this spare time seemed to be a good time to relax and wait for everyone else to arrive.

A young man with an overactive imagination was resting beneath a tree when he took a temporary leave of absence from this family reunion and was soon riding down a very steep hill on a bicycle without brakes.

Earlier this morning he had joined with a group of other men riding their bikes to the picnic area to be with the family. He had been having trouble with the sprocket chain coming loose on his bike.

They were getting close to the picnic area when the chain broke and there were no brakes on his bicycle. It seemed to be certain death for this rider of the brakeless bike. His life was saved when he guided it into the river.

Father, help us to think about this dreamer, as he was revived with a fresh bucket of cold water. Coming back into reality can be chilling. We are on a downward course of eternal separation from God. Our runaway sinful lives can be saved by grace if we emerge ourselves into the river of God's love, amen.

A Crack in the Frame
August 26

Building inspectors recently discovered small cracks have developed in the frame of the building. We all know that once a crack appears, it will grow larger until the structure is no longer stable and will eventually collapse. Cracks that are repaired in time can add many years of life to any building that would otherwise be condemned. Lives will be saved.

Engineers have been called in for a final analysis and to make sure the infrastructure has a solid frame capable of supporting this structure. Instruments were brought in for stress tests and to evaluate the overall strength and firmness of the steel beams. Repairs were recommended.

After completely going over the entire building, it was decided the metal frame is strong but there are a few weak spots that definitely needs to be repaired as quickly as possible. A temporary evacuation of the people is necessary to bring the building back up to stability status.

There were also safety concerns about the location of the hotel as it was in a residential area surrounded by other businesses. Traffic was constantly moving by the hotel and the streets were always crowded.

If the cracks are not welded, the fracture lines would grow and eventually the infrastructure would collapse to the ground. The welding crew began working immediately on the cracked seams. After several weeks of bonding the metal together, finally the frame was stable.

Father, our lives will also vary in strength according to the small sins that have developed in the framework of our souls. Small sins can be fatal to our spiritual lives if they are not repaired. They are just tiny cracks that are barely noticeable. Buildings with weak frames collapse. Sins welded with a reinforcement of God's love can prevent a fall from grace.

Revisit Old Sins
August 27

We are going to venture into a very dangerous territory. There have been many travelers who have gone back into the dark valleys of despair. Unfortunately, all of them did not return to the safe haven of peace and contentment.

This journey is way too hazardous to go by any normal human routes. We have decided the best way to go back in time is to get connected to the imagination travel agency. A visionary of our past lives will recall sins that have long been forgotten.

Most of the time our imagination has been successful in their retreat efforts. However, there were times that we barely escaped by suffering severe wounds and near death experiences.

What makes this adventure so dangerous is that we have to go back in time before we met Jesus. We will be walking the streets of the outcast and entering into the towns of corruption. A short visit is long enough for us to be arrested and placed back in the shackles and bondage of sin.

This trip is a long journey for some of us. Let's take a short cut and go through the fields of unrighteousness and visit our old sins along the way. The transgression towns will not turn us away. Cares of the world lure us into the temptation trap.

Father, we have gone far enough, let's all go home. I didn't realize how miserable we were until we traveled down the imagination highway. Oh, the door seems to be locked and we cannot get back into our refuge in Christ.

There is no guarantee we will make it back to the safe haven and peace with God. A sigh of relief came over us as the door was unlocked and Jesus our Savior was waiting for us to come home. Thank you, Jesus for giving us another chance, amen.

God will make a Way
August 28

Explorers have gone into many interesting places and every once in a while, we hear about accidents where people lost their lives. There have been many occasions where someone or a group of people was trapped in caves because of a rockslide.

We are going with other adventure seekers to a different cave. This would be a good time to go exploring in a new cave that has just been discovered. It is on a mountain slope surrounded by thick brush and rocks. Anticipation was running high with this first-time endeavor.

One of the explorers that were in our group tied a line outside to a tree. This would be our guidance system to help us find the outdoor entrance. As long as we could hold this string, we could follow it safely outside.

We had been in the cave about an hour when we heard this unfamiliar rumbling sound. It was on the outside of the cave and we suddenly realized a rockslide was beginning to come down the mountainside.

Three of the men barely escaped as large rocks had just started blocking the exit. One man did not make it. He was trapped on the inside with very little oxygen to keep him alive. There was no escape.

Immediately the first responders were called to save this young man's life. They were about to give up when this trapped explorer came walking down the mountain. He told them how he survived by following a glimmer of light. This led to another escape route to the outside.

Father, there are times when we are surrounded by our problems. It seems as though there is no way to resolve them. The only solution is blocking the way. When there is no way, God will make a way. Let's not forget the power of prayer.

Keep the Stream Flowing
August 29

The valley is dry and the cattle will soon die if they do not receive fresh water from the mountain stream. It has been noticed that the water supply is gradually disappearing.

Farmers in the valley depend on the flow of the creek to keep their livestock and gardens alive. They also need water for their own personal lives. There have been a few good rain showers and this has been a real blessing for those who live in the valley. The main water source is the mountain stream.

Farmers held a meeting. One man who lived on the side of the mountain said there is plenty of water where he lives. His home was right next to the stream. There was so much water that it was flooding his property.

After a careful investigation, a dam was discovered about halfway down the mountain. Nature's architects (beavers) were involved in landscape development.

There are times in our spiritual journey when an unintentional barricade is built with some small sins that become larger over time. Access to the Father is hindered.

Heavy equipment of grace is needed for sin removal. This construction project of development in our lives must begin immediately before the current of God's love will cease to flow.

These corruptible things will separate us from the main source of God's mercy and change the moral landscape of holiness to ungodly living. Repentance is the best sin removal.

Father, there is no reason for us to keep our lives cluttered with sin. When Jesus gave His life on the cross, He was breaking down all barricades, removing all obstacles, and forgiving all sins. If we do not have access to God, it is because we have not asked Jesus to cleanse our hearts, amen.

The Time of Departure
August 30

This is a trip that has been planned well in advance. We are going to meet at the airport and we will be leaving first thing in the morning. It is very important to arrive early for security reasons. The flight schedule was listed with the departure time.

A boarding pass was processed with a time, day, and month stamped on it. Any time after the appointed hour would completely void the contract with the airport. Watching a plane leave is very distressing.

Passengers who are own time have peace and contentment as they board the plane. Early arrivals are not in stressful situations like those who come late and run through the terminal to catch the flight.

There are many sorrowful hearts, as they walk sadly back to their vehicles, wishing they were more time efficient. Opportunities lost for life-changing events may not ever be recovered if the flight is gone.

If we are late coming to the airport and the plane is already airborne, we will not make it to our preferred location. Get up early, be at the airport on time, just one more thing, and please don't oversleep. We cannot afford to miss this flight.

Father, we are traveling to our home in heaven. Jesus told us to watch and pray. There is coming a time when the careless, unwatchful, sleepers of the faith will miss their flight as Jesus comes in the clouds.

If our time on earth is wasted, we will have to forfeit the pleasures of heaven. The appointed hour is not yet fulfilled, as Jesus has not yet descended in the clouds. This would be a good time to have our luggage packed and for us to be waiting for our flight. There will be rejoicing in heaven as we walk through the gate. Let's be on time or have deep regrets, amen.

Entangled in Sin
August 31

This was a good time to spend the day at the river. It was reported that minnows were being used to catch Largemouth Bass. These men had already been to the creek where minnow nets were used to catch the fast-moving fish appetizers. Enthusiasm was running with this new fishing adventure.

There was concern about the weather conditions. A long time ago these fishermen had been caught in an electrical storm, which almost cost them their lives.

Soon they arrived at a remote spot where some trees had fallen into the water. Seaweed vines were hidden along the bottom of the riverbed. After several hours of fishing, it was time to go home. None of the men were aware of the vines that had gradually wrapped around the motor.

The boat was held fast by the underbrush. One man had to get out of the boat and cut the vines loose. While he was cutting the vines, some of the wrap-around weeds had also managed to get a strong grip on the fishermen's leg.

There was also more danger as a strong current developed which was life threatening to this struggling fisherman. Finally, he cut himself free and the men made it safely to their homes.

Father, there are times in our lives when we will be entangled in the cares of this world. Our sins are like the seaweed that wraps around us, cutting off our circulation. Jesus is the only one who can set us free.

Once Christ has delivered us from sin, He does not want us to go back into the places where we will be entangled all over again. If for some reason we slipped back into our old sinful ways, we need a rescue. Jesus is able to break the grip of sin and save us if we will just call out to Him, Jesus, Jesus!

Sinners Transformed by Grace
September 1

An old flower vase had been purchased at a flea market. The woman who bought the flower container was real anxious to get home and show it to her family members. There was nothing special about this new item except a beautiful array of flowers was painted on the side of the vase.

This ceramic piece was not very expensive, as the price had already been marked down to fifty percent off. The flea market vendor was even thinking about throwing it away. He did not want to load the flea market items back into his vehicle because he finally had room in his garage to park his car.

Soon this woman would find out by accident the real value of this intended throwaway. She removed the dirt that was packed inside this worthless container and to her amazement a bright shiny object was gradually uncovered. A beautiful diamond ring was imbedded in the clay residue.

The excitement almost caused her to break the vase, which was a collector's item, as a date was uncovered on the bottom of the glass. A few moments were needed for her to fully recuperate and regain composure.

Let's think about this story and the valuable object that was found on the inside of a vase. No one knew that it was there. Who would want to buy an old worthless vase with mud still caked in the bottom? When this worthless item was bought, the value exceeded all expectations.

Father, our lives are similar to the lost item in that we were in the miry clay of sin. Who would even consider paying the price for our ungodly, worthless lives? The answer is plain to see as Jesus hung on a cross with His arms spread wide. This much is how much He loved us. When Jesus paid the price at Calvary, he knew the luster of the diamond would shine in our lives. He saw sinners purified by His blood and transformed by grace.

Salvation's Exit
September 2

Our travels in life will take us down the road of corruption, a daily routine of living with immoral values. We will cross the bridge of sin. This is a continuation from one place to the other. The roads we travel will take us past the exit of salvation. All of us have been on this road traveling as sinners.

There were many opportunities that we had to make peace with God. These are the times when Jesus was dealing with our hearts and trying to get us to change course. We drove right on through conviction without receiving grace.

Let's think about the situations in life where our living process takes us through various resources of travel that will affect our eternal concerns.

Sins highway is the one that always takes us away from heaven. Different locations are on our earthly journey. Sin is a constant companion unless there is a roadside eviction.

As sinners we continued to live day by day. Our routine was pretty much the same as driving down the road. We were consistent in our sin endeavors. The road traveled would end in tragedy and we would have to suffer the consequences of sin.

Ungodly living was the road we traveled many times, always past the familiar surroundings. We kept passing the exit of salvation. There seemed to be more important things for us. Cares of the world, sin in abundance, and unrighteousness kept us on a really tight schedule.

Father, before we pass the last exit, travel arrangements need to be made for eternity. The highway of life shows certain exits we need to take in order to reach our destination. We could keep on driving but what is our profit if we fail to make it home? An exit from sin begins a new life in Christ and it gets us on the glory land road to heaven. Amen.

House of Neglect
September 3

Let's take a few minutes to visualize a home that had been neglected over the years. There was this family that lived in a beautiful house on a hill. The children moved away, leaving their parents there alone. Daily maintenance of the home was avoided because of more interesting activities.

One of the promises the father always made was that "There is plenty of time, or I will do it next week." Activity usually begins when a stern voice is heard from the kitchen.

There was never enough time for a fresh coat of paint or shingles on the roof. Tomorrow seemed to be his favorite saying. It was always a false promise. A new calendar was posted for more time efficient activity.

When the roof started to leak and water was dripping in the living room, he promised to fix the roof in a few days. Well his wife couldn't let old habits of neglect ruin their lives. He was starting to learn pretty fast as His wife watched him mop up the excessive amounts of water.

A house of neglect will soon be a place of ruin. Those who live inside will have to face the terrible consequences. This man could have made the repairs if there was only enough time.

After a while a house of neglect will deteriorate into the dust of the earth. The storms will come and a collapse of the structure will be the final result. If there is a little bit of time to restore the old house, we had better work quickly before the demise of the family residence.

Father, we have the same effect in our lives if we neglect our souls. Sin moves back into our hearts and the love of God deteriorates. Our only hope is to be restored by grace. Please don't use the old saying, "I've got plenty of time," "I will take care of the needs of my soul tomorrow." Where is the mop?

Drifted Away
September 4

The men were in a boat far out to sea, drifting away. Their eternal destiny fades with the evening sun. The bright hopes of heaven vanish into the night. Heartfelt memories also disappear as the boat drifts out of sight.

This story is told for those who loved God with all their heart, soul, and mind. But somewhere along the way, they pulled up the anchor of His grace and slowly drifted away from Him. Disgraceful living is not far behind.

Now they are lost without a guiding light to show them the way. They are all alone in a perilous sea. The fear of death has returned because the security net of God's grace, love and mercy was left behind.

A separation from God does not have to be a permanent thing. There is still a glimmer of hope that these men will be restored to life, fellowship with God. As long as they are breathing, there is a possibility of a family reunion.

Choosing the day when salvation will be in effect is not in our power. Our accepted time will be as the Holy Spirit brings conviction. A time of repentance with cries of mercy can be heard far and near.

God still loved them even though He was forsaken. He reached down to hold the crew in His arms; He gave them a strong, loving embrace. It was more than the men could handle. They all broke down with tears in their eyes. How could God still love them after the way they treated Him?

Father, your love is never-ending and it never fades away. These men drifted away in life, but they came back to God with repentant hearts and were saved again by grace. Drifted away, it is time to come back to Him. It does not matter how far we have gone, cries for mercy are still answered, amen.

An Old Fire Escape
September 5

Fire escapes are built to help us escape a fire. Building inspectors are scheduled to visit the local hotels and high-rise buildings to make sure all safety equipment is in excellent condition. These inspections are planned ahead of time so there will not be any tragic accidents. All of us would agree prevention is a real lifesaver.

Let's go to a hotel where a fire escape was built on the side of a hotel. The life expectancy of this unit was about ten years. If the maintenance were performed on a regular basis, then it would last a lot longer. Inspections should be more frequent especially on older equipment.

Over the years this strong fire escape began to diminish with weakness in the frame. The upkeep was poorly done and no one took the time to paint or oil any of the retractable parts. Rust and grime had weakened the support system. Residents of this hotel would not be able to escape.

Notice was given to the hotel owner to build a new fire escape. This one was just too dangerous to be used in an emergency. A person or group of people trying to escape would die in the process or be severely injured. Accidents can be avoided with diligence to the repair effort.

We need to inspect all of our spiritual equipment to make sure our personal lives are safe and secure from any fires that may occur. Personal observance and compliance removes all risk of a tragedy.

Father, if the Chief Inspector (Christ) finds that our lives have deteriorated, He may suggest an upgrade in our present living conditions. Neglect will have eternal consequences. All of us must realize that we have a choice of Heaven or Hell. If we choose Jesus as our fire escape method, then we will have the blessed hope of going to heaven. Save us from the fire, amen.

Falsely Accuse
September 6

Let's revisit the scene where a diamond ring was lost many years ago. The house was searched several times for this valuable piece of property. Some hide-away places like couches, under beds, and the worst culprit seems to be our favorite recliner. This chair sits silently in the corner, not revealing any types of disclosure of criminal activity.

We try to recall the last place we had the item. Frustration and anxiety starts to disrupt our normal peaceful composure. Family members are called to see if we had accidently left the diamond at their place of residence. A time of sorrow has a firm hold on us that will not let go.

After hours of deep thought, the owner of the diamond remembered that while she was working in the garden, she lost her ring. It was recovered and placed back on her finger. Roses were cut for a new vase that she had just bought. She was unaware that the ring had slipped into the pot-soil.

The ring was not found. We are going to go from a terrible situation of a personal loss of a diamond, which is very expensive to a more serious charge of theft. Sometimes being in an area at the wrong time can have devastating effects.

At the time this diamond was lost, robberies were frequent in the neighborhood. A young man was taking a nighttime stroll when a burglar, fleeing the scene knocked him down. When he arose from the ground, he was arrested and charged with the theft of the diamond. Conviction occurs without any evidence.

Father, this imaginary thought should help us to understand that lives can be ruined if we bear false witness. The diamond was found years later in a flower vase. This jewel owner went to the police to get a pardon for the inmate. Let's be very careful before we falsely accuse, as we cannot undo years of damage. Help us! In Jesus' name, amen.

Keep Running
September 7

Our Christian journey will have us giving victory speeches before the race is won. Personal acknowledgement is at the end of the race. A crown is not given until we cross the finish line.

A vision might have all of us going through the lonely valleys, by the troubled waters, we continued on by God's grace. We endured the storms and trials of life without wavering from our faith in Christ. It is too early to claim the victory.

Today is a good time to have a reality check up to disintegrate the word all. Each of us will have our own personal victories to claim. The glories of heaven have not yet been attained as our heavenly journey continues.

There were times when the cross was too heavy to bear and we laid it down. Jesus came by to help us pick it back up and continue in life's race. Crosses will be laid down along the way.

The lonely valleys of heartbreak, grief, and distress kept us in a distressful mood until Jesus stood beside us and healed our broken spirits. Some storms were so powerful with unrelenting force; we could not go on, unless Jesus would calm our troubled souls. "Peace be still."

We are still running, but it is because of grace. When we fall, Jesus will pick us up and help us the rest of the way. If we sin, He will forgive us so we can start again. The glory crown has not yet been obtained. Let's keep on running; the finish line is only a short distance away.

Father, the reality of life is that some of us stumbled and fell from grace. Jesus had to lift us back up so we could continue our journey. The stormy trials left us weak in need of a Savior. Sins crept in unawares and without Jesus our souls would be lost. Help us to be aware that our boastfulness is for our journey to end before we can say, "We kept the faith," amen.

Oil for the Lantern
September 8

One day while camping in the mountains, we needed a few things from the store, as our supplies were running low. It was almost dark and the food market was about half of a mile away from our campsite.

If we took a shortcut along the mountain ridge, it would not take near as long. One man decided he wanted to go down the rocky trail. We told him it was too dangerous to walk along the ridge at nighttime.

An oil lantern was hanging on a tree branch nearly empty of fuel. This man took the lantern and started walking through the woods. The reason he wanted to take the shortcut was because the store would be closing soon.

A short while later, he arrived at the store and bought the necessary supplies. The storekeeper was really concerned about this person returning to camp and told him that he should go the long route, as it was safer.

Back at the camp his friends were anxiously waiting for his return. Their worst fears were realized when they picked up an empty lantern from a rocky ledge. He had fallen to his death. His lamp had gone out, no oil in the container.

As we travel through life, preparation is needed for survival. Making the right decision is crucial when we only have a little bit of time. Advice or warnings can alert us of the consequences of neglect. One of the best ways to avoid a tragedy is to have a good light source and plenty of fuel.

Father, we cannot make it safely to our heavenly home if we venture to close to the ledge of sin. Our journey in life requires us to keep oil in the lantern. A bright light shining reveals everything that would hinder us along the way. If fuel is running low, this is a good time for a refueling of grace, amen.

Throw out the Lifeline
September 9

We have heard about cruise ships traveling on the ocean. Every once in a while, someone falls overboard. All efforts are utilized to save the victim. If the person stays under water too long, the rescue attempt will be in vain. Let's go on an adventure where we use our life saving skills.

Our travels today will take us far out to sea. This will be a voyage on a cruise ship. We were out on the deck one day and the warning system alerted the crew that a man had fallen overboard into the water. A rescue depends on the quick recovery efforts. Victims can drown in a matter of minutes.

Crewmembers gathered at the place where the accident occurred. A lifeboat was quickly lowered into the raging sea. We could hear his frantic cries for help. Every time he went under, his resurface time was longer. Although there were some favorable conditions of saving the man, it looked like this rescue operation would not be successful.

The two men in the lifeboat were too far away to reach the drowning man. There was only one chance to save his life. If they could throw him a lifeline, he could be saved, but was it too late? This man was under water longer this time. Finally, he resurfaced, probably for his last gasp of air; he grabbed the floating device and was barely saved.

Father, rescue operations are ongoing throughout the world. There is not a day that goes by without distress calls being broadcast on the airwaves. First responders and citizens come to the rescue and they risk their lives to save the victims.

Heaven is on high alert and any distress signals will be answered immediately. It is our responsibility to throw out the lifeline of God's love and mercy. Souls are daily sinking in their sins. Lives will be saved if they take hold of the Savior's hand and put on the lifejacket of God's amazing grace, amen.

A Thief in the Home
September 10

All was quite in the neighborhood as everyone had gone to sleep. There was one family that lived in the country. Recently they loaded up the van and went on a vacation.

This family was unaware of some crooks that had been watching the family. These men were waiting for the right time to break into the home and steal the valuable merchandise. Thieves are watchful and are well prepared to evade someone's property for personal benefit.

Most of us have special things in our homes that are very sentimental. We care deeply about our private collection of memorial items that were given to us by family members.

These thieves are already in the home, tearing the place apart. Looking for jewelry or anything of value, they will not stop until the home is completely ravaged. There is no empathy or any concerns for precious memories, family heirlooms, or any item that is held close to one's heart.

Our enemy (Satan) uses the same tactics to steal from our personal lives. His evil intentions have absolutely no interest in moral values. The Bible even warns us about him. "The thief cometh not, but for to steal, and to kill, and to destroy" (John 10:10). His visit is one of destruction.

Normally thieves will come by when no one is at home. Our lives are disrupted in terrible ways when a break-in occurs. Thieves will rob us of our personal treasures, but our peace with God remains intact.

Father, material things of the earth will be taken from us. Let's be aware of thieves that will come without warning. Valuable objects that took a lifetime to require are instantly taken away. Help us to realize the peace we have received in Christ is secure from all worldly effects, amen.

Foxes Spoil the Grapes
September 11

Grapes are ripe and ready for the laborers to harvest this fruit of the vine. This vineyard is a reliable source of income for a man and his wife who own it. It is a family business that has gone through the inheritance cycle many times.

Hired laborers went home for the evening. First thing in the morning, the grapes would be picked and taken to the markets. This crop would be used to stock up on groceries and pay the mortgage on the home.

The farmers woke this morning and they were real excited about the harvest of many grapes. They could hardly wait to get started. Soon their joyful expectations would be replaced with distraught feelings of remorse.

These pleasant thoughts of food on the table and bills paid would be gone at the rising of the sun as the laborers see the garden of devastation. No one was aware of little foxes that lived in dens a short distance away. While the harvest crew was sleeping, these little fury creatures came out of their hiding places to ruin the family investment.

All through the night, the little varmints were destroying the vineyard. It is hard to believe these little foxes could cause so much damage to the grapes. The destructive force of little things often bewilders us as to how something so small could create such havoc in our personal lives.

Father, little foxes will walk among the vines and eat these delicious grapes. When morning comes, the harvesters are really depressed at the sight of mangled grapes and barren vines. This family was terribly disheartened at the loss.

We need to be aware of the little sins that we think are not harmful. Small sins have big appetites like the foxes and they can spoil our lives. Help us to be alert! In Jesus' name, amen.

Plane Lost at Sea
September 12

Our journey today will take us on a flight into the regions of the unknown. We will have to use a little imagination mixed in with the truth of a jetliner missing at sea. Occasionally visionary thoughts will come into effect to fill in a story when we cannot recall all of the facts.

The airplane took off at the scheduled time. No one was aware of any danger. Communication lines were open between the plane and the airport tower. All of the equipment was working properly, at least for the first hour in flight.

It was required of someone in the cockpit to contact the flight navigation team every hour for security reasons. This was a regular routine for all aircrafts. Safety of all passengers was the highest priority. At the time of the call there were no security violations.

Signals from inside the plane to the command tower were essential in guiding the plane to its destination. Somewhere this flight lost all communications. This airplane with 239 passengers disappeared without a trace in March 2014. Time has gone by and the plane has never been recovered.

The radar system is used around the world to track planes and to keep them on the right flight plan. This high-tech scanning system was ineffective in the search.

Father, there is danger in our lives of being lost eternally by lack of communication to heaven's flight tower. God knows where we are at all times. If there is any doubt, please sound the alarm with cries for mercy.

If we do not approach the throne room of grace, our fellowship is broken until we earnestly seek God. We will find Him when we search with all of our hearts. Sinner's lost and found is a good report. Search today, in Jesus' name, amen.

Walk Away
September 13

There comes a time in life when we have to walk away. Sometimes visionary thoughts of a plane crash will help us to appreciate life and to realize how blessed we are when we can walk away from a life-threatening event. God spares our lives so we can finish earthly tasks.

An airplane crashed in the field surrounded by trees. A pilot, his wife and two small children were riding this plane as they encountered a storm. Lightning flashes and turbulent winds were too much for this small twin-engine airplane. The pilot told his wife and children to brace themselves as they were going to make a crash-landing in the field.

After a few horrifying minutes of colliding with trees and other types of shrubbery, the mangled plane finally came to a complete stop, the passengers regained consciousness and managed to get off the plane. The husband's wife tried to get him out of the plane; her efforts failed.

There were not any casualties in this terrible accident, at least not yet. The plane was very close to igniting in flames. A rescue unit was on the way. Hopefully they would get there in time to save everyone from this horrible crash. The pilot was trapped in the plane. He could not free himself because his leg was broken and it was wedged in the wreckage.

First responders arrived at the scene and the man was rescued from the plane. This family received medical care at the hospital. Later they were released from the emergency care unit and they all walked away, praising God.

Father, we need to come back into reality where real life walk away situations will determine where we spend eternity. Sin is like the plane crash. Rescue depends on how soon we make the distress call. It is a blessed day in our lives when Jesus saves us and we walk away from our sins, amen.

Our Best is not a Fraction
September 14

The corn is ripe and everything is ready for the harvest. This will be a day of hard work for the farmers. The old wagon has already been hooked up to the horses.

It will take all day to gather in this crop. So we began early this morning. It is very important to pick all of the corn today, as it is supposed to rain the rest of the week.

A team of horses that had recently been broke to harness was used to pull the wagon. They were fast walkers and we had to work faster to keep up with them. Most of our time was spent walking when we should have been picking corn. Time is essential but wasted effort has no benefit.

If we work at a slower pace, the corn will be ready for the market. Finally at the end of the day when our work was finished, fresh corn will be transported to various places. A higher rate of pay is given when the wagons are full.

Sometimes in life, we are just too busy and we cannot get very much done. There are so many activities that we just cannot do them all. We are so fast that our labors of love are like the empty wagon. Give a little here and more over there. How can we give our all, when each job requires our best and only receives a fraction of our quality time?

Father, as we work for you in various activities of church, we know that you do not want a fraction of our time; a full commitment is preferred with love and devotion. If we are bound with so many activities, a partial investment may lead to a reduction in our heavenly inheritance.

If too many things separate us from real fellowship with God, we need a revaluation of our spiritual priorities to control our activities. An empty wagon may be a sign of wasted grace. Help us to be more selective with our endeavors, amen.

A fall from Grace
September 15

Each of us has a responsibility to help those in need. If we are walking at the park, a person accidently falls to the ground. Our response should be to offer assistance. We should treat others the same way that we would have them treat us.

Sometimes a fall has caused serious injuries. Perhaps the help of an emergency unit is needed to transport the person to a hospital. A bicycle accident has caused injuries that require doctors to perform surgery on the affected areas of the body.

A really bad fall would be the one where death claims the victim's life. Occasionally a person will be walking a mountain trail, slip on a rock and go over the cliff. A grave will be the final resting place.

Falls influence our lives in many ways. A casual fall is where no harm is done and it does not require a doctor's care. If we are on a stage in front of a lot of people, a fall can be an embarrassing moment. It may take a few minutes to recover and red cheeks to return to normal.

Runners in a race have had the misfortune of falling when they were about to cross the finish line. Awards were given to the other athletes. Frustration is not a good reason to stay down, as all of us will have falls throughout life. Those who claim the victory will rise to the occasion.

Father, we see how devastating falls can be in our lives. Some falls are more critical than others. Medical attention helps in some cases. Words of encouragement help us to recover.

There is one type of fall that we have not mentioned. This is the worst one of them all, as it will affect us throughout eternity. We want everyone to be aware that a fall from grace will separate us from God's love. Cries for mercy will lift us up. In Jesus' name, amen.

Friendship Club
September 16

Our journey today will take us along a mountain ridge. This will be extremely dangerous, as we have accepted a challenge to walk in the dark to a certain location.

We want to join this friendship club that is just now forming. Loneliness and desperation for friends will have us going to great lengths to be accepted into a group, even the risk of life.

We must realize the initiation process is really very dangerous. Before we can participate in the group activities, we must be accepted and approved by the members. A word of advice is given about friendship invitations, as they do not always have our best interest at heart.

The cost of friendship should never be at the expense of pain or even death. If this were the payment for receiving honorary group privileges, then it would be far better if we never met these so called, friends.

I feel like a warning is necessary for this rocky ledge endeavor. Most of us who venture down the treacherous mountain trail will not make it back home. Those who are successful have joined a group that is hateful. Before we accept the challenge, or these the kind of friends that would stand beside us in troublesome times and even die in our place?

Father, help us to be aware of friends who would have us risk our own lives to prove that we are worthy of their friendship. If we find ourselves walking through the valley of loneliness, this would be a good time to meet Jesus.

He is God's Son and He proved His love for us by dying on a cross. Crucifixion has claimed the lives of many people. What separates the death of Jesus from others who suffered the same way? Jesus is the only friend who could take our punishment by giving His life to save us. Thank you, Jesus, amen.

In the Lions' Den
September 17

We are going to a place today where our chances of survival are very slim. Many of us have been at zoos where wild animals are kept. There are lions and tigers enclosed in cages or running free in a fenced in area.

If a roaring lion approaches the car, this would be a good time to exit the confined space because the lion has probably escaped its cage and is looking to solve some hunger pains.

Today we are going to be on the inside of a den. Hungry lions will be there with us and it has been days since they had a good meal. If it will make everyone feel more comfortable, Daniel will be the main character in this drama scene.

We will be more like invisible spectators in the lions' den. It is easy to be brave men and women when we do not have to confront the wild beast.

Courage manifests itself more in a crowd when there are sufficient back-ups with sticks to take care of all aggressive animals. Crowd inspiration is not needed because one person and God is able to accomplish great and mighty things.

Daniel is with us in the lions' den because he prayed to God, disobeying the king's orders. All through the night hungry lions were walking around.

The deliverance of Daniel from the hungry lions came into effect when he obeyed God rather than man. Prayer brings us into fellowship with God and He is the one who will give us the victory.

Father, we know that you had rather have obedience than for us to yield to the ways of the world. We might be cast into the lions' den for our beliefs. Stand strong and be vigilant, as it is better to obey God than to betray Him with disobedience.

Adopted into the Family
September 18

Today we will be running in a race for a special project. The money raised for this outdoor activity will go to build an orphanage.

Children who do not have any guardians will be the winners of this event. These little ones want someone to take care of them and a home of their own. They need parents whose love is unconditional without any restraints.

An administrator of the old orphanage was at the race with two orphaned little girls. We saw them standing there with joy in their hearts. Their hopes for a new life were seen in the tears that trickled down their cheeks. Tender hearts have a deep longing to be loved.

Finally, the race was over and enough money was raised to begin the building process of the new orphanage. My imagination couldn't resist an opportunity to help the two girls. They were adopted that very day and a short while later they went home with their new parents.

Adoption papers were in order as the court approved the man and wife as legal guardians. Background checks were complete as no criminal record was found on either party. The judge brought forth the papers and the signature sealed the deal. These two little children found a home that day and loving, caring parents to help them throughout life.

Father, there are children around the world without homes. Parents have died and their kids are left without guardians to attend to their needs.

Some of the children are placed in orphanages where they wait for someone to adopt them. Heaven also has an adoption program. Help us to be aware that God is waiting with a loving embrace to welcome His sons and daughters home, amen.

Oil in the Lamp
September 19

A small flickering flame will only give light for a short distance. When the wick is low, the shadows of darkness creep closer. The dangers increase by each passing hour. Strangers appear; we do not know if they are friends or the enemy.

While we are focusing on the distorted things in view, there is a greater danger on the pathway we trod. Soon it will be total darkness. One misstep and we will fall into the ravine.

On the other side of the camp, the campers are rejoicing in pure delight. Flames of hope are glowing, dispersing the shadows far and wide. A light will reveal the people approaching are friends. Calmness prevails in our lives when anxiety and fear are no longer a threat.

The lighted pathway gives comfort from a distressful night. There is oil in the lantern and the flame is glowing bright. A path is easy to see when there are no dark shadows.

No one is stumbling in the dark or falling by the wayside. Flames grow stronger as the wick is raised higher. Those with oil in the lamp are safe and secure all the night.

We have a lantern that is supplied from the throne room of grace. When we give our hearts to Jesus, He ignites the flame of love that is all enduring. The lantern of hope shines brighter still, when we live by faith according to His will.

Father, when the fire begins to sputter, the flame is gasping for air, no more oil in the lantern. If we walk in darkness our fate will be a grave of sorrow.

There is still a little time to refuel the lantern and hold it up high, as a bright flame spreads far and near. A fresh supply of grace from the throne room is always available. Let our lives be a light that shines throughout the night, amen.

Train Derailment
September 20

I have heard about trains that went off the rails for one reason or another. Recently there was a passenger train that derailed. Some of the people died in the crash. It is never known when a derailment will take more lives. Disasters will happen in our lives when we least expect them.

A train derailment can happen at any time. Natural disasters have caused many trains to go off the rails. Hopefully these occurrences will not interfere with our future endeavors.

The conductor at the station was calling for the people to load the train. "All aboard." After hours of visiting the tourist attractions, it was time to go home. While we were on this train an emergency situation was developing in front of us.

We were going down the mountain and leveled out in the valley. Some of the rails were loosened by a huge rock that rolled over the tracks. The loose rails would cause the train to derail. It is a good thing we were going slowly when this accident occurred. Unfortunately, there were deaths. This train derailment was a tragic accident.

While traveling on the rails of life, there will be times when we are unable to get to our destinations. Everything is going well, when all of a sudden sin causes a derailment in our lives. Visions of our heavenly home fade, as repairs hopefully will be made to correct the problem.

Father, we know that this is a very dangerous situation, off the rails and in a dangerous area. Unless we take immediate action to correct the derailment caused by sin, we will miss our flight to heaven.

Let's lay down some new crossties so the secured rails of God's love and mercy will have us back on the track of forgiveness. "All aboard," heaven's flight is on schedule, amen.

Lion on the Prowl
September 21

This was a special day in our lives, as siblings would meet with their parents for a family picnic. All of us were supposed to meet at the national park for a time of enjoyment and fellowship with one another.

An urgent warning had just been announced over the airwaves. A lion escaped from the local zoo and it is very hungry. Everyone is advised to use extreme caution in all outdoor activities. Please warn the neighbors to stay off the streets and be vigilant to avoid the danger.

A concerned citizen called the Police Department to inform them about a family picnic at the park. They do not know a lion is on the loose. "Please warn them!" The elderly man and his wife were patiently waiting for their children to arrive. The charcoal grill was already fired up and the smell of fresh hamburger meat was lingering in the air.

The policeman was quick to respond by driving down to the park. While he was driving, he received another call that the lion had just been spotted a short distance away from the unsuspecting couple. There was doubt if this rescue would be successful as the police unit was too far away.

Warnings were constantly announced over the radio and the television networks. While this father's son and his wife were riding down the highway, they heard the report of a hungry lion on the prowl. Immediately a call was made to the parents. When they heard the news, a retreat to the shelter saved them. The lion was recaptured and returned to the zoo.

Father, help us to realize how this family was saved from this vicious attack. Let's think for a moment about the man's son who heard the warning on the radio; "A lion is on the loose." Warnings are given so that we will be saved from impending danger. "Except we repent, how shall we escape?" Amen.

Thin Ice
September 22

Winter came a little early this year and the temperatures have already dropped below freezing. Throughout the night the snow continued to fall. After a while the ground was covered with about twelve inches of snow. This was a beautiful scene with icicles hanging on tree limbs.

One young man was more concerned about a frozen lake that would be an excellent place to try out his new ice skates. However, he never took into consideration the possibility of losing his life that day. He thought this would be a really good time to go skating. Without telling anyone where he was going, he headed across the field to the thin ice disaster.

A failure to make precautionary plans can be devastating with the high risk of death. It is really dangerous for a person to be alone on a thin layer of ice. Along the edges of the lake, the ice is thick, as the water in the shallow area freezes a lot faster.

The danger signs were all around, but he did not heed any of them. When he was part of the way across the lake, the ice began to crack. This was a warning that caught his attention, but it was too late. He found himself struggling to stay alive. All of his efforts were in vain to save himself.

Sin is like the frozen lake; it lures us past the shallow areas with sinful pleasures. When we are too far from shore, the ice breaks and we fall into the icy cold water. This is a good place to have farsighted vision as the consequences of sin may have us in a lake of fire of deep regret.

Father, our only hope is to take hold of Jesus' hand. Invite Him to come into our lives and He will give us the blessed hope of life eternal. Spiritual foresight will see the dangerous areas before we have to call for help. If we are already in the deep places of sin, Christ will respond quickly to the cries for mercy and save us, amen.

God Never Abandons
September 23

As we drive down the road, thinking about the place where we used to live. We notice old houses along the way that have been forsaken. This is a time in our lives when we want to refresh our memories of the wonderful life we had while we were growing up in the country.

Families have moved away and building inspectors have condemned these dwellings. Finally, we came to our old house that had been abandoned many years ago. We need to be careful as we walk through this deteriorated building, as the rotten boards are unstable and extremely dangerous. Memorable experiences are better without pain.

When our parents passed away, there was no one to take care of the home, as the children had grown up and moved away to have families of their own. Everyone who lived in the old homestead was living many miles from this present location. No one lives there now, as it has been condemned by the state inspectors and is considered a safety hazard.

There is no glass in the window sections and the doors are barely hanging on. The roof with rotten rafters has collapsed into the interior of the home. This dwelling was abandoned many years ago. There is no hope of restoring it. The decay has gone deep into the timbers.

Homes are forsaken for various reasons; neglect has caused many of these dwellings to deteriorate for lack of maintenance. Facilities that cannot be restored have to be abandoned.

Father, when our lives were in decay, deteriorating from sin; God never gave up on us. Jesus did not come to condemn but to save us. Over the years the upkeep of our souls was neglected and our relationship with God was lacking in love and devotion. It is so obvious that we needed to go through a restoring process, which required a fresh layer of grace, amen.

Too Close to the Edge
September 24

We were standing near a mountain ledge, enjoying the scenery. Pictures were taken of the beautiful landscape. Everyone was having a really good time. It is never a good idea to take photos when we may end up losing our lives. Walking and focusing a camera can be fatal.

Borderline security would have helped to avoid an accident. This extra bit of safety precaution on a lookout sight could have been a lifesaver. Little children and adults had a better chance of survival if only a barricade was erected along the cliffs edge before this terrible incident.

The tourist guide had warned us not to get close to the edge. We were following his instructions, at least for a while. More attention was going to the photography than to the safety of our lives. This peaceful day was about to turn into a tragedy. We did not realize how close we were to the edge of the cliff.

A family portrait was going to be the last picture. The photographer was trying to focus the camera while moving gradually backwards. Suddenly without warning, he made one step too many and began to fall from the cliff.

No sooner had he started to fall, when the guide grabbed hold of him and pulled him back to safety. His life was spared just in time. An accident was prevented and a safety hazard resolved with a new wall.

Father, there are times in our lives when we might stand too close to the cliffs of sin. We might be so far away from God that we do not realize how close we are to the edge.

Our focus might be on worldly cares while we are moving further away from God's love and mercy. Let's refocus and keep our eyes on Christ while walking away from the sins that would have us fall from grace. In Jesus' name, amen.

Self-Inflicted Wound
September 25

A self-inflicted wound takes time to heal. We cannot blame others for our own display of honor. I admit my guilt of using a false impression; all the shame belongs to me.

Deep down in my heart, all I wanted to do was honor the veterans on Memorial Day. A self-portrait can cause a lot of grief if the image is distorted and a resemblance is a lie.

Some of the church members were putting together a video. They wanted a picture of each veteran for this time of honor. At the time, I did not think I had a picture, so I created a self-portrait using some of my military photographs. Computers are really remarkable for photo creations, but they are not accountable for clip and paste recreations.

This was my self-inflicted wound. I was very sorry for my false impression. The following year I gave them a real photo to replace the old picture. Shame is not easily erased and sometimes we have to bear the guilt for many years.

The injury I inflicted was my own. My good intentions turned out to be a lie. The veterans were still honored, but I had lost mine. Jesus saw that I was hurting on the inside.

He came by and wrapped up the wounds in bandages of love. Honor, dignity, and self-respect have been restored and I stand proudly with the other veterans of America.

Father, false impressions take time to heal. This was not a physical injury that needed bandages to stop the bleeding. The pain of self-inflicted wounds, no one else can feel.

Our best assurance of a clear conscience is when Christ removes the guilt and heals the wound. His love is the healing balm with eternal effects. Help us in life to portray an honorable image without false effects, in Jesus' name, amen.

Peace in a Storm
September 26

Weather stations had been announcing for a week that a severe storm was approaching the area and we were all advised to prepare for this monster storm. An evacuation was in process at some communities and the people were informed to stay away until further notice.

Throughout the night the snow continued to fall. We awoke to the sound of state trucks plowing the snow. Warnings were given to stay off the highways, as they were slick from an accumulation of snow and ice.

A strong wind was blowing and every once in a while, we would hear the cracking and breaking of tree limbs. The yard was cluttered with fallen branches. Vehicles that were parked under trees had to be relocated so that any falling debris or trees would not damage them.

The news media was broadcasting over the TV'S and radio about the intensity of the storm. State Police and other law enforcement agencies had reported many accidents. We saw live videos with cars and trucks sliding into one another.

Power lines were heavy laden with a thick layer of ice. Thousands of people were without electricity. The list of horrifying events continued to accumulate.

There seemed to be no end to the mass destruction from this blizzard that was destroying property, uprooting trees, and smashing them into people's homes. Casualties were reported.

Father, it is a blessed time in our lives when the storm is over and we are able to resume our daily task. Turmoil and trials come to an end when the sun shines and all is well with our souls. This will only happen when we make peace with God. The storm continues to rage until we surrender our hearts and lives to Christ. Give us peace all the days of our lives, amen.

Escape, Sparks of Sin
September 27

The more wood that is added to a fire will cause the flames to grow higher. Wood that is added to the fire will cause intense heat. we will be burned If we stand close to the heat source.

Some of us have stood too close to a fire with the result of scorched eyebrows and singed hair. Sometimes a good retreat is better than a bad stand.

There are some safety requirements that we need to follow to keep from having severe injuries. Fires are very dangerous and they have caused many casualties. A good way to avoid these life-threatening experiences is to stay a good distance away from the red-hot flames.

If we are burning brush, we have to get close enough to put more branches on the fire. We do not have to stay there while the flames have been intensified with sparks drifting off into the treetops and surrounding area.

One very important safety measure that I forgot to mention has probably caused more runaway fires than anything. It is never a good idea to have a fire when a drought is in the area. I am sorry I didn't give this warning earlier. After the fire is out of control, it is too late for a weather report. It looks like it is time to get a new fire instructor.

Sin indulgence is like putting wood on the fire, the flames grow higher and the heat more intense. When sins are drawing us closer to the flames, we had better turn and run. How close do we have to get before we realize that we have gone too far? Singed eyebrows are too close.

Father, there is another fire and we are giving the warning now so that lives will be saved before it is too late. A rescue is possible from the sparks of sin if we ask Christ to save us. In Jesus' name, amen.

Drifting Away from God
September 28

Remember the days when we were on the peaceful shores of God's grace and mercy. Time has gone by with the precious memories left behind. We do not have time to pray, go to church, or have fellowship with Him anymore.

Our joyful days of serving Him are special moments of the past; they also are gone. There were no goodbyes as we drifted out to sea. We followed the deadly currents of sin to disgraceful living.

Peace we once had with God is no longer the anchor of our souls. Drifting away every day, far out to sea in the darkness of despair with no hope of heaven anymore.

The fulfillment of a sinful life will bring us to ruin as our ship drifts more out of sight. Our ungodly living will bring us closer to the grave, eternal separation from God. It will be too late to return to His love and mercy when death seals our fate. Heaven's gate will never open again.

Imagination shows a person who died at sea with sin as his burial marker. He left those words in a note on the ship. This captain, who was on the same destructive course, broke down in tears after he read them.

He ordered the men to turn the ship around. "Where are we going, they asked?" "We are going back to the peaceful shore of God's grace and mercy." The gates of heaven open wide as sinners come home.

Father, if we drift away from you, we are going into enemy territory. Let's get back in the current of God's amazing grace and reset the anchor of commitment to love God with all of our hearts. It's not too late to go back to Him. Time is running out, that is true. Peace will be restored when we return to His loving embrace. In Jesus' name, amen.

Unexpected Grace
September 29

Visualize for just a moment, a wildfire is burning out of control. Trees block the roads. There is no escape for the campers; it looks like they will all die from the intense heat. Dark smoke hinders us from going in the right direction.

The campers were warned about the danger of having fires. Warning signs were posted throughout the area and the forest ranger came by on a regular basis to enforce the restrictions.

There was a lookout tower in the distance where a group of people was constantly watching for lightning strikes, small fire flare-ups. Being in a drought increased the chances of an uncontrollable forest fire.

A forest ranger's worst nightmare was about to take place as lightning had struck a dead tree trunk and quickly ignited into flames. The fire was growing at a rapid rate and consuming everything in its path.

Flare-ups were developing throughout the forest. All the campers were trapped inside this horrific circle of fire. Firemen were called to the scene. However, a rescue seemed impossible because of high flames. This area was not accessible by fire trucks because of fallen trees.

Without a miracle from heaven these campsite adventures would lose their lives. Dark storm clouds suddenly appeared and within minutes the earth was saturated with rain. Many lives were saved that day as prayers ascended to heaven. Death was seen as the final outcome, but God gave them life.

Father, sometimes when we least expect it, you bring the showers of blessings to satisfy our spiritual needs. We may be going through the fiery trials, but we know that you can and will extinguish the flames. Unexpected grace deserves a shout of praise. In Jesus' name, amen.

Never Castaway
September 30

Our story today is told of a runaway who left his family. I believe he wanted to be with a relative in another part of the country. His travel methods were beyond comprehension and his behavior was irrational.

Otherwise, he was a normal kid but had a strange way of accomplishing his goal. There are lots of teenagers that leave home for various reasons.

I have never heard of any of them that wanted to fly on the underside of an airplane. Please don't be astonished, as this story is quite perplexing. This adventure was far more life threatening than the home he left.

Flying on a plane is probably the fastest way to get to a certain location. His transportation methods were not the best. Since he did not have a ticket or boarding pass, there were not many options left. Travel arrangements were not made in advance. His entry was in secret.

We do not know the circumstances why he left home. There might have been an argument or disagreement with his parents or a relative. This might have resulted in him being a castaway. Let's say he is a runaway and then he will be a stowaway. He has chosen a place on the plane where no one would find him.

This young man is determined to get on this flight. He climbed up into the wheel-well and stayed there until the plane landed. He is very fortunate to be alive. Several times he passed out for lack of oxygen.

Father, it was really quiet a miracle that he survived. He was so determined to get away. Finally, the plane landed and he was rescued. We try to escape from various situations. I'm so glad that in our relationship with God; He will never cast us away. Christ coming in the clouds is a time for us to flyaway.

SOS, Call for Mercy
October 1

There were four fishermen in a boat and they were having difficulties getting to shore. Finally, they had to swim for their lives and eventually they all made it to a safe haven on land.

This was a deserted island; no one lived in this remote part of the country. Their chances of survival were slim as the damaged boat drifted upon the rocky shoreline.

When these men set out to sea on a fishing trip, they did not tell anyone where they were going. They are stranded on a desolate island, starving and growing weaker by the day.

One of the men swam to the sandy area and wrote SOS in large letters on the sand. While he was scribbling the words for a distress call, he realized that this message would be invisible from the sky.

After thinking about the signal for help, he decided to use palm branches for the letters. A short while later all four of the men were rescued in time.

We have the blessed assurance that whether we are in perilous conditions or in peaceful circumstances, we can call on God and He responds immediately to our prayer request. He listens attentively for the cries for mercy. There are no hesitations in His rescue efforts.

Father, we may not ever be on a stranded island, seeking a way of escape, but we need to know our distress calls will be answered. Time is always a factor in a successful rescue operation. Tomorrow's signal cannot save lives today.

The most important need we have in life is the salvation of our souls. We need to make things right with God before life on earth expires. This would be a good time to send up an SOS signal. A distress call for mercy will get better results, amen.

A Fresh Outpouring of Grace
October 2

An old well has supplied water for a family many long years. We think about the good old days when the well was full of water. Some of the neighbors would come over with their drinking utensils because their wells had gone dry.

If the water is shared with those in need, the people around us will have better attitudes and they will all work together to solve their thirst problems. Refrain from giving a drink and see how quickly tempers flare. The peaceful nature of humanity becomes more aggressive.

Water that is not given will be taken when the kids are begging and crying for a drink of water. Those days are gone when our well was the only one that was supplying the needs of the drought-stricken families.

All of the well diggers were having doubts about any more water being found in the area. They were thinking about giving up. Families are in distress for lack of water to drink.

Neighborhoods were shriveling away because there was not enough rain to replenish the earth. Some of the families moved away. After a while the new well was full of water and rain filled up the lake. A community that was dying was revived when the rain saturated the earth.

The dry spell has ended with abundance of rain. Cloudy skies and stormy weather refreshed the creeks and filled up the wells. Kindness returned, as there was now plenty of water; apologies were accepted.

Father, earthly wells run dry; the need of humanity is a fresh water supply. We think about our spiritual needs and without a refreshing shower from above, our fellowship with God will be as the withering plants. Please send down the rain, a fresh outpouring of grace will revive us throughout life, amen.

Reflection of Christ
October 3

There are times in life when we are walking by the riverside and see our reflection in the water. This is a good time for us to meditate. We just want to have quite peaceful moments with God and let Him speak to our hearts in His own gentle way.

While walking by the water we think about the sacrifice of Christ when He died on a cross. His love was beyond comprehension. God's only begotten Son bled so our sins could be washed away. Jesus died in our place to break all the bonds of captivity.

If the Son of God sets us free, we are free indeed and with the blessed hope of life eternal. Salvation cost Christ His life. This does not mean that we are automatically saved. The pardon goes into effect when we repent.

"If we confess our sins, He is faithful and just to forgive us, and to cleanse us of all unrighteousness." There is more to think about as we look at the reflection in the crystal-clear water. We are created in God's image.

Throw a few rocks into the water and see if the reflection changes in any way. No matter how many pebbles we throw into the river, our image never fades. Large rocks will not change the reflections we want to portray. Rocky trials do not distort the image of Christ in our lives.

Father, we are thankful for this time of meditation at the riverside where mercy is so real. A reflection in the water has many wonderful qualities that are revealed in our outward appearances. A more lasting impression is in our hearts where Christ abides.

Our best reflection is not in the water, but in our lives where daily living reflects Jesus Christ our Lord, a living Savior. Thanks for this reflective moment. In Jesus' name, amen.

Tear Down the Old Fence
October 4

Cattle on a ranch in Texas were gradually disappearing. It was discovered that the old fence needed some repairs. The strands of barbed wire were broken in several places.

A few ranchers were sent out to check the fence line. They noticed that there were areas where the cows could easily wander into other grazing fields. There were no signs of cut wire or any personal involvement.

A meeting was held between the ranchers and farmers about the bad fences. This fence line separated the two groups, but they decided to work together to repair the fence. Immediately the fence was torn down and a new one built. Differences are resolved when calmness is in effect.

After a short while the new fence was used to secure the livestock. The best thing about this situation was the ranch-hands and farmers became the best of friends. Unity prevails when the same goals are achieved.

There is a fence in our lives that separates us from God. This one is not made of wire, but there seems to be barbs of sin that keep us in alienation. A repair is definitely needed to improve our family relations. If the wall of sin has never been torn down, Seek Christ immediately for eternal benefits.

Father, broken wire is not evidence of theft. Suspicion of sins is not a conviction. The truth revealed is proof that we are guilty without any possibility of doubt. Peace will prevail with a new resolution to love God with all our hearts.

Let's tear down the old fences where sin abides and build new ones reinforced with God's love and mercy. Replace the barbed wire of ungodly living with God's amazing grace. We will have peace with God and all of us will have praising rights. In Jesus' name, amen.

Prepare to meet thy God
October 5

Before the end of life's journey, we had to prepare ourselves for special occasions in life. It seems as though our livelihood from the time we were children to adults was spent planning for activities of interest. Some of our decision-making was voluntary and other times we didn't have a choice.

Let's briefly go back down the road and travel back in time to where preparation was the normal routine. Some of us would go to college to further our education. This decision was voluntary, as most of us were not made to go against our will.

There have been times in life when we were forced to do something that took our free choice away. All of us who went through the draft can relate to this mandatory participation. Our time in the service was because some one else made the decision for us.

Some voluntary situations can have eternal benefits. Our decision to accept or reject Christ will determine if we go to Heaven or Hell. The decision to delay death is not our choice.

We are going to prepare to meet God. Planning on doing something in the future can have devastating results. How many people have said, " I am too busy, I've got plenty of time, don't bother me, I will get saved later."

Let's go all the way to the end of our journey where the preparation plan is almost complete. Throughout life we have had opportunities to make things right with God. Death may be knocking at the door, but there is still time to repent.

Father, help us to realize the days of planning will be over when we are laid in the grave. There is still a little time to get ready. The final sunset of life will disappear into the horizon. It will be too late to make peace with God when there are flowers on the grave, amen.

Search Diligently
October 6

There are many real-life situations where people of all nationalities have been on a mission to find Christ. Their search was not in vain as those who found Him were set free from sin with the promise of everlasting life.

Let's travel the imagination route today so that we can visualize a person seeking Jesus. This young lady wants to meet Him before she departs this life.

Her family members have joined in the search. Her friends and neighbors are also searching diligently to find Jesus before her eyes close in death.

Those who know Jesus as Lord and Savior, they know where to find Him. Our pastor met with us and we went to the hospital. Jesus makes personal visits on a daily basis to minister to our needs.

As we walked into the room, the girl seemed disappointed, as she did not see Jesus with us. The pastor assured her that God is a spirit and those who worship Him must worship in spirit and in truth. "Blessed are they that have not seen, and yet have believed."

This young lady still did not understand. The pastor asked her if she would pray with him the sinner's prayer and she agreed. "Lord Jesus, come into my heart. I believe that you died and rose again. Please forgive me of my sins. I accept you as my Lord and Savior." Right before she died, a smile came over her face; Christ was found just in time.

Father, The reason for this search is that Jesus is the only one who can bring us into a relationship with God, as our Heavenly Father. Oh, that we would be so intent on finding the Savior. He is not very far from any of us. Where can He be found? We will find Him when we search for Him with all of our hearts.

Break the Bonds of Sin
October 7

One dark night the peaceful tranquility of a family would be interrupted by a disastrous situation. There had been a number of break-ins the past couple of weeks.

A man and his wife lived out in the country by themselves. Their children lived in other parts of the state. Later that night a thief had broken into the home.

This couple was awakened by the intruder and confronted him. A fight resulted and the thief subdued the man and his wife. They were tied and left to die.

The mailman came by that day and noticed the glass in a window had been broken. He discovered two people tied up and he released them. Later the thief was caught and arrested.

It is a terrible thing when a thief breaks into homes and takes valuable merchandise. A worse situation is for the people in the house to be bound with strong ropes. There was a possibility of death if they did not receive any help.

Family members rejoiced because their parents were safe. This could have been a terrible tragedy if the mailman did not find the couple.

Let's think about our spiritual journey. We are bound by our own sins. The elderly couple was in a different situation. As a result of the robber's sins, the couple was bound to a chair. Our freedom depends on our cries for mercy. Jesus is the only one who can set us free.

Father, help us to realize we are responsible for the sins we have committed. People from around the world can pray that Christ will break the bonds and set us free. However, if we do not make personal pleas for mercy, our sins will hold us tight. Salvation is on an individual basis with Christ, amen.

A Runner has fallen
October 8

Let's wait a little while longer. We will pass over onto the other side. The glory land is in sight and soon the gates of heaven will open for the redeemed. Our hopes of eternity will materialize when we finish the race and a crown of glory is won. Please don't give up; we are almost home. A warning alert has just been sounded that requires attention.

While running in this race, a runner had fallen. He was so close to the finish line but he was unable to keep going. His injuries were not of the physical kind. A spiritual collapse is worse when we fall from grace.

Personal injuries can be healed with medical care. Sometimes splints and bandages will help to get us back in the race. Occasionally a cast will keep us sidelined for a few months while we receive our healing. The severity of the injury requires different types of treatment.

Some of us stopped running to give assistance to our fellow runner. We helped him to his feet, but our efforts were not sufficient to get him back on life's track. His healing needed a special kind of attention from the throne room above.

Christ normally intervenes to our healing needs. This was a good time for us to have a good Samaratan type experience. Compassion goes a long way to help those who have fallen.

Sins were too many and they were holding him back. We told him about the times in our lives when we too had fallen and God still had mercy on us. This man was revived in spirit and restored to fellowship.

Father, we are in a race and the finish line is just ahead. If one of us happens to fall in the race, it is no disgrace for us to stop and help the person who has fallen. Compassion keeps us from leaving anyone behind, amen.

In God we trust
October 9

We have a very special project that we are going to be working on today. If anyone has any good wood carving tools, please bring them to the woodworking shop. This project will require us to carve a wooden nickel.

Maybe a craft of this sort will give us a better understanding of the words inscribed on the nickel. Hopefully it will cause us to enjoy this craft experience. Our great nation wanted the whole world to know that the United States of America strongly believes, "In God we trust."

It is no secret that some individuals were offended in those words that are on all of our coins. These people tried desperately to have this logo removed, but to no avail. The words remain but what matters the most is our complete reliance in God whom we trust with all of our hearts.

This carving of what seems to be a worthless nickel will develop our creative craft skills and we will realize that we can depend upon God as one who will never let us down and stand beside us throughout life.

There are some very important words engraved on all of our coins and printed on the currency. Let's get started. The first word to be carved is, "Liberty." This refers to our freedom.

Let's move on to some more words, "In God we trust." He is the one who has complete authority and rule over us. "God bless America." Our coins remind us of our personal dependence and our complete trust in God.

Father, this trust we have for you will keep us safe throughout life, no matter what the situation. We will be victorious in battle and peace will prevail as we yield whole heartily to you. A carved nickel is not so worthless when you receive the glory and honor. In Jesus' name, amen.

Life Raft Rescue
October 10

We will need all of our survival skills to make it safely home. A terrible accident would take place causing us to be stranded in the forest.

While leading our horses through the rough terrain, we accidently came upon a grizzly bear. Panic stricken horses bolded in fear and ran away.

One young man was injured by a fall when he was running away from the bear. While lying on the ground, the bear was moving in quickly for the kill. However, one of his friends shot and killed the giant grizzly.

The man who tripped and broke his leg needed immediate attention. He was also suffering from lacerations and other serious injuries. Since the horses were no-where to be found, his hopes of survival were slim, as a trip down the mountainside would kill him.

An old wooden raft was seen in the raging waters below. These men pulled it onto the bank and took the rope and bound the logs tightly together.

This was their only chance to ride the rapids to one of the main base camps. There were times when all of their lives were in danger, but the raft held together and all survived this terrible ordeal. These men would soon be at home with their families.

Father, our spiritual journey in life will find us in need of a rescue. We have sustained many injuries by trying to escape the pursuit of sin. Today is good time to get in the current of God's love and mercy.

Life rafts are good for earthly adventures. However, we will perish in the turbulent waves of sin unless Jesus comes to our rescue. He is waiting for the cries for mercy, amen.

Home Fires Burning
October 11

Recently a friend of mine went on a summer vacation. She had a special request for us to keep the home fires burning. This seemed like a very unusual thing to say because it was in the middle of summer.

It is hard to imagine anyone going out to the shed this time of year and carrying an arm load of wood into the house for a fire. Before we see smoke coming out of the chimney, we need to realize that she was not talking about a real fire. She was implying for us to be actively engaged so that when she returned from her trip, everything would be ready.

If the house was cluttered with unwashed clothes, the floor in need of cleaning, and just an overall look of total disaster, she would utterly be quite disturbed. A new type of fire develops when anger flares-up. Our report today is one of joy because the home fires had not gone out.

We are expecting the Lord to come in the clouds of glory. When He comes will He find the home fires burning and oil in the lantern? There is still a little time to trim the lamp and gather more firewood. Please don't take too long as He might come today. No oil and a fireless faith will not be a welcome sight. The comfort of heaven will be denied.

When the flame is flickering, the fire will not last much longer. If the fire of life is burning low, the faith flame is about to go out, go quickly to the throne room of mercy where there is an abundance of grace.

Father, a strong flame burning is a good indication that we are looking for Christ to come and believing He will very soon. When He returns to earth; will He find home fires burning with faithful stewards watching and praying, actively engaged in holiness, godly living, and righteousness? Add another log on the fire; Jesus is coming, amen.

A Shortcut to Heaven
October 12

Finally, the big day of the race had arrived. Awards and cash prizes would be given at the finish line for first, second, and third place winners. We can be victorious in life if we run with a pure heart, holy, undefiled, and without any evil intentions to cheat along the way.

This was a cross-country marathon and all runners were required to stay on the designated course. However, there were three men in this race that was determined to win, no matter what the consequences.

They were familiar with this area and they knew of a shortcut that would eliminate about half of an hour off of the finish time. Their plan was to start out last and then they could easily disappear from sight and reappear in the front position.

The race has begun and about one hundred men and women were participating. Three men took the detour as planned and then came back into the race at the precise moment. Winners can still be losers.

They had just crossed the finish line to claim all three prizes. The policemen were there to present the awards. All three men received silver metals, bright shiny handcuffs and a special escort to the county jail. It is better to lose a race with respect than to win with no honor.

As we journey towards heaven, there are some shortcut runners in our midst. They use lies to cover up the truth. Cheaters and deceivers will never win an honorary prize.

Father, we need to think about the runners in the race that thought they could win by taking a different route. Handcuffs are bad rewards. There are some people that will try to make it to heaven by some other way than Jesus. Help us to realize a shortcut does not have the benefit of life eternal, amen.

Without Christ
October 13

Our adventure today will take us back in time to a place where settlers were getting a fresh start on life. These pioneers left their old homesteads to travel in covered wagons, which would be their temporary homes on this journey. They did not have the conveniences of modern day heaters. Their only source of heat was from a wood fire.

This is a good time to think about their survival methods while traveling hundreds of miles without a refrigerator or a freezer to keep the food frozen for weeks and months at a time. There were no fast food restaurants, which would be a relief from the daily baked bean routine.

While we are still wondering how they survived without any of our modern conveniences. We must realize that they had to have fresh drinking water for all of their animals and to satisfy the thirst of all the people.

Since we have already seen some of their difficult times in life, this trip back in time would not be complete unless we are aware of their power source. There were no electrical lines to supply electricity. They did not know the meaning of a power outage, as light bulbs had not been invented.

Pioneers made many sacrifices as they traveled across mountains and rough terrain in their quest to begin a new life. Snowstorms and freezing temperatures caused the pioneers to build temporary homes. Even in the worst weather conditions, these brave families continued to press onward.

Father, as we journey towards our home in heaven, we pray that you will give us the same determination as the pioneers to keep going. We must be able to endure hardships in order to make it to the glory land. There are many things we can do without on our journey. None of us can make it to heaven without Christ, amen.

Ashamed because of Drought
October 14

Cloudless skies have plagued the area with many days of a drought. Grief stricken farmers call for a community meeting to discuss the ever-growing problem of despair at the market place where the vegetable baskets are empty. Orchard trees bare no fruit and there are no apple and peach pies to satisfy the ever-increasing hunger pains.

This is probably not a good time to think about dessert, but a little bit of humor keeps us from distressing and worrying ourselves to death. A plea was given for prayer to ascend to the throne room of heaven.

The drought affected everyone's lives in this local community. There was no forecast of rain. Grass has changed from a bright green to a hazy brown. Mechanical equipment is also affected by the lack of rain. Lawnmowers are kept in sheds and fruit trucks or idle in the garage.

Before the farmers closed the meeting, everyone was urged to pray. Something really spectacular began to take place as the residents were down on their knees. This was the first time they prayed in a long time.

God is not slack concerning His promises, "what things so ever ye desire, when ye pray, believe." A small cloud was forming in the distance. The sound of thunder rumbled in the air and everyone ran outside. Dark clouds hovered above and it began to rain. Soon the lakes were full and the streams flowing again. The orchard is thriving and fresh vegetables abound.

Father, the grass is green and the sound of lawnmowers is in the air. A fresh apple pie is in the oven. We think about our earthly desires, while our souls are lacking for prayer. We should be ashamed because it took a drought to bring us to our knees. Help us to keep the prayer lines open, amen.

Stir up the Coals
October 15

Coals that have not been turned in a while will cause us to have suspicions of doubt. There is no evidence of a fire until the coals are turned over.

Embers that are still active will have a dull red glow. Stir up the coals and discover the fire is still alive. A passionate fire is burning and everyone in the room can feel its effects.

When we see all the people shivering and trying to get warm, we would probably agree, there is no fire. If our hands were cold and we had to wear coats on the inside of the house, the evidence would show a fireplace that had grown cold.

Let's all walk over to the coals and see if we see anything that reveals life. While we were standing there, no flames were burning until one person took a poker and stirred the coal.

Immediately red sparks flew into the air and they slowly faded away. Then we all saw the bright embers beneath the coals. After a few minutes, the flames were burning higher and more lumps of coal were added. Now we have a really nice fire.

A small spark is all that is needed to rekindle a cold lifeless fire. As the flame begins to grow, stir the coal a little more. Soon flames will be higher and our faith will actively remove all doubt. If flames are not activated, it is impossible to please God until the fire is burning.

Father, sometimes there is doubt if our fire of faith is alive. If it has been a while since the coals of belief have been active, move them around. It won't be long before the shivering effect is gone and lives will feel the radiance of a new flame aglow.

Let's revive the flames so a glorious light will shine and others will feel the warmth of God's love. If the coal is not turned, the fire will die. Help us to keep the flame of our hearts alive.

Unload the Wagon
October 16

Several years ago, wagons and horses were used to transport the produce to the markets. Farmers have been working in the fields, getting ready for the trip to town.

This is probably the best watermelon season they have had in a long time. Those who work hard enjoy the benefits of their labors and are able to provide for their families.

After the wagon was loaded we realized that it was too much weight for the horses to pull up the steep incline. It requires more effort to climb a mountain.

We were afraid the horses would be overly burdened and would be injured in the process. Soon another wagon was loaded and we were ready to begin our trip to the market. Safety precautions allows for future benefits.

It was a peaceful day, as the farmers rode down the dusty road enjoying the scenery. The horses were still pulling a heavy load, but it was easier for them to get over the mountain because of the weight distribution.

This would be a good time for us to prepare for a journey to heaven. We will be traveling across the hills and through the valleys. Sins will prevent us from living holy lives and will keep us out of heaven.

It is time to lighten the load. Jesus bore the weight of our sins on His shoulders at Calvary. Since He took the burden and set us free, there are no sins to carry.

Father, we know that if we keep carrying the weight of sin, there is no way we will be able to cross over onto the shores of eternity. Let's unload the wagon for eternal profits. If we are so determined to carry a heavy weight, why not let it be a cross that can be exchanged for a crown? Amen

All is well with my Soul
October 17

Recently a weather report was given on a broadcasting station about a terrible storm forming with the possibility of snow, sleet, and freezing rain. Warnings were given constantly over the airwaves to alert the people of the danger.

These weather predictions were expected to affect most of the East coast. This was really bad news for all the people who had to travel in these awful conditions. Tractor-trailer drivers who had to make deliveries were at a greater risk of injury.

There has been many times when traffic was backed up for miles because an eighteen-wheeler could not get enough traction to get over the mountain. A worse situation is when the truck is coming down the mountain and the vehicle begins to slide, causing the trailer to jackknife.

We do not always have the opportunity to stay at home. One young man was driving a big rig, returning from a delivery. He was many miles from home on slick roads. His wife and children were constantly looking out the window, praying that he would get home safely.

Family members became very worried when that heard a tractor and trailer slid off the side of the road and overturned. Reporters were on the scene and they showed a picture of the wreck on TV.

It was the young man's mangled vehicle. He called home and His wife answered the phone, expecting to hear the tragic news. Her husband spoke and said he was all right.

Father, there are times in life when we are warned about the hazardous conditions of sin. Heaven or Hell is our choice. Our response is to accept or reject Christ. Hopefully at the end of our journey each of us will say, "All is well with my soul." In Jesus' name, amen.

Wait on the Lord
October 18

It was a beautiful day as the hikers followed the trail through the mountains. A young couple was lagging behind the group when they strayed from the hiking trail, as they failed to see the guide marker.

Darkness of night is not a good time to be wandering through the mountain, as there are many unforeseen hazards that will cause injury or even death.

The sun had already set on the horizon and it was pitch dark. All of the other hikers had made it safely to their destination and they set up camp for the night. After a short while the camp leader noticed the two missing teenagers.

Early that morning a forest ranger brought a couple of bloodhounds for the search. After several hours of walking through the mountains, the dogs picked up the scent and were hot on the trail. The couple was found with cuts and bruises they received when they fell down a steep slope.

This couple spent the night in a shelter and waited patiently for a rescue. It did not take them very long to realize they might not get out of the mountains alive. Despite their fears, there were high hopes of being found by a rescue team.

Let's go back to the camp now that these two individuals were found. Occasionally we will find ourselves in a situation that requires us to wait until help arrives like these two hikers. Rescue is on the way, but we have to wait a little while longer.

Father, when there is an emergency, the responders will get there faster. We have many life or death situations that require immediate attention. The moment we cry out to God, His Son comes to the rescue. Help us to realize if we want to be saved, we need to stop running away. If we wait on the Lord, the rescue attempt will be successful, amen.

Stay on Course
October 19

Our adventures will take us to many wonderful places. We are going to be sailing across the ocean and each of us will be in our own vessel of life. This is a personal journey that will reveal our leadership skills. The position we fill will be of captains and our objective will be to stay on course.

Let's begin our voyage across the wild blue yonder. Sails have been unraveled and the anchor is back on deck. A strong wind is blowing. It will not be long till we cross over to the other side, provided we stay on course.

There are many things along the way that will interfere with our eternal plans. Pleasure seeking towns will try to lure us into corrupt situations. It is really sad, but we have already lost many in the fatal waters of unrighteousness. Keep going and resist evil temptations.

Remember we must stay on course and be on time. Those who have turned aside have to catch up. But first they have to forsake all sinful conditions. It is good to know that if we ended up on the islands of remorse, we might get back to a safe route if we live long enough. Death causes us to evaluate our plans.

Let's say there are survivors and the captain waved the flag of truce. He would once again be on the correct route to heaven. It is really dangerous when we veer off course. There is no guarantee that we will make it safely back into the current of God's love. This time pleas for mercy were accepted.

Father, it is better that we stay focused on the shore of eternity. We are crossing the ocean blue. If we keep our eyes on Jesus, heaven will be our reward.

We are just about home. Soon we will be rejoicing as we step on heaven's shore. Stay on course in life and at the end of our journey we can say, "Thank God we made it." Amen.

Don't Give Up
October 20

A baby bird had fallen from the tree to the ground. It had not yet learned how to fly. Evidently the small wings were able to create enough motion to briefly defy gravity for a safe landing.

Actually, there is no way the bird could survive a fall from limbs in the top of a tree. Perhaps we should change a fall to a whirly bird descent with a shaky landing.

Another problem seemed to exist, as the nest we thought the bird fell from was actually closer to the ground. How is this little bird going to get back into the nest for the next training session in flight aviation?

This little fellow had already learned a very important lesson. We can excel to higher heights when we learn how to rise up when we are down.

Nature has a way of overcoming obstacles. We are going to speed up the process with a person gently placing the bird back into the nest. The mother bird with her aggressive flight behavior interrupted our efforts. Finally the small bird was back in the protective custody of its flight instructor.

We thought the bird was in danger, when it could have been the first flying lesson. Sometimes we interfere with nature and slow the learning process down. A bird that seems to be immobile flies high into the sky.

Father, help us to learn that our endeavors in life may be unsuccessful at first. A little more encouragement can have us claiming the victory. We think about the little bird that had a difficult landing.

A give up attitude will keep us from soaring above the situation. Several attempts at accomplishing our goals are not reasons to quit. Perseverance helps us claim the crown, amen.

Grace does not exalt
October 21

Our journey in life will have us fulfilling different positions. Some will be lawyers who have dedicated their lives to defending or prosecuting victims.

These officials search for the truth. They will spend their lives in courtrooms, resolving personal problems, criminal offenses, and different types of lawsuits. This type of work requires long hours of preparing and gathering material to present to the jury for a verdict.

Colleges offer a variety of educational programs. Some of the students have chosen a career as lawyers. These individuals made a personal choice as to their type of employment. This position of seeking justice can be very distressful if the lawyer's client is found guilty and will have to die.

Lawyers go to college for several years and then have to pass a bar exam. Some of these individuals have spent thousands of dollars to go to law school. Those who are able to go into the profession usually make enough money to pay off their mortgages and financial obligations.

Successful careers will find these men and women with beautiful homes, living in nice neighborhoods, and driving the most expensive cars.

Father, we need to realize that some of the lawyers were not able to pass the bar exam. The same amount of money was spent for their college education, as it was for the successful lawyers. Those who failed the test will not be accepted in any type of lawyer activity.

When it comes to the salvation of our souls, we all have the same eligibility rating. It does not matter if we are rich or poor. We have the same benefit of forgiveness when we accept Christ. Grace does not exalt one person over another, amen.

Steadfast like a Tree
October 22

The storm is over and the old tree is still standing. Down through the ages in all kinds of turbulent weather, the forces of nature could not make it yield.

Today the tree stands strong with roots in the ground; they go deep into the earth and hold fast to rocks. Its strength comes from beneath the earth with roots that hold like anchors.

Severe storms have lifted houses from their foundations. However, a tall oak only anchored to the ground by an overlay of roots is still standing. The house is completely demolished by the strong winds.

This old tree withstood the rage of many storms and still stands steadfast, unmovable, it defies the elements with enduring strength.

Once it was a little thing, swaying in the wind. The storms came with a vengeance, but they could not loosen the hold of this young tree. Over the years it continued to grow without wavering or falling in defeat.

The tree stands strong in the field with limbs of praise to the creator for all the victories won. A tree is an example of endurance and steadfastness.

Father, oh, that we would become as strong as the tree with our lives grounded and settled in Jesus. Help us to understand that endurance is the strength of our souls that will never let go no matter how severe the situation. If the force is greater than our resistance, we grip the Savior's hand tighter and hold on for dear life.

Our strength is in Jesus who endured the worst storm when He gave His life on a cross. Let's praise Him with arms lifted high and give thanks for His amazing grace, amen.

Force the Door Open
October 23

Let's take an imaginary trip to the country where an accident took place inside of a home. One person was hurt from a fall and needed medical attention. Hopefully he would be found before it was too late.

An elderly man, John was taking care of the farm. He lived by himself out in the country. A friend of his came by every once in a while, to visit with him and share the events of the day.

Jim drove up to the house and saw John's old truck parked in front of the farm. While they were together, John talked about Jesus standing at the door, wanting to come into our lives.

They always had a good conversation and the two would part company. The Holy Spirit had brought conviction upon John, but he would not ask Jesus to come into his heart.

One day John was inside of his home, painting the ceiling when all of a sudden, the stepladder shifted and he fell to the floor. No one was there to help him. Jim just happened to come by for a visit.

He heard the cries for help from inside the house. Jim responded quickly by calling out to John and then he forced the door open, ran up the stairs to help his injured friend.

When John was released from the hospital his friend met with him again. Somehow the conversation went back to the locked door and how that force was used to save him.

Father, Jesus is knocking at the door; He will not force His way into anyone's life. The Holy Spirit was drawing John again, but this time he opened the door of his heart and accepted Christ into his life as Lord and Savior. Help us to realize that Jesus hears our cries for mercy. This is the open door for us to make peace with God. In Jesus' name, amen.

316

A Light on a Hill at Night
October 24

On a cold wintry night an airplane was flying over the mountains and the plane crashed. Four passengers and a pilot were on board when it went down. Everyone survived the crash. These victims would require medical attention.

Those who were monitoring this plane crash new the exact location of the plane before it lost altitude and disappeared from the radar screen. No one knew how far the plane flew before the crash occurred.

Meanwhile the flight victims left the damaged aircraft and went to search for a shelter to keep from freezing to death in the bitter cold temperatures. Soon a cave was found where the victims would stay.

A box of matches was found in the emergency pack. Although hands were cold and numb, finally matches were lit and a small fire was burning in the cave.

First Responders were dispatched to the crash sight. Helicopters flew overhead but the crew could not see the people in the cave or the fire that was hid from view.

These victims would die unless a fire could be started on the hill. Helicopters were circling the area again and this time the crew spotted the fire and made the rescue.

Father, you have already given us a warning in the Bible about hiding our light in under a bushel. We can relate this to the survival in the cave. A light that is hid will not help those who are searching and there is no benefit if no one can find us.

This rescue was a success because two fires were burning, one in the cave for warmth and the other outside as a signal. Let the warmth of God's love in us be a light shining for those who are lost. In Jesus' name, amen.

Dream-Catchers
October 25

While working on the farm, sometimes we have to go on errands to the mall. We have a supply list of all the things that are needed. The buckboard wagon is ready to roll.

This is our regular shopping time. All of the needful things for daily living will be purchased on this trip to town. The want-a-bee's will remain on hold until wishful thinking becomes a dream-catcher or a reality replacement.

Today is Ralph's birthday and the family has decided on the gift they want to buy him. So Amy and Jill headed toward the hardware store. A nice plow was in the building next to the display window. The cost was too high for a purchase.

However, the store clerk was a kindhearted fellow with a generous heart. He reduced the price to a non-profit sale. Occasionally emotions outrank business endeavors.

Ralph would be really surprised and overjoyed with this new piece of hardware. Since his old plow was worn out and broken down, this new one would be a great replacement.

We cannot even imagine the joy when Amy and Jill took their father to the barn and showed him this brand-new plow. Overflowing with heartfelt thankfulness, he broke down in tears and hugged his children.

Father, your grace always abounds and all of our needs are met according to your riches in glory. Blessings come to us on a daily basis. We know windows of heaven are always open for our eternal profits.

When we have a desirable list, God is also compassionate in His giving for His adopted children. Please don't be surprised if He helps us become dream-catchers of our heart's desire. In Jesus' name, amen.

Goliath and David
October 26

We are going to go back in time to a major battle where a giant will be fighting against a youth to the death. David is the person who will be fighting Goliath. The outcome will prove that there is a living God who is able to deliver.

This is certainly not a fair fight. These brave warriors will not be in a cage with a wire mesh enclosure like a wrestling arena. Championship belts will not be given for the one who defeats the other man in battle.

There will not be any bells ringing on the sideline to control the time and duration of the fight. One thing is for sure death will be the final outcome. War cries from the giant seem to echo throughout the valley.

I suppose this battle will be considered a no-holds-barred or anything goes in this death match. The giant will have all the military accessories of a man of war. Practically his whole body will be covered from head to toe with steel plated armor.

Let's take a brief look at his opponent, David. He is not big in stature like the giant. There is no heavy armor that will protect him from an aggressive attack.

His frail body is unprotected from a man yielding a sword. This battle seemed to be impossible for David to win. We must realize he was not defenseless because God was on his side.

Five smooth stones were taken from the creek and now both men were prepared for war. One stone from David's slingshot and Goliath the warrior was dead.

Father, help us to realize that our battles will be fought and won if we go in the name of the Lord of host. If we stand alone without God, we will not be standing very long. Our God whom we serve is able to deliver, amen.

Big I and Little you
October 27

The battle between Goliath and David has helped multitudes of people down through the ages be victorious in many types of battles. We recently learned that if we try to accomplish things by our own strength, we would fail. Jesus has promised to go with us all the way. There is no good reason to fight alone.

This is a good time for us to enter another war with the same two characters, Goliath and David. We will refer to the giant as the "Big I" and David will be the "Little you." This is a war where the giant with all of his pride thinks he is stronger than his opponent David who has humility.

Let us look at the profile of these two opponents. The first one is the giants profile; he is a man of war from his youth. He is a man that takes pride in his size and strength. His main features are arrogance, conceit, and superiority. We call him the "Big I," and he is looking down at this youth-humility with disgust and he would like to crush the little you.

The second one appears to be weaker in strength. He is just a youth, not even old enough to be in the military. His qualities are meekness, gentleness, and kindheartedness. This little you will represent humility.

I know there are spectators among us that are wondering if this is a real battle with bloodshed and the loss of lives. Who would send a boy to war? In a few minutes we will find that one opponent will die on the battlefield. I's may be bigger and more in number, but less in power.

Father, the war was about to be decided by these two individuals. The "Little you" approached the "Big I" and killed him with a stone to the forehead. This is a good time to realize that it is better to have humility than pride. I wish I were more like you. In Jesus' name, amen.

Let the Lifeboats go
October 28

A ship out at sea was taking on water and sinking rapidly. The men on board feared for their lives as turbulent water splashed over the ship's side.

All of the people on board would be saved, but they had to let go of the lifeboats. Since it was Paul who told them to release the boats, they obeyed this man of God.

Lifeboats drifted away and planks from the ship were floating in the water. Some of the men were holding onto pieces of the wrecked vessel, struggling to get to shore.

Finally, they made it, and the people on land took care of them. The promise came true, as no one lost his life. Shelter and food was also given to the survivors.

The lifeboats of our sinful lives let them go, or we will crash on the rocks of destruction. If we refuse we will suffer the consequences of sin.

Sometimes we have to let go of our self-sufficiency before we will trust God to deliver us. Take hold of His hand. Soon we will be on heaven's shore.

Think about this thought for just a moment. We are in a perilous sea with the possibility of losing our lives. The only thing that can save us is a lifeboat. Paul received orders from God to release the boats.

Father, our only hope of surviving is now drifting out to sea. Without these lifeboats to save us we will surely die. Reliance in our own abilities is not God's way of deliverance.

We can be saved if we yield whole heartily in obedience to His divine plan. He is our only hope. If we keep holding onto sin, what is our profit if we are cast into Hell? Let go of sin, amen.

Sparks from a Propane Torch
October 29

The home is a desolate place when the water stops flowing, no fresh water to drink. Dirty laundry keeps piling up and the closets have empty hangers.

Sinks are full of grimy pans. When tragedy strikes we have to make a few changes or adjustments to allow for the inconveniences in our lives.

It was on a cold wintry day when this disaster took place. My home was not the only one affected by this calamity. There were many unfortunate victims in the neighborhood. Freezing temperatures with wind chill factors well below zero created a dangerous environment.

Sometimes we have to go outside in the bitter cold and thaw out the pipes with some type of heating source. A propane torch is very dangerous because the flame beneath the pipe is actually sending up sparks into the wood. If we drive away, we may return to a house fire.

Pipes thaw out and we go inside the home, thinking everything is all right. Before we fall asleep, we smell smoke and immediately head outside to the frozen pipe area. Tiny sparks had developed into a flame. Fortunately, our lives were saved; we were able to put out the fire.

Father, there are many situations that will put our lives in danger. If we don't take necessary actions to prevent these terrible disasters, it will be too late to call the fire department when the house is burnt down.

We need to be aware that sin can be like those small sparks from a propane torch. These little sins are not harmful; there is no need to worry about them. This is a false delusion because sin draws us closer to the fire. It would be far better if we were drawn closer to God by faith in Christ, amen.

Meet at the Crossroads
October 30

A special meeting is planned for today. It is not very hard to find this place. When we tell someone else about a certain location, we try to point out the best way and the shortest route. Normally our instructions will include road signs, traffic signals, and local or interstate highways.

Our directions are as precise as we can remember them. Even though we are familiar with the area it is still easy to give misguided information. We don't realize the error until the person has already driven away.

While they are leaving a guilt complex suddenly overshadows us as we realize a false statement will interfere and disrupt their travel plans.

We think about those times in life when we needed someone to help us find a hospital, or a medical facility that offers a certain type of treatment. After receiving instructions, we would proceed to the designated place. It is always a relief when we arrive on time, especially for a hospital appointment.

We are going to meet at the crossroad of life. This is where decisions are made to either accept or reject Christ. Please pay attention because we do not want anyone to be lost, as this will be a very costly mistake.

There may be some concerns about the travel arrangements. Since this invitation is to meet at the crossroad we do not need an airplane or any other transportation vehicles, as this will be a personal journey. Let's cancel all flights, voyages, and any other means of transportation.

Father, I am thankful this is not a road trip because too many of us would have difficulty finding the correct location. Actually, there is no travel whatsoever. A decision for Christ can be made wherever we are receptive to God's mercy, amen.

Follow Jesus
October 31

We need to be careful whom we follow on the pathway of life. Many lives have been swayed by the influence of actors, movie stars, and professional entertainers.

Deception makes its way down through the channels of the wealthy and the poor. Leaving a trail of discouragement, disillusioned lives, and a distorted view of a real-life image hid behind the walk of fame.

It is possible that we will imitate a special character on TV and pick up some habits that will cause bodily harm later in life. Occasionally the false impressions of someone's life will lead us astray.

Passion to be like a-make-believe-star is like following a dream that quickly fades out of sight. The final results will be a starless crown and empty pockets.

Movie stars are some of the most influential people in leading others astray. Recently I heard about a famous person who died from an overdose.

A short while later, her young daughter followed the same course of action. We are sorry for them, and we are fearful of the followers who are walking in their very same footsteps.

Father, the best choice we can make in life is to follow the Son of God. Jesus will never lead us astray or give us a false impression. There is nothing fake about Him; He is the Christ, the Savior of the world.

Those who follow Him will not walk in darkness but will walk in the light and we will have the hope of life eternal. A decision to follow Christ will be without regrets. There will be no deception and our lives will reflect His image of holiness and godly living. Where He leads, we will follow, amen.

Fox in the Henhouse
November 1

Recently a storm with strong winds came through the area, causing a considerable amount of damage. Trees were down and some of the windows were broken from the flying debris.

During this cleanup process, another problem developed that was a real mystery. One of the hired employees met Bill in the driveway and told him about the disappearance of several of the chickens. Also, a lot of the eggs were destroyed.

Days went by and there were no disturbances in the barnyard. Bill called off the visual search and the farmhands returned to their daily routine. Disgruntled neighbors who did not have eggs for breakfast went back to their homes to wait for new laying hens to fill the menu.

After a while the criminal activity continued and the villain always left clues on the floor of the hen house. There would be broken eggshells and chicken feathers lying all around. No one noticed the broken window in the henhouse, which the egg snatcher used as an entry and escape route.

One day the culprit trapped himself in the fence. This would be his last free meal. All of those delicious chicken meals increased the size of the fox. He became so big that he could not get through the small hole in the perimeter fence.

The fox was able to escape for a brief length of time. He was fed daily and the chickens were the ones that suffered the most. Well the farmers were also hurt by the fox's appetite. This was a loss of revenue in the sale of eggs and Chickens.

Father, many lives are affected by sins that creep into our lives like a wily fox. Our own sins will be the ones that affect us the most and we will have to suffer the penalty. Little sins grow into larger ones, which will prevent an escape unless we repent. In Jesus' name, amen.

Endure the Trials
November 2

The mountains are covered with snow and ice crystals hang on the trees. Fallen limbs are scattered on the ground. These are miserable conditions for people living in the mountains or traveling on the highways. Slick roads are very hazardous for driving conditions.

Let's take an imaginary trip to a time when a father was on his way home from work with sad news for his family. His job was terminated. He was laid off from his place of employment with about three hundred other employees.

This was bad news with Christmas just around the corner. It looked like the shelves would be bare, as there would not be any money for groceries. Steve's wife and three children would not have any presents this year and this family would probably be homeless.

While driving home on slippery roads, he lost control of his car and slid over an embankment, crashing into a tree. When he awoke from being knocked unconscious. Steve was really surprised that he had only suffered minor injuries.

There was only one way that Steve might make it safely home and that was for him to walk all the way. A strong determination and a resolve to not turn back, kept him going until he was at home with his family.

We are on a heavenly journey, enduring the trials of life. Faith in Christ motivates us to press onward. Soon our trials will be over and we will exchange them for a crown. There is no turning back to our old sinful ways.

Father, Help us to realize there will be many trials, but we can make it home if we are persistent in our heavenly endeavors. Take one step at a time and soon we will be walking the streets of glory. In Jesus' name, amen.

Sneak out the Backdoor
November 3

Mountains have fresh snow and the ski slopes are already open. After driving all day, we finally arrived at the lodge. During the night, the snow continued to fall.

Mother nature was generous in her efforts to make sure the sports enthusiast was not lacking for snow. She may have made a mistake because there was too much snow accumulation. It is unusual for a ski resort to be closed.

There were four of us in our group and we were warned not to go out into the snow, three of the men sneaked out the back door and started up the mountain on the faded trail.

None of them had snowshoes so they could walk on the snow. Somewhere along the way, they got off the trail and were knee-deep in snow. No one was there to help. The temperature was dropping; these men could freeze to death.

Back at the cabin, the fourth man had told the resort owner and soon a rescue unit was searching for the three men. Finally, the men were found and they were barely alive. They were rescued just in time.

We have been warned about the effects of sin. Some people are sneaking out the back door, thinking that they will not be caught. However, sin has a way of tracking us down.

Sin is not just a sneaky occurrence that will just happen in privacy. When we told the ski resort owner that we would stay inside. One little lie would develop into many more and put us in danger of losing our lives.

Father, warnings are given to keep us from suffering the consequences of sin. It does not matter if it is private or public. Sin keeps us out of heaven. Forgiveness releases us from the penalty of hell. Thank you, Jesus, amen.

Life Expectancy
November 4

Life expectancy, who can count the days, how long on earth will we stay? Each of us has a different lifespan. A few years or many it is not in our control. A chart is displayed that shows the approximate age that we will die, or how long we will live.

We are not interested in insurance policies right now, as there is something far more important than the money that is distributed to our heirs. Our main concern is what happens to us after we die. Let's take a quick look at our lifespan. A small child or an adult will not be turned away from funeral arrangements.

A coffin is made in all sizes for all nationalities. Gravesites will accommodate small children, adults, and even the rich and poor. We are just passing through; our time on earth is limited. All the good we can do, we had better do it before we die. There will not be any more opportunities after death.

Let's not waste any more time; we will not pass this way again. Our existence here is only temporary. We will not be granted an extension to prolong our lives into the future. Live for today, tomorrow may never come. It is time to stop worrying about when life on earth will be over.

Father, we are just passing through a temporary lifespan to one that is eternal. The gates of heaven will open wide for the believers. We will be rewarded for our kindness. Life on earth is short compared to eternity. Before life ends we should have already made peace with God.

When we depart this world by death, our eternal resolutions by faith must be accepted before we die. Since none of us actually knows the date of our departure, a prearranged agreement is made with Christ for our heavenly concerns. Pleas for mercy are acceptable and we will be reimbursed with everlasting life. In Jesus' name, amen.

Jail Time
November 5

Several years ago, a young man had a bad habit of visiting the county jail. It was more like free room and board. He didn't come voluntarily to see anyone special.

Most of the time it was for minor offences like fighting or disorderly conduct. Randy would usually stay a day or two in jail and after he sobered up, the sheriff would let him make one call. This jail visit usually occurred on Saturday nights.

The crimes seemed to be getting worse and jail time was even longer. Tom and Mary would not give up on their son. Every night they prayed for him and on Sundays requested prayer.

We can't always see the results of our prayers for our loved ones to be saved. Let's patiently wait while the Holy Spirit brings conviction and guilt of sin.

One night the phone rang at Tom and Mary's home, they expected the worst. It was Randy on the other end and he told them they would never have to come and get him again. While he was in jail, Jesus saved him.

When Christ comes into our hearts, there will not be any more jail time, unless we are visiting other inmates to tell them about God's mercy. The jail cell incident was imaginary to help us think about real life events.

It is always terrible news in our lives if we hear that our children are locked up. Our immediate response is to go to the sheriff's office and pay the bail. Sometimes family members will have to stay all night behind bars.

Father, as sinners we are also guilty of many offences. We don't have to be in a jail cell before you will help us. The cries of a repentant heart will not go unanswered. Let's make the call that will change our lives for eternity, amen.

Shelter of His Love
November 6

Frank and his wife Jane had gathered resource material so they could plan a vacation in the mountains. The place chosen was in the Shenandoah National Park.

This would be a good time for Frank to try out his new camera. Photography was one of his favorite hobbies. Jane loved everything about nature. She wouldn't pass up an opportunity to add driftwood to her collection.

The planning was over as tents had been set up in the park where other tourists were camping. Frank and Jane woke up earth in the morning to go hiking through the mountains. They checked in with the recreational department, as a precaution in case they got lost in the mountains.

Before they left the park, instructions were given for them to not stray very far from the trail, as this would create a safety hazard. Well Frank and Jane couldn't resist the temptation of a mountain stream photo with blue skies. After a while the marked trail was nowhere to be found.

While walking through the woods, a bear and cub appeared suddenly from the brush. The mother bear quickly became aggressive to protect her cub. She stood on her hind legs and was growling furiously.

Frank and Jane were now running away from the bear. Their only hope of survival was to cross a narrow swing-bridge to a shelter on the other side. They survived the attack.

Father, when you look down from heaven, may you find all of your adopted children walking on the straight and narrow path, following Jesus. Let's immediately seek shelter in Christ where we will be kept safe from any impending danger. If any of us have gone astray and we cannot find the trail, cries for mercy will be answered from above. In Jesus' name, amen.

See You in the Morning
November 7

The saddest words are spoken at the end of life's journey. Tears roll down the cheeks of the parents as they say goodbye for the last time to a wonderful son or daughter. Whether it is a loved one or a close friend, the pain is unbearable.

There seems to be no end to the sorrow. It takes a long time for grieving hearts to heal. A love chain is temporally broken, but only for a short length of time. Strong bonds of love cannot be separated by death.

The affections of our hearts never die. We think about the wonderful times in life when various activities drew family members together. Precious memories follow us on our journey. Bringing back the joyful times of life when a loved companion was standing close by our sides.

All those who knew and loved the deceased offer their condolences. The Pastor comes by to offer his sincere sympathy and to lead the family in prayer. "Our Father and our God, we come into your holy presence in the name of Jesus Christ.

We pray that you will lay your holy hand upon the family. Comfort their hearts and give them peace. Hold them close to you with a loving embrace. Bind each one together with the blessed hope of being united again in heaven, in Jesus name, amen." We will meet loved ones again in just a little while.

Life comes with unexpected announcements that will leave a trail of tears. A loved one is at the end of life's journey. This departure brings grief to the family. Sorrow is for a season, but joy comes in the morning.

Goodbye is one of the saddest words on earth. We are not going to let that word be the final closure of a dying loved one. As we stand beside them in the final hours of life, emotional words are said, "See you in the morning."

Grace compels us to win
November 8

The athletes from around the world have gathered on the track. Everyone is waiting in anticipation for this sporting event to begin. Men and women take the starting position and wait earnestly for the signal.

After a while some of the participants are lagging behind. They are running at a slower pace and a few of them have dropped out of the competition to win the prize.

Some runners cannot win because they are now carrying a heavy burden. Various situations affect our running abilities. Something in the past may have resurfaced causing the runners to lose their enthusiasm and determination to win.

A word of encouragement is given to help those who are thinking about giving up and dropping out of the race completely. The past tries to interfere with our endeavors. But if we concentrate on the things before us, the memories will fade and we will be victorious in life.

The glory crown is just ahead; keep running to the finish line. Never turn back to the old sinful ways. It is really hard to win a race if we are looking back and not forward. Let's cast all sins aside and run to win.

Those who quit have fallen from grace and feel like they cannot finish the course. It's not too late to get back in the race. Winners will be awarded the crown of life. We may not be able to catch the runner in front of us. However, we can still claim the prize of life eternal. There will be many winners.

Father, Life in Christ is the blessed hope of going to heaven. We are running for the glory crown. If by chance the cross is laid down, a fresh supply of grace compels us to lift up the cross. This renewed energy revives our faltering spirits so we can win. In Jesus' name, amen.

Tragedy at the Circus
November 9

Recently there were flyers being posted throughout the community, telling us about a circus that was coming to town. TV stations and radio programs were making the announcements. This was a yearly event.

We were looking forward to this traveling road show. It seemed as though everyone in town was excited and couldn't wait to see the circus performers using their special abilities to entertain the crowd. The third day there was an accident.

Thousands of people went to the circus that day. A terrible tragedy took place in the arena, as nine acrobats were injured from a fall. The apparatus that was holding them broke loose.

These professional entertainers were not using a net. They fell about thirty or forty feet to the ground. The injured were rushed to the hospital for medical attention.

There are some things in life that we would trust to hold us, especially if we commit our lives to them. The acrobats felt like the metal framework was trustworthy. They did not have any doubts about this metal structure holding them.

It is possible that strong chains were also used to support the apparatus. The circus was closed until an investigation would reveal the cause of this tragedy.

There are many situations in life where we have to hold on until someone can rescue us. The object we choose may not be the best choice, but if it is a matter of life or death, we will take whatever is available.

Father, when it comes to spiritual matters there is a possibility of us falling from grace. The best way to keep this from happened is to keep holding the Savior's hand. His strong grip will keep us from falling, amen.

A Wild Man's New Life
November 10

Today we are going to visit a real-life character that was known by his violent nature. We don't know anything about how he lived after his encounter with Christ. Let's travel down the imagination highway and spend some time with this man so that we will get to know him better.

He was well known around town and throughout the community. All of his neighbors spoke well of him and the little children loved to be with him. A day would not go by without him helping someone along the way. No matter if it was a little child or an elderly person, he loved each one and was always doing good deeds. Godly living touches many lives.

Every Sunday he would be at church worshiping and praising God. We just imagined the life of this man after he met Christ. Let's see what kind of man he was before he met Jesus. Please don't hold the past against him and use it to dishonor and discredit his good behavior. Once we reveal his name, please don't go and get the kids and hide in fear.

His name was Legion because he had many devils. No one wanted to be around him for he was a wild man. Little children were scared of him and the people would go out of their way to avoid being in his presence.

He didn't live in a house, but in tombs. They bound him with chains and he would break the fetters. Jesus cast the unclean spirits out of the man and gave him a new life. Ungodly living is replaced with holiness.

Father, it is a blessed day in our lives when Jesus walks by and touches us. He gives us peace and forgives our sins. Our wild sinful nature is replaced with loving-kindness. Sometimes we need to go back in time and think about our deliverance. We need to recall how we lived before we met Jesus. Let's thank Him for giving us a new life, Thank you, Jesus, amen.

Veterans' Day
November 11

This is a special time in our lives when we honor the veterans of our great country, America. These brave men and women answered the call to serve in a variety of positions. We think about hospitals where patients were treated for their wounds.

Their call to active duty could only be filled with love and compassion. Many long hours were spent at the bedside of severely injured patients fighting to stay alive.

Medical care was not restricted to buildings inside a secure area, as there were mobile units that would travel with convoys into battle. Another place for these emergency care providers was on the front lines in the heat of the battle. Their calling was not to fight but to heal.

Veterans day is a time to honor all those who served. We all needed one another in order to survive. There was no position without honor. Whether in war with bullets flying all around, or in a medical unit, caring for the wounded, our fight for freedom was the same.

Men and women across the land have answered the call to fight against hostile forces. These brave soldiers have left homes and families behind, little children crying as their parents went to war. Days turn into years on the battlefield.

The call for service is one we cannot deny for it is our patriotic duty to defend or die. Our love for country compels us to answer the call to fight for freedom.

Father, we hold in our hearts deep respect, love, and the utmost appreciation for our men and women of the armed forces. America is the greatest country on earth because of the sacrifices made by true patriots who fought in the past and for those who are fighting today. Honor is given with respect to the Veterans. In Jesus' name, amen.

How much do you love me?
November 12

We have a very important question that each of us would like to ask Jesus. "How much do you love me?" They say that actions speak louder than words. Jesus dyed on a cross.

Listen very closely and maybe we will hear the crack of the whip that brought lacerations to His body. He was beaten with a whip (a cat of nine tails) thirty-nine times. Many of the victims died before they even got to the cross.

Jesus, God's beloved Son was placed on the cross with His arms spread wide. This can be interpreted as a loving embrace to show how much we are loved. The depth of Christ love required His blood to be spilled.

Sounds of a hammer are heard in the distance as nails are driven into His hands and feet. Love in action can be heard around the world as Jesus was crucified and died for our sins.

A crown of thorns piercing His brow has no sound effect except for the moans from the suffering of Jesus in excruciating agony. Blood was flowing from His wounds.

Some people would say that no one cares about us. Our response would be that they had never met Jesus. His love brings us into fellowship with God.

Father, let's return to the question we asked in the beginning. "How much do you love me?" Let's go back in time and see how the answer is revealed. He was beaten with a whip. A crown of thorns was forced upon His brow. Spikes were driven into His hands and feet.

He stayed on the cross because He loved us. We asked a personal question. The arms of Jesus were spread wide on the cross. "This much, and He died for us." Receive from Him a loving embrace, amen.

Distorted Vision of Home
November 13

A journey in life will have us traveling from one place to another. Sometimes we will be on company business where we will be flying high in the clouds. Interesting things on the earth have caught our attention.

Looking down from above, we see a panoramic scene, as if we were viewing an image through a 3D mirror. Everything is out of proportion.

Another course of action has us taking a trip on a cruise ship. We will be traveling on the deep blue sea, admiring the beautiful scenery along the way. The view is different than our flight across the blue skies.

Our vision reveals everything from an artist perspective. Each picture captures the imaginations of our hearts with shoreline excitement. A water crest disappears on shore, highlighting the trees with a beautiful array of colors, red, orange, and yellow. As much as we would like to stay, we have a deep-down longing in our hearts to return to our homes.

The trips so far have been with different types of landscapes. This time is a little different because thoughts of home will be out of focus. We are driving down the highway and enjoying the beautiful scenery along the way.

A hitchhiker is just ahead, trying to catch a ride. Normally we don't pick up strangers. He seemed like someone we could trust. However, with a little bit of deception, he persuaded us to take him to sin city. Once we were there, sin caused us to lose sight of our heavenly ambitions.

Father, help us to realize as we travel on our journey to heaven, Sin will distort our vision and keep us from going home. Let's enjoy the scenery while keeping our eyes on Jesus. The grandeur of heaven will be a glorious sight, amen.

AWOL from Prayer
November 14

Problems of life can be many when we do not take the time to pray. We have no divine direction from the throne room above. The course of life becomes a disaster when we start out alone and need help along the way. Remember we began the day without prayer.

No time with God will leave us defenseless in the trials of life. When we pray, He will give us strength to be victorious in battle. Please don't forget to have fellowship with Him. Peace is far better than turmoil.

There are many dramatic things that can happen in our lives. If we fail to take the time to pray, our journey through the day may be a disaster. If we prayed, those terrible things might not have happened.

Even if those events were unavoidable, peace would prevail. Problems may be eliminated altogether, or they may create a stronger alliance with God.

Today is the first day of employment, but we slept a little longer than usual. We hurried out the door and the glass broke on the way out. This day was getting off to a bad start. At the time we didn't relate it to our lack of fellowship or being AWOL from prayer duty.

Once we were outside and about to get in the car when we noticed a flat tire. Our dirty hands and soiled uniforms were not a very pleasant sight. We were fired that day. Prayer can make the difference of joy or sorrow and can reverse a loss of a job to full time employment.

Father, one of the greatest needs we have in our lives is fellowship with you. We know that the welcome mat is always on display. God will send us on our way with a loving embrace. Take the AWOL sign down and rejoice in His presence, amen.

Prayer and God's Presence
November 15

This sure is a busy world with high-tech machines that can send data around the world in a matter of minutes. A few clicks on the computers and family members can be connected thousands of miles away. This would be a good time to follow the trail from personal visits to the technology of vocal sounds.

Conversation was on an individual basis. If we had something important we wanted to share with family or friends, we would travel many miles by horseback and maybe spend a day or two before we would return to our homes. It was always good to visit and transfer the information.

When the telegraph came along, this opened new channels of communication. Those people who contacted family members by this new invention wanted a talking conversation, as no voices were heard on these devices. I would say each click was reassuring with the knowledge a message was in process.

Conversations were improving as the people learned how to break the silence barrier. Telephones came into existence and the joy of talking with family members, and loved ones, was once again bringing people together just like in the old days before the telegraph. This type of communication has been around for many years.

Computers came on the scene with high-speed technologies. It seemed as though the cyber web influenced the world. New phones were created with text messaging. Silent conversation has replaced the vocal sounds. One thing is evident, without correspondence, loneliness would prevail in our lives.

Father, we need to think about our communication system of how we approach the throne room of mercy. Personal encounters are not made by telegraph, telephone, or any text messages. Prayer brings us into God's presence. Whether we talk or silent, He gives us a loving embrace, amen.

Escape from Sin
November 16

Felons have many ways to escape capture. Bloodhounds are used extensively to track prisoners who have escaped their confinement areas. A piece of clothing or some personal effect is used to activate the sensitive membranes of the dog's nose.

The dogs tracking skills have saved many lives. Sometimes a trail is cold and the scent is gone. An escape for the prisoners is possible when the trail is covered by water. Human scent that is in the air dissipates quickly. A foot trail will be easier to follow as the scent is on the ground.

These trained canines follow the trail for long distances. Occasionally a person will be missing from the neighborhood and these bloodhounds will be used to search wooded areas in an attempt to find the victims.

Mechanical devices are used to help solve crimes and also to track fugitives who are trying to escape the law. Helicopters are good examples of surface to air surveillance. Heat sensors are used to locate escaped prisoners.

Let's think about a certain type of criminal activity where bloodhounds and helicopters will be ineffective in the search. We are looking at a different type of crime where an individual breaks into our bank accounts by the Internet.

These lawbreakers have devised ways to escape punishment by shredding any evidence that would convict them. This is not full proof as bits of paper have brought convictions.

Father, our personal data can be completely erased, if it was only that easy in our sinful lives. We have a more permanent way to delete sin and that is by forgiveness. There will not be a paper trail to convict us. Trackers and sky observers can find escaped convicts, but has no effect on sin. An escape from sin is possible but we must repent. In Jesus' name, amen.

Strong Current of Sin
November 17

One morning two men were going to go fishing at the river. This time of year the current was stronger than usual and the water more turbulent as a result of strong winds and excessive amounts of rain.

These fishermen had a fairly large boat and they thought it was safe enough to use in the water. So, they loaded it up with their supplies and fishing gear. After a short while, they realized the water was too rough.

Later that morning they were going down the river to a more peaceful place where the water was calmer and the fishing trip would be more enjoyable. These men were about to enter a life-threatening situation. Prevailing winds were calmer. There was still one more place in the river that had strong currents. This is where the accident happened.

The boat turned over and the two fishermen climbed on top of the hull. Eventually the boat floated free from the current and the men were rescued. Some campers saw the incident.

We are traveling through this life and not necessarily going fishing, but there are some places we need assistance to get through the rough places of turbulent times. Trust in God will enable us to weather the storm.

The worst conditions are sinful living. This is a really strong current that will cause us to perish, unless we are rescued by a first responder, Jesus Christ. If we are in sins current, we should cry out for mercy.

Father, some of us may have been like those fishermen except we were drifting in the strong current of sin unable to save ourselves. All of our efforts were in vain as there is only one way for us to be saved and that is by Jesus Christ. Let's climb back on the boat. Help is on the way, amen.

Earthy Riches
November 18

A family was having problems with their financial obligations because of a desire for a new oil well, which had already drained their bank accounts. Wealth is a non-profit adventure when it robs us of daily living expenses.

Well diggers were out in the field every day, working from sunup to late in the evening. The low cash flow was not enough to keep the money-collecting agency from inquiring about delinquent accounts.

The cost of this new well was tremendous as a father and mother of five children had invested all of their retirement savings into the prospect of striking it rich.

Dreams can be so big that they will cause hardships that will affect future endeavors with unattainable results. Poor investments will cause us to depend on others for bread.

Foreclosure papers have been written and tomorrow is the final day. Early the next morning, the bank officials met at the farm and were starting to sign the paper.

All of a sudden there was a lot of commotion in the field; horns were blowing and men shouting. Oil was gushing out of the ground. Sometimes big dreams fulfill life's expectations.

All of the money in the world cannot buy the one thing that is needed the most in our lives, peace with God. "What shall it profit a man, if he shall gain the whole world, and lose his own soul" (Mark 8:36)? We can be poor or have a surplus of money and still have no treasure in heaven.

Father, many lives are ruined because of worldly riches. The wealthy and the poor have some things in common, they both need salvation for their souls. It does not matter if the wallets or empty or full, we cannot buy our salvation, amen.

Locked in the Past
November 19

There seems to be no escape from the dark ages of the past. The days and years are gone, but the memories remain. It is a terrible thing to be locked in this confinement area.

The past visits with us while we are walking at the park. This intruder does not stay long as he just came to interrupt our peaceful and serene thoughts. We try to escape his influence by running, but the past always catches up to refresh our memories. "Remember what happened a long time ago." The past keeps guilt alive.

Our heart's long for the day when we don't have to look back over our shoulders and see if we are being followed. We have had some days where we almost escaped. If we looked back, he was always on our trail.

The violator of our conscience will not let us rest. No matter how fast we ran or tried to hide. We were always found and held captive by our guilt complexes. This evil stalker and peace invader is the past.

If it were possible we would lock the past in cages of steel and throw away the key. We would walk away and just think about the present and visualize the future. The things that happened many years ago, we would erase them from our minds and never be bothered again.

There is a way of escape that will set us free from the haunting effects of the past. Jesus is the answer to clear our consciences of guilt oppressors that have been disturbing our peaceful nature. Sin forgiven is the best past eliminator

Father, when we keep looking back, we see the things behind us. Look straight ahead to Jesus and there will be no image of the past. We pray that the love of God will be so strong in our lives that old memories cannot break through the wall of grace.

Water is contaminated
November 20

Recently a warning was given on the broadcast stations that the water was contaminated because a hazardous substance leaked from a storage tank.

Everyone that heard this emergency alert was told to go throughout the community and warn all the residents of this deadly chemical. If there was any water consumption, the hospitals were on high alert to offer emergency care as quickly as possible to save lives.

Chemical engineers were on the scene and they were taking water samples from the river. There was a high content of bacteria in the water and it was poisonous. The purification system has put in chemicals to purify and disinfect the water, but it may be too late.

A policeman drove by to warn these residents of the chemical leak. Bill immediately went inside to tell his family that the water was not safe to drink. His daughter told him that Sarah was down at the lake getting fresh water. Bill and the officer ran to the lake.

A short distance away, Sally was seen lying on the ground with a tin dipper and water bucket by her side. She was taken inside to receive medical attention.

An emergency helicopter unit arrived on the scene and would have given an antidote for the chemical poison. But she began to recover on her own. Wild berries made her sick. My imagination breathed a sigh of relief.

Father, many warnings are given about the pollution of sin. This is a far worse disaster than a storage tank spill. Medical assistance will not help in purifying our lives. Antidotes have absolutely no effect. The remedy is a pure heart by sanctifying grace. In Jesus' name, amen.

An Empty Bucket
November 21

The master of the house wants two men to go on an errand. Billy and Frank are given empty buckets. They are told to go to the river and fill up the containers. Instructions were given so that the full buckets of water would be distributed to anyone on the trail that needed a drink.

Billy, he quickly filled up the bucket, but Frank left his empty. It is a dangerous thing to deceive the master because He knows all things. Neither of the two men used their talents to quench anyone's thirst.

Although the people were begging for water, some of the people they passed along the way were dying for lack of water. Billy was so careful with his water pale that he didn't even spill a drop. Frank didn't even bother to fill up the bucket. The master was not pleased with the results.

He decided to give them one more chance. Billy carried a full bucket home just like last time. Frank had a change of heart. He filled up the bucket and was delivering it. There were some children along the way that were very thirsty.

Frank gave each one a drink and his bucket was empty again. Many lives were blessed by Frank's kind deeds. The master was well pleased with Frank because he used up the talent.

Along the pathway of life there will be people in need of water. The Lord has entrusted to us a full bucket of water by the way of talents. When we meet people who are thirsty, begging for a drink, we stop and give them some fresh water.

Father, we know there is a need or you wouldn't have sent us on an errand to help others along the way. A full bucket of water returned to you is a wasted talent. Many lives could be helped if we only took the time to share. Let's keep filling up the bucket so that many lives will be refreshed, amen.

Amnesia on Thanksgiving Day
November 22

This is a special time in our lives when we give thanks for the many blessings that God has given us. Thanksgiving Day came to us when the Pilgrims and the Native Americans gave thanks to God and recognized Him as the sovereign creator.

Let's think about this day as a time to remember and to thank God for all of His blessings. Thank Him for His abundant mercy and goodness, which continues throughout the ages. His grace always abounds with love. He keeps His holy hand upon us and gives a loving embrace.

One man loved this time of year to be with the family and have a thanksgiving dinner with them. Jim our imaginary person always prayed over the meal. The Holy Spirit visited us in this prayer time.

We are going to go down the imagination highway and travel back in time to a place where an accident occurred causing a young man to be injured while horseback riding in the country. His horse bolted and threw Jim to the ground.

Jim could have died there that day from the fall because he hit his head on a rock and was knocked unconscious. His injuries required hospital treatment. The doctor said he had amnesia and that he might not ever fully recover.

There was a slight chance his memory would be restored. Jim's life was spared that day. This was a good reason to be thankful. A loss of memory was completely restored when Jim began to pray.

"Our kind and gracious heavenly Father, we come before your presence in the name of your Son, Jesus Christ. We want to thank you for the many blessings that come down from heaven. The bounty of your love touches our souls. Hearts are filled with gratitude for your loving, kindness, amen.

Bloodhound on a Cold Trail
November 23

We are going to investigate the disappearance of a young girl in the neighborhood. A call was received at the office of imaginary crimes where victims or suspects will be tracked down with bloodhounds. This method of locating a person has been in use for hundreds of years.

When a missing person report is turned into the police, bloodhounds will be used in the search. This is a good way to find those who have disappeared from homes or people lost in the mountain. These dogs are well trained to follow scents. There is no guarantee of the final results.

Ronda lived with her parents in a home in the country. She was eighteen years old and loved the great outdoors. It was starting to get late as the sun was beginning to set on the horizon.

The mother was frantic and convinced the officer to bring a search team to look for their daughter. Shortly a K9 unit arrived with bloodhounds to follow Ronda's trail. Immediately the dogs picked up the scent of the girl and these trained trackers were hot on the trail.

A short while later the trail was lost at the creek. It was dark now and the men were thinking about calling off the search until morning. Just as they started to leave, they heard Ronda's cries for help. Soon she would be safe at home.

Father, help us to realize that no matter how fast we run, or if we have the best hiding place around, our sins will track us down. Sins are relentless in their pursuit.

We don't need bloodhounds or high-tech equipment to track us in the mountains or anywhere in the world. The best thing we can do is having the blood of Christ wash our sins away. A cold trail is where sin meets with forgiveness, amen.

Sin is the Culprit
November 24

Throughout the neighborhood crimes have been on the rise. A day does not go by without someone being affected by these awful conditions.

There seems to be an ongoing trend of ungodly living. People everywhere display acts of aggression against God. Who or what is this villain that corrupts society and even demoralizes us spiritually?

Some acts of violence have been in the daytime in people's homes and in public places. Is there no escape from this menace that is active day and night?

The courtrooms are full of victims who committed crimes. There have been numerous arrests, but the administrator of all these disgraceful acts is still creating turmoil.

This intruder affects families around the world; no one is safe. Law-breakers are on the rise. Transgressions invade every person's life without end.

This life invader is a threat to society and must be stopped at all cost. His aggressive tactics are swift as a river overflowing the banks and consuming all of humanity with its behavior. No one is excluded from the vast destruction that is engulfing mankind with corrupt hearts.

Father, before we can rid ourselves of this character demoralizer, we must identify this intruder and then take all necessary actions to alienate it from our lives. After careful observation we have come to a conclusion that sin is the villain.

We must become actively involved in telling others that Jesus forgives sin. He is the antidote for this contagious disease. Take down the quarantine signs and replace ungodly living with holiness. The demise of sin is the result of amazing grace.

Faith's Battery Recharged
November 25

While we were sitting in a safety class the instructor was talking about the maintenance of our vehicles. There may come a time when there is a life-threatening situation that requires us to respond as quickly as possible. A delay in fixing problems can be extremely disastrous.

It is very important to keep our cars in the best running condition. He told us many accidents could have been avoided if certain things had been checked out before relying on the vehicle for transportation.

A good battery can save our lives in emergency situations. If someone has to go to the hospital for an illness or from an accident, the last thing we want is a dead battery. This decreases the chances of survival dramatically. If we keep the battery fully charged, lives would be saved.

We should have checked the battery before we went on vacation. While we were at the campsite a storm had set in overnight and it rained for three days.

A camp official came by and told everyone to leave the area. Mudslides are forming and it is too dangerous to stay. As usual we were the last ones to leave, the engine failed to start and mud was coming down the mountain.

If we could not get the motor running, we would die. Battery cables were hooked up to my car from the boat. The engine started and we drove to a safe area.

Father, there are times in our lives when we have difficulty escaping the problems of life. We are in a safety class, dreaming just like our careless campers that ignored all the warning signs. Meanwhile our faith battery is on a low charge or there is absolutely no energy to revive us. A power surge of grace revives stalled lives. In Jesus' name, amen.

Last Opportunity
November 26

Let's go down memory lane and refresh our memories with one-time events. There are many occasions in life where we just have one opportunity to accomplish certain things. We may be going for an interview for a job. It is our desire to make a good first impression.

Once we leave the office it will be too late to make any corrections in the job interview. While we are driving home we wish that we had said something different. There is no turning back to talk with him again. All we can do is wait by the phone and hope that our interview was successful.

A call is made to the company with inquiries about the applications we summited. We were told that two other people were more qualified for the job. The manager said there were no more vacancies at the plant. Most employees hired for this company stayed on until retirement.

There are special times in life when something happens along the way that causes the door to open again. In the mean time we are looking for other places of employment. A few weeks later in our unsuccessful attempt to be hired at other industrial companies, we felt like giving up.

While we were in a state of despair, the phone rang from the first place we had an interview. We were told that the two men who were hired left the company because of personal reasons.

They asked us if we were still available and if we wanted the job; we could go to work immediately. The following week we were hired for employment.

Father, help us to realize that when we have an opportunity to make peace with God, we should respond immediately. Heaven or hell was offered to me. I accepted Jesus that day. We need to choose before life expires, after death, no more chances.

Power Failure
November 27

A powerful storm moved through the area and it left a terrible path of destruction. Power poles are down; live wires are dangling in the air. Driving is extremely dangerous with high voltage lines on the ground.

This winter storm continues to cause catastrophic damage. Snow mixed with freezing rain and sleet continued to fall. Robert and his wife, Jill lived with their two children in a cabin in the mountains.

There were no other residents living in this remote area. After a while a power outage caused this family to be without electricity. Their only source of heat was the fireplace. The wood supply was slowly dwindling away. After a while the fire had gone out.

This family cuddled together in the cold damp air, trying to stay alive. A few burning embers rekindled the dead fire. There was no way to get outside to bring in more firewood. Death seemed to be whistling in the wind.

The power company was busy restoring the electricity to the community. A rescue unit was trying to get up the mountain to the family, but the sleet and ice made it impossible to climb the steep slope.

There was only one chance of saving their lives. The power line was connected miles away from the home and a miracle took place. Heat was restored and this family barely survived this near-death experience.

Father, we think about our spiritual journey to Heaven and for some reason or other, our personal faith lines has a power failure. Our belief system is in need of repair. Jesus is the only one who can save us by connecting us back to heaven's power source. The love of God is a current with eternal effects, amen.

Time of Departure
November 28

The days of our lives fade with each passing hour. When the sun sets on the horizon or it rises at the break of dawn, no one knows the time of our departure.

If the time and date of our death was marked on a calendar, we would still be unable to prevent the dark shadows from crossing our paths. We do not know when death will occur.

Those of us who have an early date schedule would probably be attending church regularly. We would use every opportunity to make things right with God. Knowing that our time on earth was limited, cries for mercy would be heard day and night.

Let's suppose the death date on the calendar is at a much later time. It is possible that we would spend our lives in riotous living, thinking we've got plenty of time; there is no need to hurry. The death date is in the future.

I doubt very seriously that the people would be looking up for the coming of Christ in the clouds of glory, as there is still a lot of time before death. An unknown departure keeps us alert and living godly lives.

The time of our departure is an unscheduled event that no one knows the time when life on earth comes to an end or when Jesus will descend to earth.

Father, if we are waiting for the last few days of life to repent of our sins and make peace with God, Jesus may come while we are unprepared to meet Him.

Accept Christ while there is time. Heaven's roll call will be minus some names for those who think we've got plenty of time. Choose Jesus today; there is no time to waste. Help us to be ready before our names appear in the obituary, amen.

Overcoming Hurdles
November 29

All along the pathway of life, we will have many obstacles that we have to overcome. They are not always the same size and the larger ones require more effort. Small hurdles allow us to have more speed and a better time score.

The race has already begun and the runners approach the first hurdle. A young girl, Sharon accidently fell when she was going over the obstacle. She quickly rose to her feet and continued down the track. There was still a possibility to win.

If she gave up at the beginning of the race, this failure would hold her back in life until she could overcome the emotional stress of giving up. Some runners have fallen and accepted defeat; they never raced again. One hurdle and a fall, but it was too many to get back in the game.

Sharon went on to finish the race; she still had a good score, but it just wasn't good enough to win. However, that did not stop her from entering other races. A winner is one that knows how to lose gracefully. When we walk away or call it quits, we have higher hurdles to overcome than if we stayed in the race.

If we fall at the first hurdle or some other place in life, get up and keep going. Accepting defeat will keep us from wearing the crown. A hurdle that is knocked down is not a good reason to stop running.

No one has ever gone through life without having a fall. A fall can hurt us physically with broken bones and other injuries. We heal from those things in time. One of the worst falls is having a give up attitude.

Father, our spiritual journey will have many obstacles in our way. Some of them will be difficult to overcome. These are the times when a prevailing attitude helps us to cross the finish line. Press onward, we are almost home. In Jesus' name, amen.

Arise from the Shadows
November 30

We are going far away into the mountains where the eagles build nests and raise their little ones. This will be an adventure that will help us to rise above the shadows of despair.

When the eagle is hungry, she will descend to the lower heights so she can see a rabbit playing in the field. This mother bird has a family to feed.

Sometimes an eagle will perch on a tree and look out across the land. If there are no animals to be found, a flight over the water may produce a salmon.

This eagle found that it was a good day for fishing. Returning to the nest with the catch of the day, but to the eagle's dismay, a baby bird was missing from its resting place. A frantic mother eagle was terrified over the disappearance of the little eaglet.

She searched intently all around and finally saw the little one on the ground below, hiding in the shadows. A swift recovery saved the little one from impending danger.

The baby bird was not hurt, but it way crying for its mother. A rescue took place and the eagle lifted the little one out of harm and flew back to the nest. It is now safe and secure beneath the wings of an eagle.

God takes care of us on a daily basis. He is more than concerned about our physical needs and He satisfies the longings in our hearts for heavenly things. It is His good pleasure to richly bless His children.

Father, we know that you want to keep us safe and make sure no harm comes to any of us. If our lives are in the shady area of sin, a lift to higher ground will give us peace forevermore. Let's rise from the shadows with praise in our hearts, amen.

Wagon Wheels keep turning
December 1

We are going to travel on a wagon train to go out west and build homes in the valleys and on the mountains. There will be rivers to cross and rough terrain along the way, but each of us has a strong desire to begin a new life.

Traveling in the summer time was difficult, not knowing when it would rain or where to find the next river. We never gave up, as the hopes of a new life kept us going.

Autumn was a good time to travel, but the terrain was really hard on the wagons. We had to fix broken wheels ever so often, but nothing would stop us from conquering the elements.

Wintertime came and we had to stop for a while and live at the fort until the weather cleared. Winter was just about over when we started again on life's adventure. Soon we would be tilling the land and reaping the harvest of vegetables and fruit.

Visions of a new life kept us pressing onward. Spring came with budding trees and the beauty of wild flowers everywhere. We all rejoiced as we crossed the last river and no more mountains to hinder us on our journey.

The pioneers traveled across the land to build new homes and raise their families. They had to endure all kinds of hardships. Traveling for days on rough terrain and hazardous situations.

These pioneers were determined to have new lives out west. They continued their journey without any thought of turning back. Oh, that our zeal for heaven would be so strong that the wagon wheels of faith never stop turning.

Father, this is a good time to think about our spiritual journey to heaven. Before we can enter the gates of pearl, all of our sins must be forgiven. This is the beginning of a new life. Soon we will be in our heavenly home. In Jesus' name, amen.

355

Shameful Humiliation
December 2

Let's go back in time and think about candles as the main source of light. We will have to do without the modern conveniences of electricity. This will be a painful experience because all activities will be performed in the daytime.

We noticed the candle supply was running low and would not last through the night. It is already pitch dark outside, but we need to go to the store and buy some new candles.

After about an hour of stumbling and tripping over things in the dark, we finally caught the horses. We still had to hook up the harnesses. This is not easy on a moonless night.

The people on the farm were used to nights without electricity. These men watched us as we fumbled around in the dark. They never said anything when we started down the road, but one man told us to not forget the matches.

After a short while we arrived at the store so we could buy more candles. I don't guess we had been so embarrassed in our entire lives. Remember we are still living in the dark ages without any electricity. The store was closed all night.

While traveling back down the road to our previous location, we just couldn't face those people who were grinning from ear to ear as we went to the store. Humiliation caused us to stop at one of our neighbors and we told them the situation.

They gave us candles and groceries. We were determined to get the last laugh. The men at the farm were expecting us and said, "Where are the matches?" Shame has no respect.

Father, there are times when humiliation will cause us to strike back and try to get even with those who offend us. We need to be more like Christ when He was humiliated, "Forgive them." Let this be our attitude in life, In Jesus' name, amen.

The Candle of Faith
December 3

When there is no power in our homes, we have to use another source of energy. If the electricity had gone out in the day, we wouldn't have any problems of finding the candles. Daylight would be sufficient as long as we were in a room where light could come through the windows.

Accidents are more likely to happen at night when we don't have a light to disperse the darkness. A little candle is in the window and the flame is burning low. The flickering fire cannot last much longer.

It gives just a glimmer of light to keep the dark shadows away. Even a sparkle, a little light from a dying candle will keep us from stumbling in the night. There have been many falls in the darkness and they have caused serious injuries. We cannot find our way if the flame goes out.

Let's say we are visiting a friend and we have been asked to stay all night because of bad road conditions. We were told that our rooms would be upstairs and that we were to be extra careful because the banister had been removed from the staircase for remodeling purposes.

It was late at night and my friend decided he wanted to get something to eat from the refrigerator. His hunger pains might mean his last meal. He found a small candle with a short wick. While he was approaching the stairwell the flame went out.

Everyone in the house heard the screams and they thought for sure he fell to his death. Candles were lit so the room would have enough light to reveal this terrible tragedy.

Father, when we let the fire of our faith dwindle away, we are in danger of falling from grace. Faith is like that flickering candle that needs a bright glowing flame to keep us alive. If a fall occurs, seek Christ immediately for help, amen.

Deep Water Rescue
December 4

A special life-saving class was in progress at the recreational area in the park. Videos were shown with life-saving techniques as well as swimming demonstrations for those who have not yet learned how to swim. Telling someone how to swim helps in a lot of ways. The best teacher is a real-life water experience.

We cannot stay in shallow water and learn how to swim. Chances of drowning are very slim in shallow areas. Sometimes it takes a catastrophic event to move us into the deeper elements of life. A young man was fearful of the water. His friends would come by and ask him to go swimming. As much as Jim wanted to go, he was just too fearful.

Several times Jim would walk into the shallow water, but as soon as he got waist deep he would begin to panic. He would calm down when the water was below his knees. One day he was walking by the riverside, enjoying the scenery when he heard cries for help. A small boy who was swimming alone was having cramps in his leg. He was drowning.

Jim was the only one who could save his life. The cries for help inspire us to leave the peaceful shores and go out into the deep waters to rescue the perishing. This was a successful rescue and both boys were now safe on dry land.

Father, there are times in life when those around us are crying for help. Fear will keep us in the shallows when souls are sinking deeper in sin.

Let's go a little deeper with prevailing love to bring the perishing to Christ. Shallow waters are full of regrets. Deep waters: sins forgiven, souls saved, and lives are blessed. Perhaps we need to think about those times when we were the ones drowning in our sins. Our lives were saved because someone went into the deep water. In Jesus' name, amen.

Faith Comes by Hearing
December 5

A few days ago, a dramatic change came over the neighborhood. Faith seemed to be a prevailing factor. The good news spread and the crime rate dropped to an all-time low. Let's search for this power source that changes lives.

Surely the hard-working people in the community and those who are doing good deeds would know how righteousness is replacing ungodly living. Once again, the discussion ended with no results. Church is next on the list.

When we go to church or Sunday school, we hear some very important things that help us along the pathway of life. Every time we hear a sermon or the Word of God is read, we receive something very special in our lives. Stay with me a while longer; we will find the power source.

It is very important that we listen very carefully to the words that are spoken. If we want to go to heaven, we had better pay attention. We don't want anyone to miss heaven for a lack of interest or hearing loss.

It appears to me that we have entered into a mystery of hearing the Word of God. We all would like to know, where does faith come from? I have already given a number of clues. The reason people's lives were changed is that an Evangelist was preaching the Gospel. Wherever the Word of God is present, we will find the power source is with faith.

Father, we need to listen more intently to the words that are spoken. When we have faith, we will trust and believe in God. Suspense has gone on long enough.

Where does faith come from? It "Comes by hearing, and hearing by the Word of God." Now that we know where to find faith, let's go to church on Sunday morning. Faith will be activated and a risen Savior will walk among us, amen.

Letter from Heaven
December 6

The postal service has been in operation for hundreds of years. Our thoughts today will have us thinking about a letter of a different kind and sent from a place where there is no mail service or delivery trucks.

This imaginary journey will insure that our communication lines are still open with God our Father and there is no break in our fellowship with Him.

We all know that God deals with each of us on a personal basis. He does not use the mail to communicate with us. He responds immediately to our prayer request.

Suppose a letter came in the mail sent from the throne room of grace. It should have arrived in the mailboxes around the world. No one was excluded from this personal invitation of receiving Christ as Savior.

The address of each individual was carefully chosen to ensure no one was left out. There has never been any letter like this before and sent from Heaven's Distribution Center. Read it carefully as it pertains to life.

Since this is a personal letter, Jesus will deal with each person individually. Each of us will have a chance to respond to His salvation plan. Replies of acceptance are best given on our knees in prayer.

Father, if we accepted Christ as Lord and Savior and for some reason we slipped back into sin, He will not turn us away. Notice on the envelope, "Return unto me."

God wants us to come home and He is giving another opportunity. Acceptance comes with a loving embrace to welcome us back into the family. This is a special delivery with heaven's request for life eternal. In Jesus' name, amen.

Trapped in the Mine
December 7

Occasionally we hear about safety violations in various situations, which have caused people to lose their lives. Equipment that had defective parts was still in operation.

Mines should have been closed down until replacement parts could be brought in to repair the machinery. Some accidents could have been avoided with good maintenance procedures and a daily evaluation of all safety conditions.

Mechanical problems and air quality is not always easy to detect. These safety problems can occur right after an inspection officer checked everything off the list and gave a 100% approval rating.

A terrible tragedy occurred in a mine, trapping the men underground. The miners went to work one day unaware of the horrific incident that would claim about three hundred lives. It was at the beginning of a shift change as the men were going home and others were coming to work.

Media outlets reported that a vast number of victims were still trapped inside the mine. An electrical unit exploded, causing the accident. Special equipment was brought in to help in the rescue operation.

There was still a slim chance for others to be rescued but the possibility of a successful rescue was becoming less with each passing hour. Some of the men survived while others died in this tragic accident. Finally the other men were rescued.

Father, help us to realize that the people trapped in the mine were at risk of losing their lives. A way of escape was made for them by an excavating crew and with a fresh supply of oxygen. Our journey in life will find that we are trapped in the confinement area of sin. This is not a permanent enclosure. It is getting late; a rescue is not possible without Christ, amen.

Keep our Eyes on Jesus
December 8

It was a normal day at the park; athletes were practicing for a soccer match. One person seemed to be having more difficulties than the others.

She would kick the ball but it would not go in the intended direction. Janice tried a few more times and she was getting more frustrated with each attempt.

Finally, a coach who was standing by gave Janice some encouraging words. He saw that she was very nervous and took her eyes off of the ball right before she kicked it. There was not anymore time for practice, as the soccer match had begun.

The scores on both sides would vary by a few points. Trophies would be awarded at the end of the game. It was the last one of the season.

Janice went onto the field to replace the top kicker, who had sprained her ankle. Janice's team needed one point to win. Only a few seconds was remaining in the game.

The players moved down the field and the ball came to Janice for the last shot. She kicked the ball and it went straight into the net. Everyone was so proud of Janice, as she held up the trophy. Faith believes and most of all achieves.

Father, The competition of life will be discouraging at times. We need to realize that all of our attempts will not be successful. Achievements in life are the result of continued efforts. Failure will not persist if we know that one good score is a confidence builder and a life changer.

Throughout life we can be victorious in various events. There is one thing required in order for us to be successful on our heavenly journey. We must keep our eyes on Jesus and the end result will be a crown of life, which fades not away, amen.

Enter into His Holy Presence
December 9

Think about our Father's love as we enter into His presence. He is glad to have fellowship with us. We are always made welcome with a friendly greeting. God welcomes us with a holy embrace. His loving kindness is manifest in His adopted children and throughout the world.

Take a few minutes to meditate on His goodness, thank Him for His never-ending love. When we take the time to pray, all heaven rejoices when from our hearts we give Him praise. He is worthy of the honor, praise, and glory.

It just takes a few moments to come before His presence. Talk with Him in prayer. He is attentive to all of our needs. Throughout the day we will have tranquility and peace because we took the time to pray.

A good time to meditate, to come into His presence is in the morning at the beginning of the day. Some people have found that noon is a good time to meet with God in prayer.

Still others have found the evening hours at the closing of the day bring peace and contentment for the presence of God all the way. We have access to the Father, day or night.

Whatever the time or the place of our special moments with our heavenly Father, we will find that grace is always abundant with unwavering love. He is never hesitant to hold His children in His arms.

Father, We come before your holy presence because you are a holy righteous God. Your merciful kindness is great toward us. We know that you are never too busy to hear our heart's pleas.

Our hearts are filled with praise for your grace that abounds in our lives and for unending mercy. There is no better place to be than in the presence of God. Give Him the glory, amen.

Peace Prevails in a Storm
December 10

We think about the calm before the storm. Blue skies and white fluffy clouds drift silently through space. This is a time when the quite atmosphere calms our troubled spirits and relaxes our nerves.

Overcast skies are soon covered with dark clouds. Thunderstorms move into the area. An outdoor activity is ruined by the terrible weather conditions. A family having a picnic ran for shelter to escape the drenching rain.

The storm was becoming more severe as the wind was also picking up. Lightning flashed across the sky and the roll of thunder was heard for miles.

Strong winds came with a vengeance and tried to rip the door from the hinges, but there was no breaking into this shelter. The storm was determined to bring misery and sorrow into the lives of this family, but it failed. When prevailing winds subsided, the cobblestone shelter was still standing.

When we trust Jesus to shelter us from the storms, there will always be peace in our hearts. "My peace I give unto you." Let not your heart be troubled, neither let it be afraid" (John 14: 27). The world did not give us this peace; neither can it take it away. Peace prevails in all storms.

Father, the shelters we build are only for a season. These temporary dwellings have a short life span and will soon collapse to the ground. There are many kinds of storms. Christ is a shelter that protects us from them. Seek shelter in Him and even in troublesome times His peace abides.

We are safe and secure for eternity. When we are at peace with God, even the storms cannot penetrate the barrier that love has built. We can withstand the storms of life if we abide in Christ, amen.

Peace before and after a Storm
December 11

A time of serenity is a fishing trip at the lake. Get away from all troubles and strife and relax on the riverbank. Whether we catch any fish or not, it doesn't really matter. Our time of meditation is to be alone with God.

We all need those special places where we can talk with God and have fellowship with Him. While enjoying the beautiful scenery, His love and mercy flows like a river into our souls and peace abounds.

Sometimes we just like to travel back to the peaceful times in life and meditate on God's serenity. Peace can be interrupted by a storm. Some of the residents were not prepared as the storm came with a vengeance and many lost their lives.

When the dark clouds begin to form, the sun takes a leave of absence. After a while the rains descend saturating the earth. It is a good thing a shelter was found.

Howling winds continue throughout the day, causing considerable damage. The storm is raging with lightning flashes across the sky and the thunder echoes down the mountainside and throughout the valleys. There seems to be no end to this storm, as it has rained for several days.

Although a storm came through the area and many of the people lost everything they owned, life for them did not end because of the storm. It took a while for the residents to heal and recuperate from this tragedy.

Father, storms come unexpectedly and leave a trail of devastation, but no matter how severe the storm, peace abides. Tranquil times prevail no matter how bad the situation. This would be a good day to return to the lake for a time of peaceful meditation. Fishing poles are not required for us to be alone with God. Come and go with me; the sun is shining, amen.

The Choice is ours
December 12

All through life we will make many decisions. Let's visit a bank. The law will be standing by with shiny handcuffs for those who have a better way of making investments. These law enforcement officers will also be in the bank to reward honest monetary arrangements with a free meal.

A customer walks into the bank with twenty-dollar bills to deposit. After a careful inspection of the money, officers take the gentlemen to a place where the meal will be served. A short while later a woman casually walked up to the counter.

She also had twenty-dollar bills and fresh ink stains on her fingers. Red flag warnings were going up all over the place. Counterfeit money is a good reason for handcuffs.

While we are at the bank let's observe some more choices. There are two people and they both need to make a withdrawal from the bank. The first one comes in and holds up the bank. Money is placed in a sack and he runs out the door to escape.

We would all agree that is not the best way to withdrawal money. It looks like he made another bad decision by robbing a bank while armed security men are present.

A woman walked into the facility and requests a withdrawal. Her ID and other types of information were in order. The security officer was called to the desk, handcuffs dangling from his side. We thought she was going to be locked up. However, the courtesy meal was still in effect.

Father, sin takes us to the bank with evil intentions and like the thief or the counterfeiter, we will be punished for our crimes. The decisions we make in life can have devastating results. Observation is over and now it our turn to choose Jesus Christ as Savior or reject Him. This choice will determine if we go to Heaven or Hell, amen.

Pure White Pages
December 13

A review of the pages of our sinful deeds will help us spiritually. We don't have time to evaluate every single person. Let's just consolidate sin into one unit, without disclosing any confidential information.

This is not a therapy group where every detail is revealed about our lives. As a matter of fact, we are not here to name all of our sins or any of them.

There is absolutely too many and it would not accomplish anything except bring back the guilt. Our thoughts today will be about sin that has accumulated over the years.

All of this sin is becoming depressing. Bear with me a little longer for white page results. A page of special interest has appeared that has caught our attention. This one is blank, what does that mean?

We had a chance to look at all the other pages and it was not a pleasing sight to see our sinful deeds displayed in a book. Feelings of guilt returned, leaving us distressed.

This spiritual thought cannot end with so much depression in the review of our lives. Wouldn't it be a wonderful thing if all of us could start out with a clean slate or a white page of righteousness and holiness?

We have some good news to share that will remove the guilt. There was one man who left His home in glory and came down to this vile sinful world. Jesus died on a cross; His blood sacrifice purifies our sinful lives.

Father, Jesus took all of our sins with Him to the cross. He died in our place for our sins. Receive Him now as Lord and Savior so that when the pages are turned, each one will be pure white. Enter into the glories of the Lord, in Jesus' name, amen.

Little Sins and Giant Waves
December 14

There were some people in a boat and it was pulling two skiers. At first the waves were very small, as the large boat was a long way from shore. After a while the two men were tired of skiing and they joined the other people on the speedboat for a little more excitement.

James and Robert had planned on spending the day at the lake with their families. This was really a beautiful day for a picnic and some recreational time to enjoy the various activities. The lake was peaceful and calm.

These two fishermen cast their lines into the water and were catching some really nice fish. Neither of them noticed the waves were getting larger and their boat was beginning to sway back and forth.

Small waves are not harmful to anyone, but when they grow in size, they can become extremely dangerous. These two men would soon be struggling for their lives. This special time with the family could be catastrophic.

Small ripples of water became larger as the joy riders came closer to the small fishing boat. Huge waves were formed. The fishermen's boat was overturned, causing the men to be thrown from the boat into the water.

Those teenagers kept going, as they did not know they had caused an accident. A short while later, the two fishermen were safe on shore with their families.

Father, we need to understand that even little sins will affect the people around us. The high speed, boat riders broke the law by creating a disastrous situation. Sins are like small waves barely influencing our lives. We do not realize that just a small ripple can have such a drastic effect in our lives, until it becomes a giant wave. Help us in Jesus' name, amen.

Glory Land Road
October 15

Let's think about our heavenly journey; the old sinful life is left behind. Our new life in Christ began when Jesus came into our hearts and saved our souls.

Someday soon we will be in our brand-new homes in heaven. We will not be leaving on a slow-moving wagon train, but on the glory land express with Jesus.

As we walk the glory land road, each day is an adventure. Our expectations of heaven grow stronger by the hour. It won't be long till we step on the shores of eternity. Soon we will feel that resurrection power.

Our Father in heaven awaits our arrival with arms spread wide to give us a loving embrace. He is patiently waiting for his sons and daughters to come home. Let's continue our journey with unwavering faith.

There will be no regrets or looking back to the days that are gone. Let's keep walking the hallelujah way with shouts of praise and thankful hearts for God's amazing grace.

We are walking through this life with peace in our hearts and the hope of glory divine. Our earthly journey to heaven is gradually coming to an end. Just a little while longer and we will be with Jesus.

Some people here have not made travel arrangements. Please join with us on the trail of life by accepting Jesus as Lord and Savior. Soon we will be walking on streets of pure gold.

Father, our journey to heaven will have us going through stormy weather with hardships along the way. This is a good time to remind everyone that peace with God will be with us throughout life. Those difficult times are only temporary because the radiant sunshine of God's love always shines.

Memory Bank Closed
December 16

We have bad news to report as some of the retail stores has gone out of business. Every once in a while, the newspaper will carry an article about the closing of a certain type of store.

It is really a terrible thing to drive around town and see signs posted on windows, "Going out of Business." Some of these financial institutions have a background history of many years in the neighborhood. A scheduled date of the closing is posted on the doors.

All of these closings bring a lot of sorrow in our lives, especially if the franchise is a grocery store, bank, or building supply cooperation. When we have to drive long distances because of these inconveniences, a heavy burden is put upon us. Store closings can be permanent.

There is a moment of joy when we pass a bank that we frequently visited and find a new sign had just gone up in the window. Bank temporarily closed for improvements. We are overwhelmed with a sigh of relief because this place of business will reopen in a short while.

Let's take a look at a different type of investment that involves our personal transactions. Some of us like to call this place of collection, "The memory bank."

Father, we deposit scripture, personal request, words of inspiration, and many other types of data to be withdrawn at the proper time of speech. These stored away items help us in times of relaying messages. Without these accessories, public speaking would be difficult.

Memory banks have to be closed momentarily for an upgrade in spiritual development. There is no reason to be alarmed because God's Word is the renewed deposit. The memory bank will be making withdrawals soon. In Jesus' name, amen.

Traffic Stop
December 17

Early that morning we started out on our journey. After we did a maintenance check on the car to make sure everything was working properly. We had a long way to go before we would arrive at our destination and we didn't want the car to break down along the way.

A flight was scheduled at the closest airport, which was about eighty miles away. This travel arrangement would have us arriving at a well-known hotel for a very important business meeting later that day.

Real estate agents and potential buyers would be there to bid on the land for future endeavors. If we failed to arrive on time, our once in a lifetime opportunity would be gone forever. Someone else would buy the property.

While driving to the airport, we were about fifty miles into our trip when we saw a road check ahead. Actually, it was a training experience for new police officers to learn the proper procedures in traffic safety and to make sure all the drivers were obeying the laws and regulations.

One officer signaled for me to drive forward and stop beside him so my driver's license could be checked for the correct date. He also wanted to see the registration, which was in the glove compartment.

A registration card was found but it had an expired date. Last year's card was rejected by the officer. The expression on his face showed that he was not very well pleased. This day was quickly becoming a nightmare and a real estate disaster.

Father, Help us to realize that we have something far more important than arriving at an auction on time. There will be no reservations in heaven if we have rejected Christ as Lord and Savior. A renewal of grace is good for eternal benefits, amen.

Change the Tires
December 18

Every year our vehicles have to be inspected for various things to make sure they are safe to use on the highways. Waiting until the last day is not a good idea.

There are too many things that can interfere with this procedure. If an accident occurred because we waited too long to repair defective parts, we cannot blame anyone for our lack of maintenance.

This sure has been a busy year with us driving five hundred miles a week, going back and forth from home to work. Tires receive a lot of wear and tear with this type of mileage. Neglect causes a lot of accidents.

There is no problem as we just had the car inspected about a year ago and everything was in excellent condition. A yearly inspection should be all that is needed to keep the vehicle in good running condition.

This is not the advice from a mechanic at the inspection station. He would more than likely tell us this vehicle is a death trap and must be taken off the road immediately or someone is going to die. Preventive maintenance saves lives, but defective parts have different results.

What happens if we wait a whole year before we do any repairs to our vehicles? Let's take on the responsibility ourselves of being the owners of these cars and trucks. Remember we've got families that we have to be responsible for their livelihood.

Father, help us to think about things we should have done and never got around to doing them. We went to church every Sunday. Somehow, we forgot the preventive maintenance of accepting Jesus into our lives as Lord and Savior. Please forgive us. In Jesus' name, amen.

Bills to Pay
December 19

Most of us are familiar with various organizations that keep a fresh flow of bills coming to our homes and businesses usually with a notice. Let's consider some of the ways these payments help us in our daily lives.

It's getting a little dark in here; maybe a good light source would help us to understand where our money goes each month. Candles do not have enough energy to operate any of the appliances. Electricity is one of our benefits of paying bills.

This summer has been extra hot with temperatures in the high nineties most of the time. It sure would be nice if we could bring these high humid levels down to a more comfortable place. Air conditioners would be an excellent choice.

Maybe some of us would rather open the windows and let some of that hot stale air circulate in all the rooms. When it comes to our comfort and enjoying the necessities of life, bills are not so bad.

Someone just drove up in a beautiful red truck and parked next to our RV camper. When they got out of this brand-new vehicle, we recognized the driver as a former co-worker at the post office.

We wouldn't dare ask the price of this luxury vehicle. The owner took us out of the mystery zone and told us that his payments were so much a month. Vehicles are purchased for our transportation purposes. There has always been a need to travel. Payments keep us out of the horse-n-buggy area.

Father, I think all of us realize how important it is to pay our bills. We know this is necessary for us to have comfortable living conditions. Help us to realize that Christ paid the ultimate price by giving His life so we would have life. This payment keeps us out of hell. Thank you, Jesus, amen.

Pleasurable and Necessities
December 20

We are going to take a journey back into the country where two families have bought homes, which are located many miles from the city.

Both of the families really loved the outdoor life. However, they did have to make quite a number of sacrifices by leaving the comforts of the big city, electricity, running water, and easy access to hospitals and other facilities.

The reason we are going on this journey is to observe the living conditions so that it will help us in our future endeavors. We are not going to choose which family we like the best. This time of research will help us to see different work ethics.

When these two families arrived, it was in the early spring. There was plenty of time to get a supply of wood for the long harsh winter months. John and Randy both went into the mountains to cut some wood for the woodstoves in their homes.

We noticed that Randy would only cut enough wood for a mild winter. He seemed more interested in fishing and resting on the riverbank. John always cut more firewood.

Winter came as was expected and the fourth snowfall was on the ground, temperature had dropped below zero. Randy's family was freezing to death. John shared his huge woodpile and all survived the winter.

Father, Jesus is soon coming in the clouds of glory. We need to have our priorities in order so we can go to our heavenly home. It would be good for us to know that pleasurable things are for our enjoyment.

The necessity things are more beneficial and they are required to sustain us in life. All of us must understand that without Christ none of us will go to heaven. Amen.

If Christ is missing
December 21

Many years ago, there was a family that lived in a small house just outside of town. Every Sunday they all went to church and worshiped God.

Christmas was a special time of year for this family. They always gave thanks to God for his amazing grace. Something happened to this family, as the cares of the world crept in unawares. Vision of heavenly things was distorted by greed.

There were never many gifts under the tree, but that didn't matter as long as they had each other. A couple years ago Bob and Jane inherited a lot of money. This is when they gradually began to drift away from God.

It seemed as though they wanted the best of everything. Soon they were living in a mansion on a hill with the most expensive cars that money could buy. Beware of worldly riches.

This couple was not going to church anymore, as there was not enough time. The family was constantly quarreling with one another. Divorce was in sight.

Father, we look at this marriage and wonder what caused the strong bonds of love to be broken. The reason they had such a good relationship for many years is because Christ was dwelling in their hearts.

Jesus is always the strong link that binds us together with God's love and mercy. When we do not have fellowship with the Father, it is because Jesus is missing from our lives.

There are times in life when we want the very best money can buy. We fail to realize that God has already given us the best gift in His Son Jesus Christ. If we want temporal things, we can go to the mall or retail outlets. If it is eternal, we had better go to the throne room of mercy. In Jesus' name, amen.

What can I give?
December 22

It's that time of year again when we go shopping for a special gift for a loved one or friend. There are a variety of things on the store shelves that interest us. The toy department is always a good place to take the kids for the holidays.

The adults have their own special needs and so we walk up and down the aisles, looking for those gifts. Sometime we have to make a return trip to the store because our first attempt did not produce good results.

Let's think about the gift for Jesus. This treasure from our hearts will not be found in Wal-Marts or any other facility where merchandise is sold. As a matter of fact, it cannot be purchased with earthly wealth.

Christmas is the time of year when we think about the birth of Christ and God's great love for us. This is a special time in our lives when we can show family members and friends how much they are loved.

We want everyone to know that no gifts under the tree have the same effect of many wrapped packages. The most expensive gifts have no more value than a drink of water that is given from the heart with love.

Father, many of us would like to know what kind of gift could we give to Jesus who has loved us so much? We would like to repay Him for the sacrifice He gave on an old rugged cross. The gift God gave cost way too much, His on Son suffering on a cross. Let's give Him what He gave us, our lives.

The gift of praise, glory, and honor is what Jesus wants us to give to our Father, but there is so much more. An acceptable gift would be for us to love God with all our hearts, souls, and minds. Love is the best gift with Jesus as our Savior and God as our Father. In Jesus' name, amen.

Best Gifts are Embraces of Love
December 23

The people in the neighborhood were getting ready for Christmas. Decorations began to appear throughout the neighborhood. Fir trees were cut and set up in people's homes.

A variety of colored lights were placed on the trees. It is always a moment of suspense when the lights are turned on for the first time. Glittering lights brings a sigh of relief.

Paul was a family man who loved his wife and children more than anything. Well, he had to go to town, which was about twenty miles away. This trip was very important to Paul, as he would do all the Christmas shopping today.

His wife and two kids watched him as he backed the truck down the driveway. Sarah told her husband to be careful. She couldn't help but feel something bad was going to happen.

It was starting to snow and Paul wanted to get home in time for Christmas Eve. He made it to town and found the gifts that his family wanted him to buy. While traveling back down the slippery road, his vehicle slid into a tree.

His wife and kids were constantly looking out the window at the blizzard conditions. Everyone in the family was worried if Paul was all right and they prayed for his safe return. He was not hurt but he would probably miss the family celebration.

The family members were having a Christmas Eve meal. This was a time of sadness for the family, as they still didn't know if he was all right. Early Christmas morning the family was overcome with emotions as Paul walked into the home.

Father, the best gifts are not always beneath the tree. Those are the things that we use to express our love and appreciation. However, it is far better to embrace a loved one. Cherish the moment and be thankful for the blessings throughout life.

God's Gift to Mankind
December 24

There are many wonderful gifts that are exchanged at Christmas time. This is our way of showing our love for family members, friends, and even people we have never met. We think about the various organizations that try to provide gifts for the poor and less fortunate.

Every year there always seems to be several angel trees somewhere in the community. Boys and girls names are placed on the trees with the hope that each of them will receive a gift from kindhearted people.

The homeless live in shelters because of unfortunate circumstances. Single individuals as well as entire families live in these places of refuge. Gifts at Christmas time have a special meaning to the disadvantaged. It is a real blessing just to know that someone cares about his or her living conditions. Bread for the homeless is received with thankful hearts.

Let's visit another place where the people are separated from their families. All of us are familiar with hospitals and the care they give to help us recover from health problems.

We had much rather be at home with our loved ones, but sometimes it is necessary to stay a while in a hospital room. Surgery may prevent us from moving around.

There are times when those in our families cannot visit for personal reasons. Jesus comes by to visit and to reassure us that love will always prevail. Christmas cards can help heal the wounds with sentimental words.

Father, help us to realize Christmas is not what we give or receive. It does not matter if there are no gifts at all. The greatest gift for mankind was not a present under a tree. God gave His Son to set us free. Jesus gave all He could give; He gave His life. Thank you, Jesus, for salvation.

The Gift of God's Love
December 25

Many years ago when Jesus was born into the world, He was wrapped in swaddling clothes and laid in a manger. The type of clothing was bands of cloth wrapped around an infant. His birthplace was a trough where the livestock ate food.

We try to visualize what it was like in those days to be born in a stable where the livestock were kept. There was no room in the inn because all of the taxpayers and local residents had to have rooms for their families.

This was a very special time for God as He looked down on His Son, lying in the manger. Mary and Joseph were also thrilled with having a baby boy born into the family. Humanity shares in the joy of the birth of Christ because He will be revealed as the Savior of the world.

"For unto us a child is born, unto us a Son is given: his name shall be called Wonderful, Counselor, The mighty God, The everlasting Father, Prince of Peace" (Isaiah 9:6). "A Savior is born in the city of David."

His birth had a humble beginning. Later as a young man He would go to the cross and die for us. He would give himself as a living sacrifice so that our sins could be forgiven and we would have the blessed hope of life eternal. God has given us the gift of salvation by faith in Christ.

Father, it is not very nice to refuse a gift from a loved one or a friend. If we knew that this gift was the very best that someone could offer, regardless of money, material wealth, or even empty pockets, we would show our appreciation. Gratitude with thankful hearts would prevail.

Help us to realize that you gave the best gift, which was your Son (Jesus) to save us. We need to accept the gift of your love and receive life eternal. In Jesus' name, amen.

The Right Choice
December 26

A terrible tragedy happened one day as a young man was walking on a path near a deep ravine. He had just drawn a bucket of water from the well and started down the narrow path. The lights of sin city and the glamour of the world on the other side of the ravine momentarily distracted him.

Suddenly he fell from the edge of the ravine and went tumbling into the rocky crater. The only thing that saved Jim's life was probably the brush that cushioned his fall. When Jim regained consciousness, a headache and a visual distortion left a hazy cloud over him.

This ravine was about twenty feet deep. However, the bucket and rope somehow got wedged in the rocks on the cliff's edge. The other side of the cliff had a large vine growing on the rough, rocky terrain; this escape route was to sin city.

Jim looked over the situation very carefully and decided the rope was the best choice because this was the only way to get back on the straight narrow path, which leads home.

Hopefully Jim is able to get to this rope in his weakened condition and climb to the top of the cliff. He piled up the brush that was on the ground and this gave him enough height for him to reach the rope.

If Jim had chosen the vine it would have been the wrong decision. Sometimes we make bad decisions that affect us eternally. Sin city is a distraction that can be avoided if we keep looking to Jesus our Savior.

Father, we need to remember that before this accident took place, we were on the straight path. Sin city caught our attention and we fell. The decisions we make in life are not always for our benefit. An escape is possible but we must decide if heaven or hell is the place we want to abide, amen.

Pay Now
December 27

There were several days in our search for an old model car before we found a classic 55 Chevy. We spent many long hours to find this car. A variety of cars are sold on eBay; this is where the Chevy was located.

The agreement was to pay now the set price or bid to the end of the auction. Once the click button is pressed to buy the car, there is no backing out of the deal. This is a binding contract.

We didn't think we would have any problem with the bank, but that was before we learned of our low credit score. The first bank we called turned us down and so we quickly tried another. Rejections kept coming, causing us to panic.

Our only hope was to contact the seller and explain the situation. He was not very happy as he was counting on this money to pay for his mother's surgery. The hospital would not perform the operation unless the payment was in advance.

After much prayer had ascended to the throne room of grace, God sent the answer by another person who was also on the auction sight but was too late in his bid for the 55 Chevy. He contacted the seller and the buyer. These men came to an agreement for this late bidder to buy the car.

When we come to Jesus and ask Him to come into our lives, He does not put a restriction on us like a credit report and wait for our financial situation to improve. Whether we have money or poor, His grace is sufficient to meet all of our needs. Prayers for mercy receive approval.

Father, Jesus has a better transaction than the Internet. A pay now is a mandatory plan that is only good if the money is available. The accept Jesus into our heart's plan is voluntary. It is best to accept Jesus now because this offer may not be available later. In Jesus' name, amen.

Early one morning a foal was born to a thoroughbred mare. This was at a horse ranch in Texas where racehorses were being trained for the Kentucky Derby.

This foal was very special as it was the offspring of the famous horse, "Bright Star." Everyone had high hopes for this new foal that one day he, too, would be crowned the winner.

Jim was the owner of this beautiful foal and he would take his daughter, Jane to the horse pasture to watch this little prankster gallop across the field, kicking up his heals as if he was already the champion.

Jane was a teenager and she loved this foal more than anything. Every morning she would go to the barn and make sure he was well fed. The family did have a hard time of keeping any carrots in the house.

Morning Glory had all the features of Bright Star with the same strong spirit and with good training he could win the Kentucky Derby.

Some of the other ranchers told Jim that a cougar had been seen in the neighborhood. John, one of Jim's friends told him that the cougar came to his ranch and killed one of his foals. The ranchers were fearful of more attacks.

A meeting was called for the men to track the cougar. Tracks were seen at some of the other farms, even reports of other animals being killed. Several days of snow had hindered the cougar's ability to find food. This animal was very dangerous.

One of the ranchers was attacked and killed by the mountain lion. All of the men were advised to keep their livestock in a secure area, and to make sure that their children were not playing outside by themselves. (Cont.)

Cougar Attack

Meanwhile back at Jim's ranch, in the late evening hours, a commotion was going on in the barn. The thoroughbred mare and her young colt were extremely terrified of something moving in the bushes.

Jane heard the noise and rushed out to the barn to find out why the horses were so alarmed. She brought with her the rifle, but to calm the horses down, she laid the rifle against the feeding trough of the stall. The cougar entered the barn and it was too late for Jane to get the rifle.

Morning Glory moved quickly in between Jane and the approaching cougar. He was willing to sacrifice his life to save Jane's.

Finally, the battle was over and the cougar was killed, but Morning Glory had sustained injuries. It was not known if this young colt would ever be able to compete in national competition. Only time would tell if the wounds would heal.

After about a year of an extensive healing process and a lot of love, Morning Glory's wounds were completely healed. He was back in training for a race that some of the people thought was impossible to win. Ranchers came from all around to watch this young colt race.

All of the horses lined up at the starting gate and Jane was having trouble getting her colt into the stall. After a few more tries, her horse was in line with the others. He still had the jitters, but ready to run.

Soon they were off and running down the track. Morning Glory was the last one out of the gate and it seemed as though there would be no way to catch up with the other horses. However, to everyone's surprise, Morning Glory was passing every horse and was getting close to winning the race. (Cont.)

Morning Glory wins Championship
December 30   (3 of 3)

A horse that was not expected to win is neck and neck with the champion. Morning Glory made one final effort and crossed the finish line to claim the Kentucky Derby crown.

Soon Jane's family and the derby winner were back on the ranch. The father and daughter watched the young colt in the field as he kicked up his heals and galloped across the pasture. He had the spirit of a champion and he proved it that day.

Remember how Jane was left alone in her father's house. The cougar was on the prowl and she went to calm the horses down. Jane was attacked but her young colt saved her life. Love manifests itself in life by a strong desire to protect others even if it requires a divine sacrifice.

Jesus comes to our rescue and even stands between our oppressors and us. When Jesus was crucified on the cross, He was standing between all the evil forces of Satan and us so we could be saved. He gave His life so we could have life. There is no greater love than what He gave for us.

Once Jesus comes into our hearts and delivers us from sin, we go through a daily training process that prepares us for the greatest race in life. When we have entered salvation's gate, the race has begun and soon we will be wearing a crown of glory that never fades away.

Father, if we had a late start or we stumbled along the way, we can win the victory crown. This is the way we are going to win. "Thou shalt love the Lord thy God with all thy heart, soul, and mind."

It won't be long till we will be walking the streets of glory and praising the name of Jesus forever. We have learned from this race that if we have a strong will and made up mind we can claim the crown. In Jesus' name, amen.

Stranded on the Highway
December 31

One morning a man and his wife were getting their old 55 Chevy ready for a car show. This was a beautiful car that had been completely restored. Joe and Jane had a special attachment to this classic vehicle.

They had it before they were married. This car was bought new and kept in perfect running condition. Many years has gone by since Joe made the first payment. It was a joyful day in their lives when there were no more monthly payments.

When this couple retired they spent their time going to car shows. Most of the time they would go to local events to display their most prized possession. However, this morning the car would be driven many miles to a mountain resort where thousands of vehicles would be on display.

People would come from all parts of the country to admire these old classic cars. Some of the spectators would try to buy this 55 Chevy, but Joe and Jane would always respond with the same words, "Not for sale."

While driving down the road in a remote part of the country, Joe noticed that the gas gage seemed to be broken. He drove about one mile when all of a sudden, the old 55 Chevy began to sputter and gasp for fuel.

A sheriff arrived on the scene after receiving a call from someone that saw the stranded couple on the highway. The sheriff offered to help and he waited with the couple until a state vehicle brought some gas.

Father, there are times in life when our fuel gage is inactive, causing us to be stranded on the road. It is always a blessing when someone offers assistance. If Christ finds us with empty fuel tanks of faith, this could be hazardous to our heavenly journey unless we receive a fresh supply of grace, amen.

Never Give Up

While I was watching TV one day, a race was in progress. One of the runners left a very strong impression in my life. This is where having a never give up attitude gives us the strength to keep pressing onward to heaven. A positive attitude overcomes any obstacles in our lives.

There was one young girl on this competition team that had a really strong determination to win. My imagination tells me that all through life she had stamina and endurance.

She stood out among her classmates as a leader and as person who would accomplish all of her goals in life. Her fellow students looked up to her as their role model. They respected her because of her never give up attitude. When physical conditions restrain us, our ability to run may be hindered, but that does not stop us from winning the crown.

The race was in process and the runners were close to the end. This young lady was in the front position, but the miles and hills bore heavily on her physical condition.

She was utterly exhausted and only a few feet from the finish line. She fell to the ground and could barely stand by herself. Rescue workers offered help but she refused. Her legs were trembling as she struggled to cross the finish line. Persistence is a trophy winner even when resistance is in our way.

This young girl did not come in first place, but she won all of our hearts. Her attitude in life will be the same one that helps us to cross over onto the hallelujah side. "Never give up, we are almost home."

Father, it is very important that we have the right attitude. There are some people with these special characteristics. They have a never give up, never quit attitude. Their example in life helps us to claim the victory. Give them the honor, amen.

About the Author

After David's tour of duty in Vietnam, he volunteered for a lifetime mission of holding up his cross to glorify God and to magnify Jesus Christ. Life changed in so many wonderful ways when he accepted Jesus into his heart. He shared the gospel with the little children in Sunday school class. Later, he worked with the youth and brought the good news of salvation to the elderly at a nursing home.

The blessings continue to come down from the throne room of mercy, as David is now writing inspirational thoughts with prayer to help others along the way.

David lives in Radford, Virginia. He attends the Dublin Church of God in Dublin, Virginia. This is where he received a very special award by the State Layman's board of Virginia. He was recognized as layman of the year. David knows that life is short; he is only passing through. His heart's desire is to be a faithful servant and a witness for Jesus Christ.